BEST
BACKPACKING TRIPS
IN Montana, Wyoming, AND Colorado

BEST BACKPACKING TRIPS IN Montana, Wyoming, AND Colorado

Mike White
Douglas Lorain

UNIVERSITY PRESS OF COLORADO
Louisville

Published by University Press of Colorado
245 Century Circle, Suite 202
Louisville, Colorado 80027

Printed in the United States of America

ASSOCIATION of UNIVERSITY PRESSES The University Press of Colorado is a proud member of the Association of American University Presses.

The University Press of Colorado is a cooperative publishing enterprise supported, in part, by Adams State University, Colorado State University, Fort Lewis College, Metropolitan State University of Denver, Regis University, University of Colorado, University of Northern Colorado, Utah State University, and Western State Colorado University.

∞ This paper meets the requirements of the ANSI/NISO Z39.48–1992 (Permanence of Paper)

ISBN: 978-1-60732-837-7 (paperback)
ISBN: 978-1-60732-838-4 (ebook)
DOI: https://doi.org/10.5876/9781607328384

Library of Congress Cataloging-in-Publication Data

Names: White, Michael C., 1952– author. | Lorain, Douglas, 1962– author.
Title: Best backpacking trips in Montana, Wyoming, and Colorado / by Mike White and Douglas Lorain.
Description: Logan : Utah State University Press, [2018] | Includes index.
Identifiers: LCCN 2018056061 | ISBN 9781607328377 (pbk.) | ISBN 9781607328384 (ebook)
Subjects: LCSH: Backpacking—Montana—Guidebooks. | Trails—Montana—Guidebooks. | Montana—Guidebooks. | Backpacking—Wyoming—Guidebooks. | Trails—Wyoming—Guidebooks. | Wyoming—Guidebooks. | Backpacking—Colorado—Guidebooks. | Trails—Colorado—Guidebooks. | Colorado—Guidebooks. | LCGFT: Guidebooks.
Classification: LCC GV199.42.M9 W47 2018 | DDC 796.510978—dc23
LC record available at https://lccn.loc.gov/2018056061

Cover photographs by Mike White.

To Claire

Thousands of tired, nerve-shaken, over-civilized people are beginning to find out going to the mountains is going home, that wilderness is a necessity.

—JOHN MUIR

Contents

PART 2. WYOMING

PART 3. COLORADO

Maps

Trail Profiles

Acknowledgments

Thanks for my projects ever seeing the light of day go mainly to my wife, Robin, without whom nothing would ever come to fruition. Also, I would like to acknowledge the now retired Joanne O'Hare at UN Press for helping to launch the *Best Backpacking Trips* series. A big thank you goes to Rachael Levay and the current staff at University of Colorado Press for all of their assistance. Thanks to Doug Lorain, my coauthor, without whom I'd still be trying to get all the hiking completed. Tic Long, Andy Montessoro, John Huston, and Devin Long joined me for the trips I contributed to this volume and their presence on the trail was much appreciated. Gratitude also goes to Claire Snyder and Ariel Koenisberg for being willing to transport us on the long journey from Cooke City to Red Lodge from their home in Billings for the Beaten Path trip.

—Mike

I would like to express my thanks to the following fine individuals, some of whom I know well and others whom I only had the pleasure to know briefly, but each of whom assisted this intrepid writer and pedestrian in invaluable ways: Ben and Jason (they know their last names), two cash-strapped but very friendly teachers from Pennsylvania, who provided companionship on the trail and the indispensable offer of a place to put up my tent one unplanned night in the backcountry of Glacier National Park; my coauthor, Mike White, for bringing me into this project in the first place and allowing me to legitimately write off the expenses of hiking through some of the greatest landscapes in North America; David Elsbernd, my partner in backpacking crime on many trips around the American West and my tent companion one hellishly long night as thunderstorms lashed our nylon shelter in the Wind River Range; and most of all Becky Lovejoy, my wife, best friend, and greatest supporter, for everything she does, large and small, to make our lives together a joy and my career as a guidebook author possible.

—Doug

BEST

BACKPACKING TRIPS

IN Montana, Wyoming, AND Colorado

Introduction

Best Backpacking Trips in Montana, Wyoming and Colorado is our third book in this series following guides to similar excursions in California and Nevada; and Utah, Arizona, and New Mexico. The idea for a destination backpacking book for the great trips of the West was birthed one summer when my best friend, Tic, found himself the victim/beneficiary of a job loss due to the corporate raiding of Rupert Murdoch's expanding empire. A generous severance package was the positive aspect of being let go after thirty-plus years of service, with a summer free from any obligations toward gainful employment. Along with a couple of other friends, Andy and John, we embarked on a nearly month-long backpacking expedition in the northern Rockies, with the added bonus of intervening forays into civilization to shower, eat, drink, sleep, and relax. After backpacking through the stunning landscapes of the Beartooth Mountains in Montana and the Wind Rivers and Tetons of Wyoming, and upon meeting several groups of fellow backpackers from across the country along the way, the idea of a comprehensive guide to the classic backpacking trips of the western United States started to evolve.

Backpacking these three trips of a lifetime in one summer was quite an exhilarating experience and a genuine blessing, especially sharing the journey with three good friends. In our fast-paced, workday world,

Pyramid Peak over Glenns Lake (from Trip 1)

the opportunity to unplug and decompress in the natural environs of the wilderness for just a week, let alone three, is quite a luxury. For those who appreciate the recuperative tonic of such an opportunity in the great outdoors, we trust this guide will provide all the necessary information to plan and execute the best backpacking trips of the western United States. For those who may have not taken the plunge into the wonderful world of traipsing through such magnificent country on foot with all the necessary essentials on their backs, we also hope this guide will inspire and encourage them to consider the possibility.

The western states of Montana, Wyoming, and Colorado possess some of the wildest and most scenic backcountry landscapes in the nation. Not only do backpackers from the United States find trips in this region highly desirable, but so do countless international devotees as well. From scenic canyons to alpine summits, and nearly everything in between, this region is a prime area for backpacking trips of a lifetime. The trips begin in Montana with two trips in scenic Glacier National

Park. The Ptarmigan–Glenns Lake–Highline Loop is an extended loop with plenty of spectacular side trips on one of the grandest backcountry experiences imaginable. Glacier's Gunsight Pass Traverse is a classic across-the-park ramble that can be done in a short amount of time. Third, the little-known Crazy Mountains Traverse offers sky-scraping peaks, splendid mountain lakes, abundant wildlife, amazing views, and even a small glacier or two. The Spanish Peaks Loop features some of the best of the state's dramatically scenic Madison Range, unknown to many but a favorite of locals due to the many gorgeous lakes, fine fishing, and first-rate mountain scenery. The last of the five Montana trips is the Beaten Path, a high alpine ramble across the lake-filled Beartooth Plateau below the range of peaks of the same name, including Granite Peak, the state's highest summit.

Wyoming has six spectacular entries on the life list of western backpacking trips. The first is the Bechler River Trail in Yellowstone Park's "Cascade Corner," a fun and relatively easy ramble that visits expansive meadows, wildlife-rich habitats, a lovely river canyon, a bubbling geyser basin, and plenty of beautiful waterfalls. The Teton Crest Trail runs along the spine of one of the most beautiful mountain ranges in the country, offering unparalleled scenery along the way. The Solitude Trail Loop offers national park scenery without the permit hassles, visiting many highlights of the towering Bighorn Mountains. The Wind River Range provides three classic backpacking trips worthy of life-list status. The Highline Traverse is the classic Wind River experience with plenty of options for trip extensions. The Cirque of the Towers Loop in the southern Winds includes one of North America's finest alpine ridge walks. The Glacier Trail transports backpackers through sublime mountain scenery to the vicinity of Gannett Peak, Wyoming's highest summit.

Colorado offers several Rocky Mountain highs with three classic high-altitude trips. The Trappers Lake–Devils Causeway Loop explores an immense and beautiful alpine plateau, visits dramatic cliff-backed lakes, and traverses a narrow ridge crest in one compact loop. The Four Pass Loop makes a stunningly scenic circuit around the picture-postcard Maroon Bells outside of Aspen. The final backcountry trip follows one of the highest and most scenic extended stretches of the entire Continental Divide Trail through the magnificent San Juan Range.

From wherever you live, these guides are designed to help you plan a once-in-a-lifetime backpacking trip to the premier routes in the western states. An attempt has been made to choose the majority of trips as ones that can be done roughly within a nine-day window, fitting conveniently within a traditional workweek bookended by weekends. This time frame usually includes a day each way for travel to and from the trailheads from most points within the United States.

We begin by helping you identify the top hikes in each of the three states. From there, all the aspects of planning a trip are covered, including travel; acquiring gear, lodging, and food; campgrounds near the trailheads; and any local outfitters serving the area, in case you prefer such service. Also highlighted for each trip is a section for any must-see attractions close by that could be easily incorporated into your adventure. Information is provided to help you navigate regulations and permits specific to each locale. Along with the customary technical data pertinent to each trip, any particular concerns or warnings are highlighted as well. Every attempt has been made to provide an accurate, up-to-date description of each individual hike. Unlike what is the case for some other guides on the market, we as authors have walked every mile of the trails described herein. We feel confident that you have the complete information you need to plan and carry out any of these trips of a lifetime.

Along with all the previously mentioned details, short, historical highlights for most of the areas have been included for your enjoyment in the hope that they will increase your appreciation for the areas themselves and for the people who were instrumental in their discovery or protection.

Lastly, personal vignettes accompany most trips as well. Hopefully, they will inspire and encourage you to, as John Muir so eloquently stated, "Climb the mountains and get their good tidings. Nature's peace will flow into you as sunshine flows into trees. The winds blow their own freshness into you, and the storms their energy, while cares will drop away from you like the leaves of Autumn."

Trail Etiquette, Wilderness Ethics, and Safety

We presume that the vast majority of people holding this book and contemplating a longer backpacking trip into the magnificent wilds of the American West already have (or should have) considerable experience with lugging around a heavy pack and the associated risks and responsibilities. (If not, *please* pick up a good how-to book on the subject and get some experience with a hiking club in your area and/or take several shorter overnight adventures before setting out on any of the trips described herein.) Thus, this obligatory section on how to keep yourself safe and the wilderness unblemished by your visit will be kept short and to the point.

In their basic form, wilderness ethics are very simple and really nothing more than commonsense principles: be light on the land (ideally nobody should even be able to tell you were there), and be courteous to other users. In practice, this means being respectful of other users and following all of the "Leave No Trace" principles to ensure that the land is undamaged by your presence. So,

- Always camp in designated sites or on harder surfaces (*not* meadows) that can accommodate a tent without being damaged.
- Never cut switchbacks.
- Build only small campfires and only in areas permitted by local or seasonal regulations. Always use a backpacking stove for cooking, which is far more efficient than cooking over an open fire.
- Never feed wildlife.
- Never use any type of soap (even biodegradable soap) in any natural water source.
- Pack out *all* of your own litter (even biodegradable egg shells and the like) and pick up any litter you find left behind by others.
- Be quiet, inconspicuous, and respectful both on the trail and in camp, as to not impact the wilderness experience of others.

- Allow horse users the right of way by stepping off the trail on the downhill side.
- Report to land managers any major problems such as trail washouts, trashed-out hunter's camps, illegal ATV damage, or animal encounters.

In other words, be a good wilderness citizen. The land and other trail users will greatly appreciate it.

You also, of course, need to keep your safety in mind. Safety issues specific to particular hikes, such as camp-raiding bears, lack of water, and extreme heat are covered in the introductory material or trail descriptions for the individual trips. As for more general safety concerns,

- Never drink water, no matter how clear it looks, without purifying it first. (At least one of the authors has had giardia, and he wouldn't wish the experience on his worst enemy).
- Fully acclimate yourself before setting off on a long trip in the high elevations of the mountains or elsewhere.
- Be cognizant of the weather and avoid high ridges and mountain peaks during the afternoon, when thunderstorms are common in the mountains.
- Be especially careful when you are hiking in areas with unstable footing—loose boulders, small pebbles, icy patches, or similar obstacles. When you are twenty or more miles from your car, even a relatively minor injury can develop into a life-threatening situation.
- Hypothermia is the number-one danger to hikers in the American West. So dress in noncotton layers, stay dry, eat plenty of high-energy snacks, and know the warning signs to look for so you can avoid this common killer.

Most important, exercise plenty of that often rarest of commodities, common sense. In other words, steer clear of anything that a disinterested third party might uncharitably describe as "stupid." If you do that, and have along the necessary gear and experience, you are much more likely to come back safe and sound and have a comfortable and enjoyable trip.

Using This Guide

We intend for this guide to be used primarily by backpackers with at least some experience under their belts, as weeklong excursions are the focus of the trips selected for inclusion. As previously stated, beginning or highly inexperienced backpackers should become proficient at the activity on overnight outings before attempting any of the much-more-lengthy trips described here. For more information about backpacking, plenty of resources are available. Many cities have local hiking groups, community colleges, or outdoor retailers offering clinics and outings. An excellent book for basic backpacking is *Joy of Backpacking: Your Complete Guide to Attaining Pure Happiness in the Outdoors*, by Brian Beffort. *Mountaineering: The Freedom of the Hills*, published by the Mountaineers, is a technical guide about mountain climbing but contains a great deal of useful information about traveling in the backcountry.

Since backpacking is considered a rigorous physical activity, participants should be in excellent physical shape. Anyone with a lifestyle of lying on a couch all day watching television and eating Twinkies should not expect to be able to suddenly rise up and accomplish even the easiest trip in this guide. The level of enjoyment one experiences on the trail will be directly proportional to one's level of physical fitness. Additionally, some of the trips require advanced skills, such as the ability to navigate cross-country, or the possibility of using an ice axe on steep, snow-covered slopes. Pay close attention to the difficulty ratings and the reason for them when evaluating the suitability of a particular trip.

Following each trip's introduction, important information will be listed and a brief explanation follows.

Days: A suggested number of days required to comfortably hike each trip is listed. This number is for the average hiker; some people will want to take more time and others less. Since all of these trips are located in spectacularly scenic areas, certainly more time could be spent enjoying the scenery. On the other end of the hiking spectrum, ultralight backpackers in excellent shape could surely accomplish these trips in much less than the recommended time.

Distance: Every attempt has been made to record the cumulative distances for each trip accurately, though you may find minor variances from time to time.

Type: This entry lists the nature of each hike. Loop trips start and end at the same trailhead. Shuttle trips start at one trailhead and end at a different trailhead, requiring either two vehicles or being dropped off at the beginning trailhead and subsequently picked up at the ending trailhead.

Scenery: As to be expected with trips of a lifetime, all of the ones in this guide are highly scenic. On a scale of 1 (lowest) to 10 (highest), we have made a very subjective rating of the trips relative to each other. More than likely, some readers may have a difference of opinion.

Solitude: Similar to the scenery category, we have listed the potential for solitude on each trip. Similarly, this is a subjective evaluation and may vary from one's own experience. Some people may inadvertently end up on a trip with a high solitude rating at the same time as a group of 50 Boy Scouts.

Technical Difficulty: Another subjective evaluation on a scale of 1 to 10, this entry attempts to evaluate factors such as condition of the trail, degree of navigation required, stream crossings, lack of water sources, sections of cross-country travel, whether or not the use of an ice axe may be required, etc., to determine the overall technical difficulty of each route.

Physical Difficulty: Similar to the previous category, we determined how physically demanding each trip might be, taking into account factors such as elevation change, trail grade, altitude, and daily mileage.

Elevation Gain/Loss: The cumulative elevation gain and elevation loss for the entire trip is listed here.

Season: This listing indicates the average time of year when the trail is open for travel.

Best: The optimum time within the open season when conditions are usually at their peak.

Maps: For most trips, the USGS 7.5-minute quadrangles are typically the best maps for backcountry travel, and they are listed here. Additionally, other maps, from public or private sources, may be equally as helpful, or more so, and are also noted where applicable.

Resources: If additional resources are available that are helpful for background information or trip planning, they are listed under this heading.

Contacts: The appropriate government agencies overseeing the public lands for each trip and their contact information are noted.

Permits: Necessary permits and how to obtain them appear under this category. National and State Parks usually require an entrance fee. Some areas do not require backcountry permits, others can be self-issued at trailheads or ranger stations, and still others require quite a bit of effort to obtain. We have provided all the pertinent information and necessary resources to aid in this quest.

Regulations: Along with permits, many agencies have specific requirements for backcountry travel. As noted in the section on Backcountry Ethics and Trail Courtesy, great care and respect should be given to the lands being used. Sometimes this will match the specific regulations listed here, and sometimes they will be exceeded by the standards of minimum-impact guidelines.

Nearest Campground: For those parties wishing to camp at a developed campground, either before or after a backpacking trip, campgrounds closest to the trailhead appear under this heading.

Nearest Airport: The closest international airport to the trailhead is noted here, with mileages to the trailheads. Closer municipal airports with commercial service are also listed.

Nearest Outdoor Retailer: In case backpacking equipment needs to be purchased or rented, the closest outdoor retailers appear here with mileages from trailheads.

Outfitter: For groups desiring to be guided on their backcountry adventure, appropriately licensed outfitters appear under this heading with contact information included. A wide range of services is oftentimes available, from simply dropping supplies at a prearranged destination to hauling gear and patrons and providing all meals.

Transportation Logistics: This category is for any specific concerns regarding transportation to and from the trailheads, including lengthy car shuttles, car rentals, public transportation options, and road conditions.

Backcountry Logistics: Symbols will highlight any potentially significant concerns you may need to prepare for on each trip. A = altitude, BB = black bears, GB = grizzly bears, FF = flash floods, H2o = waterless sections of trail, L = lightning, N = navigation may be required, PI = poison ivy, R = rattlesnakes, Sn = possible snow-covered slopes, St = stream crossings, Su = sun, Tc = ticks, W = inclement weather, XC = cross-country sections. Any additional concerns for safe backcountry travel will be noted in this section. If applicable, special conditions will be noted.

Amenities and Attractions: Since the focus of this guide is on vacation backpacking trips, we have included this section, which highlights things of note in some of the communities and natural areas closest to the trailheads. Lodging, dining, special attractions, great day hikes, and other activities are highlighted for those interested in the addition of a more civilized touch to their backcountry adventure.

Directions to Trailhead: Accurate directions are given to all trailheads.

Trip Description: Constituting the main part of each backpacking trip is the trail description, which should be both accurate and up to date.

Possible Itinerary: Following each description is a possible itinerary with corresponding mileages and elevation figures. These itineraries are meant to be suggestions only. Undoubtedly, other plans may be equal to or better than these suggestions. However, feel free to follow our suggested itineraries if they fit your needs.

Alternates: If appropriate, an alternative route may be suggested, in case, for whatever reason, plans do not work out for a specific trip.

Giving Back: The backcountry of the West is a very special resource, more than worthy of our care and consideration. For those who want to give something back, we have listed an organization involved in efforts to preserve and protect an area.

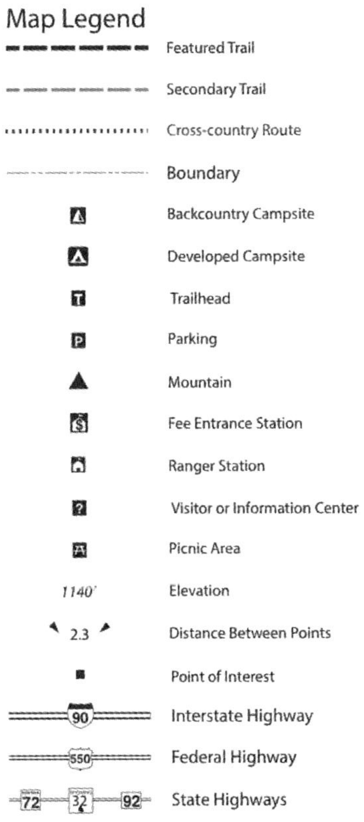

Map Legend

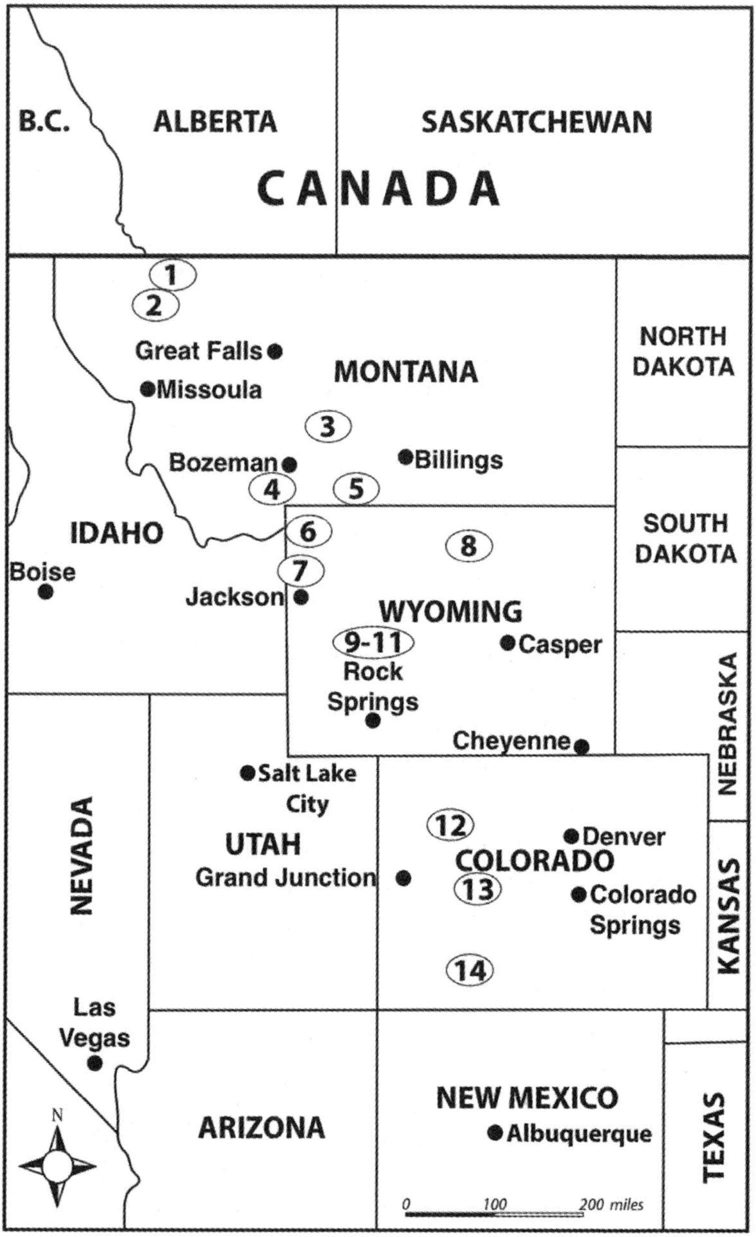

Area Map Showing the Trips

PART 1

Montana

Glacier National Park

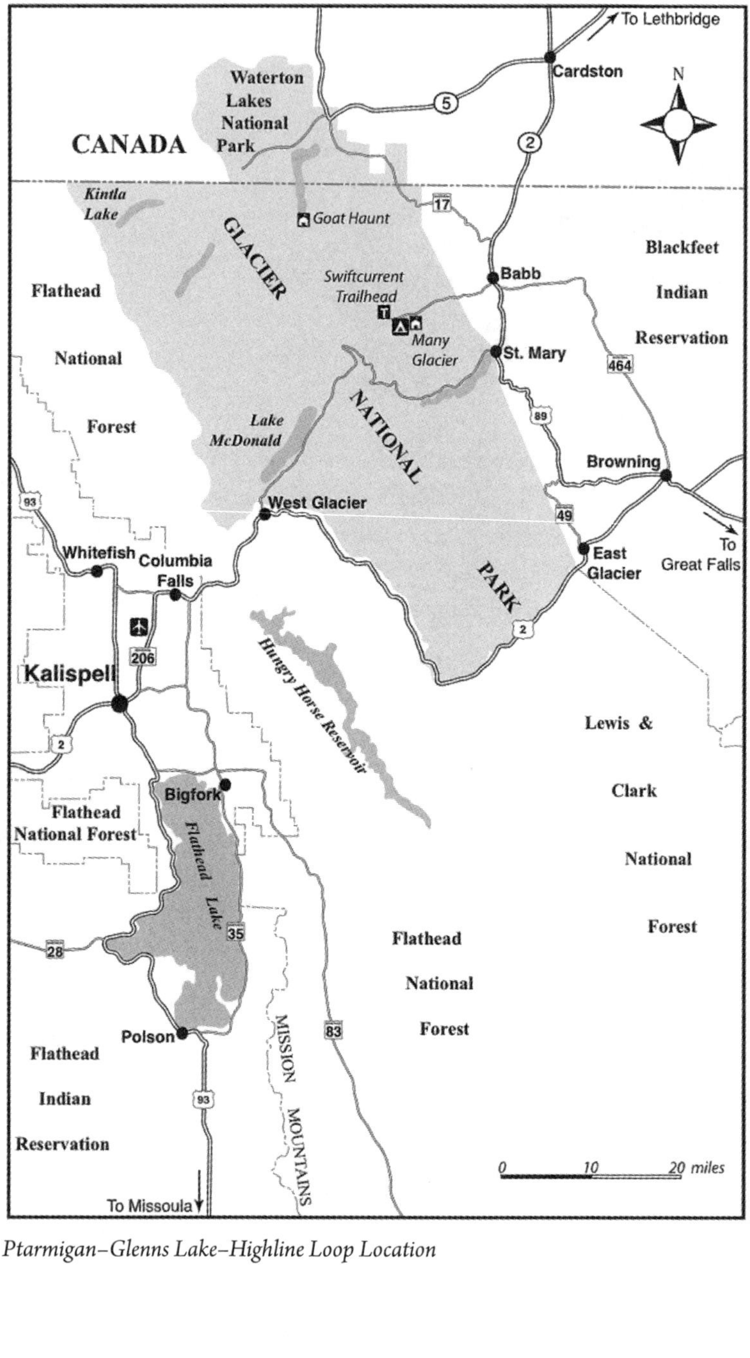

Ptarmigan–Glenns Lake–Highline Loop Location

TRIP 1

Ptarmigan–Glenns Lake–Highline Loop

> Who will gainsay that the parks contain the highest potentialities of national pride, national contentment, and national health. A visit inspires love of country; begets contentment; engenders pride of possession; contains the antidote for national restlessness . . . He is a better citizen with a keener appreciation of the privilege of living here who has toured the national parks.
>
> —STEPHEN T. MATHER, NATIONAL PARK SERVICE DIRECTOR, 1917–29

Almost every time someone publishes a survey, Glacier National Park ranks as the best national park in the United States for backpacking. And how could it not? With an abundance of large wildlife, dozens of spectacular waterfalls, hundreds of stunning alpine lakes, countless wildflower-filled meadows, an infinite amount of amazing mountain scenery, and a network of over 700 miles of hiking trails, the park offers everything a mountain-loving backpacker could want. If the authors were so inclined, we could easily include four or five extended trips in the park and still not really do the place justice. But space limitations (and a sense of fairness to the many other outstanding hiking areas in the Rocky Mountains) kept us to just two superior Glacier Park adventures, which we feel are the best of an outstanding selection.

This trip, sometimes called the Northern Loop, takes you through the incredibly scenic northeast portion of the park. The recommended

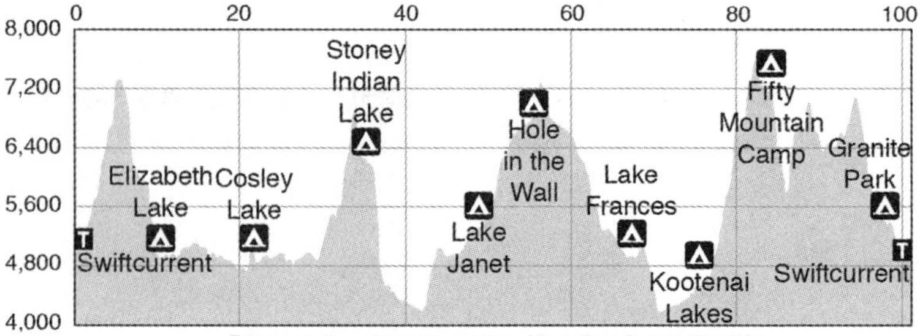

Ptarmigan – Glenns Lake – Highline Loop Profile

basic loop includes a generous supply of outstanding scenery, stunning lakes, crashing waterfalls, and just about everything else you could hope for from a classic backpacking trip. To immeasurably enrich your experience, however, take a few extra days and add several side trips, especially the very long but commensurately very rewarding adventure to scenic Boulder Pass. Regardless of how long you stay or how far you go, you'll gather enough memories to last a lifetime.

Days: 5–13

Distance: 52 miles (minimum loop); 106 miles (with recommended side trips)

Type: Loop

Scenery: 10

Solitude: 2

Technical Difficulty: 6

Physical Difficulty: 7

Elevation Gain/Loss: +10,750'/–10,750' (minimum loop), +16,200'/–16,200' (106-mile trip)

Season: Late July to mid-October

Best: August

Map: Trails Illustrated: *Glacier-Waterton Lakes National Parks*

Resources: *Glacier-Waterton International Peace Park*, by Vicky Spring; *Blood Lure*, by Nevada Barr; *Last Stand: George Bird Grinnell, the Battle to Save the Buffalo, and the Birth of the New West*, by Michael Punke

Contact: Glacier National Park
PO Box 128
West Glacier, MT 59936
406-888-7800

Permits: All advanced reservations for backpacking in Glacier National Park are made online at www.pay.gov. Starting in 2019, all reservations submitted on March 15 (opening day) will be processed in random order in a "modified lottery" system. Processing reservations received on March 16 or later is done on a first-come, first-served basis, so you should apply as soon as possible to increase your odds of acceptance. Beginning on March 15 (March 1 for large groups of 9–12), requests can be made up to seven days before the day of departure. A charge of $40 (credit card or PayPal) is levied for each application/reservation, $30 of which is refundable if your request cannot be filled. Applicants will be notified by email, which may take up to a month due to the typical high volume of requests. For more information, consult the park's website.

Without a reserved permit, you must get in line *very early* (usually by 5 AM or so of the day *before* your trip is to begin) and pray for a first-come, first-served permit. Even for the earliest risers, however, the odds aren't good, so be very flexible about where you want to go, where you want to camp, how many miles you are willing to travel per day, and how many days you can stay for your trip.

Regulations: Along park trails, camping is only allowed at designated campsites. Group size is limited to a maximum of twelve persons. Visitors are required to properly store all food and other items away from bears *at all times*, even if you are only gone for a few minutes.

Nearest Campground: Many Glacier Campground—0.3 mile

Nearest Airports: Great Falls International Airport (GTF)—195 miles

Glacier Park International Airport (KFCA or GPI)—95 miles

Nearest Outdoor Retailer: Rocky Mountain Outfitter—105 miles
135 Main Street
Kalispell, MT 59901
406-752-2446

Outfitter: Glacier Guides
11970 Highway 2 East
PO Box 330
West Glacier, MT 59936
800-521-7238
www.glacierguides.com

Transportation Logistics: There are no public transportation options, so the easiest way to reach the trailhead is to drive your own vehicle. The park's free shuttle bus over Going-to-the-Sun Road does not access the trailhead for this hike.

Backcountry Logistics: (GB, BB, Sn, St, W) Glacier National Park is grizzly bear country. Although rare, attacks do occur and people occasionally get killed. Properly store all food and other odorous items away from the bruins and well away from your tent. All official campsites have bear poles or wires for hanging your food and designated cooking areas—use them! Although not prohibited, solo travel is not recommended. Make noise while you hike, so bears are not surprised by your arrival (a potentially dangerous situation). *Never* approach a bear, especially not a sow with cubs. Stay away from any carcasses you encounter, as bears often feed on these and aggressively protect them from intruders. Always check with park rangers about recent bear activity and any closures due to bear encounters. Finally, you should carry bear spray, know how and when to use it, and keep it readily available.

The weather in any mountain environment is subject to rapid changes, a fact especially true this far north in the Rockies. Rain is fairly common, and more than once I have woken up to fresh snow on the ground in July and August. Carry rain gear, warm clothing, and a sturdy tent.

Lingering snowfields often cover the trail on steep, north-facing slopes well into late July or even early August in some years. On cold mornings these snowfields can be dangerously icy, which makes parts of this loop too hazardous for most hikers before late summer.

The park has dozens of seasonal bridges, installed as the trails open up in the summer. Without these bridges, you may face some tricky or even dangerous fords. Ask about the status of these bridges when you pick up your permit to ascertain the safety of crossing the various streams and rivers along the way.

The Glacier backcountry is understandably popular. This not only makes getting a permit difficult, but also affects your sense of solitude. All on-trail hikers are required to stay with other backpackers at designated campgrounds, which are invariably full throughout the summer. For bear safety reasons, the individual sites are usually fairly close together, and you are required to hang food and eat with the other campers in the designated food-preparation areas. Especially in camp you will never really feel alone, which is fine if you enjoy the company, but may be off-putting for those seeking solitude.

Almost all the established sites in the designated backcountry campgrounds in Glacier National Park have lots of rocks and gravel. Carry a sturdy and thick ground cloth to protect the bottom of your tent from sharp stones.

The relatively wet climate, especially on the west side of the park, means plants grow very quickly, which explains the almost ubiquitous brush often crowding even well-used trails. Generally, this is not a problem, but after a rainstorm or when plants are covered with dew in the morning, you'll get soaked hiking through the many brushy areas along the trail. Use rain pants and gaiters to stay dry and comfortable.

Amenities and Attractions: The nearest town with a reasonable array of shops, restaurants, motels, and other amenities is Browning. A more limited number of tourist facilities are found at the smaller towns of Babb and St. Mary. For a full range of services, you'll have to drive either to Great Falls or Kalispell. In Browning, on the Blackfeet Indian Reservation, history buffs will find an hour or so of their time worthwhile to tour the excellent **Museum of the Plains Indian**.

There's a lifetime's worth of natural attractions in and around Glacier National Park. Near the starting trailhead don't miss the wildly scenic (and extremely crowded) day hikes to **Grinnell Glacier** and **Iceberg Lake**. To the north, Canada's **Waterton Lakes National Park** offers dozens of outstanding hikes, most notably the trail to **Crypt Lake** and the very scenic **Carthew-Alderson Traverse**. In the southeastern part of Glacier National Park, you'll be delighted with the hikes to **Medicine Grizzly Lake** and **Triple Divide Pass**, as well as the terrific trails to **Oldman Lake** and **Upper Two Medicine Lake**. At Logan Pass, don't miss the spectacular (and spectacularly crowded) hikes to **Hidden Lake** and along the **Garden Wall**. No matter how much time a hiker spends here, he or she will be handsomely rewarded.

The Swiss-style **Many Glacier Hotel** is one of the national park system's classic hotels built during the golden era of rail travel. A night's stay will be well rewarded with the dramatic early morning view across Swiftcurrent Lake of the surrounding mountains.

Directions to Trailhead: Drive US 89 to the tiny community of Babb. Turn west at a junction at the south end of town, following signs to Many Glacier, and drive this paved road for 7.7 miles to the entrance station for the park. After paying the entrance fee, continue another 4.1 miles, and then go straight at the junction with the access road to Many Glacier Hotel. Exactly 1 mile later, go straight again where a road goes left, this time to the Many Glacier Ranger Station and Campground, and proceed 0.2 mile to another fork in the road. Go straight here, and park in the enormous (but, nonetheless, often full) lot for the Swiftcurrent Picnic Area.

One of the Fathers of American Conservation: George Bird Grinnell (1849–1938)

Seeing Mount Grinnell, Grinnell Point, Grinnell Falls, Grinnell Lake, Upper Grinnell Lake, and, of course, the famous Grinnell Glacier, a visitor to Glacier National Park can't help but ask, "who was this Grinnell guy anyway?"

"This Grinnell guy" was George Bird Grinnell, who was born in 1849 to a wealthy family in New York City, and, apart from having to grow up explaining a rather odd middle name, he had things pretty good. He spent most of his youth at a house in what was then a rural part of Manhattan Island called Audubon Park, named for its recently deceased and famous resident, John James Audubon. Lucy Audubon, John James's widow, was a friend and teacher for young George, and the grown Audubon children were good friends of the Grinnell family.

The next relevant event in George's life happened just after he graduated from Yale. He managed to land a place on a scientific expedition to the West led by Professor Othniel Charles Marsh, a renowned paleontologist. On this trip in the summer of 1870, Grinnell experienced some of the last of the classic "Wild West." He met real trappers, was chased by hostile Indians, survived rattlesnakes and prairie fires, had his train stopped for three hours by an enormous herd of buffalo, and was even guided for a time by the famous Buffalo Bill Cody. The expedition also managed to find a wealth of very significant fossils, but the adventurous happenings were what appealed to George, a young man who was now completely enamored with the West. His future course in life seemed set.

He returned to the West in 1872 to accompany the Pawnee tribe on its last great traditional buffalo hunt, and again in 1874, traveling as a naturalist with General George Armstrong Custer's Black Hills expedition. Fortunately, he declined to fill the same role in Custer's disastrous 1876 Little Big Horn campaign.

In the summer of 1875, Grinnell was the naturalist on an expedition to the newly established Yellowstone National Park. He was enthralled by the spectacular and unusual sights, but also showed his first strong concerns about conservation issues as he watched the unchecked slaughter of the area's rapidly diminishing big game, especially bison, and saw rough bands of "tourists" vandalizing the geysers and other natural features. He was dismayed that despite the area's status as the world's first national park, Congress had not appropriated a single penny for rangers or any other measures to protect or maintain the place in the first six years of the park's existence.

Grinnell soon began writing columns for a new magazine called *Forest and Stream*. After just four years he had taken over as editor of the magazine, which rapidly became the nation's leading voice on conservation issues. He skillfully used his editorials to galvanize hunters and anglers into the first important political force for conservation. He called for commonsense game laws with bag limits, hunting seasons, and licenses—hardly radical notions by today's standards. His words had some effect, and a few local and territorial laws were passed, but enforcement was nonexistent and there was usually no penalty for breaking the law, so the slaughter of the buffalo (and a host of other animals) continued. In just a decade of massive commercial hunting, the buffalo numbers went from tens of millions to a scattered couple of thousand. Very soon, the nation's entire population of wild bison resided almost exclusively in Yellowstone National Park.

Poaching was rampant in the park, and the federal government did almost nothing to stop it from happening. Grinnell's voice gradually brought together a coalition in an attempt to halt the slaughter and shame the government into action. Eventually the situation was so bad that the phrase "wildlife wars" became literal, when the United States Cavalry was sent in to run the park and save Yellowstone's wildlife. And none too soon, because at one point in 1902 the wild buffalo population reached a perilously low twenty-three animals. But pushed, prodded, and cajoled by Grinnell's insistent demands for better enforcement and punishments for poachers, the government finally took the necessary actions and the herd just barely survived. Today, thanks to Grinnell, the Yellowstone herd of wild bison numbers around four thousand, with several thousand more in other parks and preserves scattered around the United States and Canada.

While saving the bison from extinction would be more than enough for the résumé of most men, Grinnell had several other significant accomplishments in his long life. In 1886 Grinnell called for the formation of the Audubon Society, which focused on the conservation and enjoyment of birds. He named the society in honor of the man whose family he had known so well as a boy. The group grew rapidly in popularity (39,000 members after only the first year), with chapters all around the country, and is now one of the largest conservation and outdoor organizations in the United States. More significantly for the fledgling conservation movement, however, was that Grinnell, along with Teddy Roosevelt and a few other powerful people, co-founded the Boone and Crocket Club. This small group of avid hunters was the first major organization in the United States to have a stated goal of advancing legislation to protect wildlife. For the first time in history, the conservation movement had a powerful political voice. And more than anyone else, Grinnell was both the club's brainchild and most vocal spokesperson, using his platform in *Forest and Stream*. Among other vitally important achievements, Grinnell and the club members very narrowly stopped the most wildlife-rich part of Yellowstone from being handed over to the then all-powerful railroad lobby.

In 1885, Grinnell made his first trip to the mountains of northern Montana. He hunted bighorn sheep and mountain goats, and, like generations of people since, he marveled at the amazing scenery. He found the St. Mary region in the eastern part of the range particularly entrancing. Over several visits he and a local guide, James Willard Schultz, extensively explored this spectacular land and named countless of its rugged features. And if several of the landmarks ended up with the name Grinnell attached to them, perhaps we can forgive this bit of ego. More significantly, he once again employed his well-honed writing skills to use the platform of *Forest and Stream* to fight for the creation of a new national park. Grinnell was the first to describe this remarkable place as "the Crown of the Continent," and his tireless efforts led directly to the creation of Glacier National Park in 1910.

In 1925, President Calvin Coolidge said, in honoring Grinnell, that "few have done as much as you. None has done more to preserve vast areas of picturesque wilderness for the eyes of posterity in the simple majesty in which you and your fellow pioneers first beheld them." When Grinnell died in 1938, E. T. Scoyen, then the superintendent of Glacier National Park, said that Grinnell "more than any person deserves the distinction of being the father of this great park." His *New York Times* obituary went so far as to call Grinnell "the father of American conservation."

In review, he saved the wild bison from extinction; founded the Audubon Society; began the conservation movement as a political force in America; and more than anyone else deserves credit for the creation of this hiker's paradise called Glacier National Park. This "Grinnell guy" did pretty well. As you gaze across the Swiftcurrent Valley at Mount Grinnell, or visit the ice at Grinnell Glacier, take a moment to remember this important man. Glacier National Park, and the American West in general, would have possibly been very different without him.

Trip Description: ***Note:*** *This loop is equally scenic in either direction. A counterclockwise route is described here due to the spacing and abundance of campsites (especially for the first night and for first-come, first-served permits), which makes obtaining a permit slightly less difficult in that direction.*

The well-signed and heavily traveled gravel trail departs from the northwest corner of the parking lot (see map of Ptarmigan–Glenns Lake–Highline Loop [East]) and goes 60 yards to a junction and the start of your loop. The main trail (and the return route of the loop) heads left, but your counterclockwise circuit continues straight on a lesser-used connecting trail, following signs to Iceberg Lake and Ptarmigan Tunnel. After 50 yards, come to a paved road beside a rustic motel. Follow this road for about 80 yards to the small parking area for the Iceberg / Ptarmigan trailhead, where another connecting trail veers left toward Swiftcurrent Pass.

Turn right on the trail toward Iceberg Lake, and climb a mostly open slope with good views to the west of Mount Grinnell and Swiftcurrent

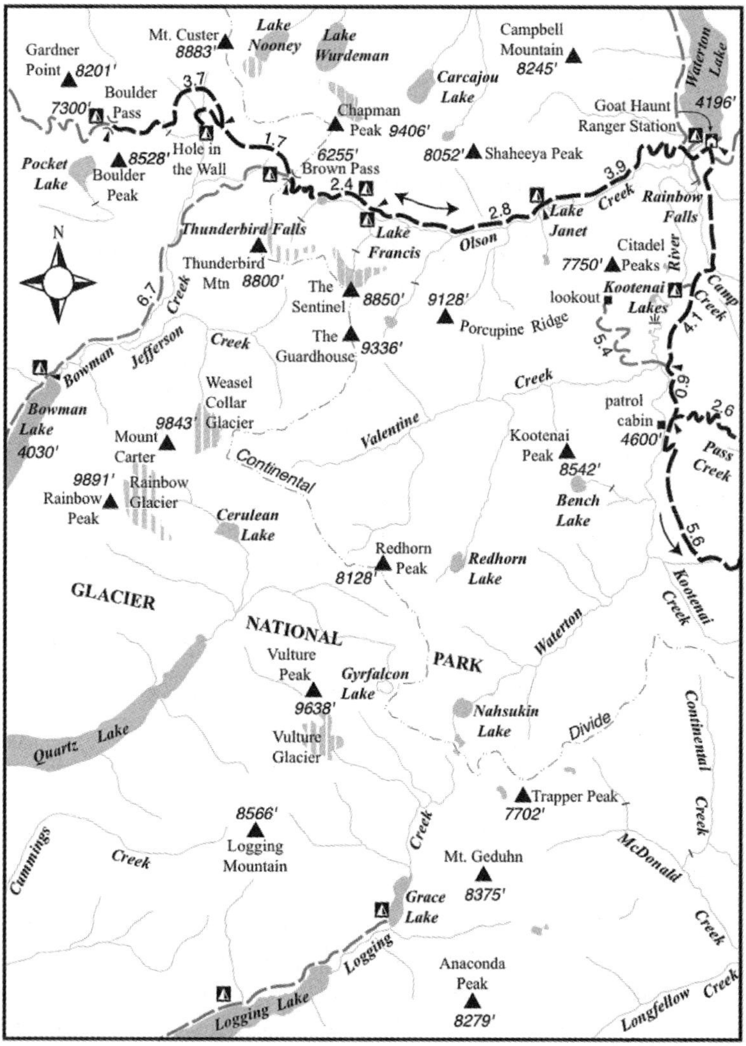

Ptarmigan–Glenns Lake–Highline Loop (West)

Mountain. In midsummer this sun-drenched slope is covered with wildflowers, including yarrow, harebells, birchleaf spirea, horsemint, and aster. After 0.25 mile, turn left at a junction with a trail on the right heading toward the Many Glacier Hotel.

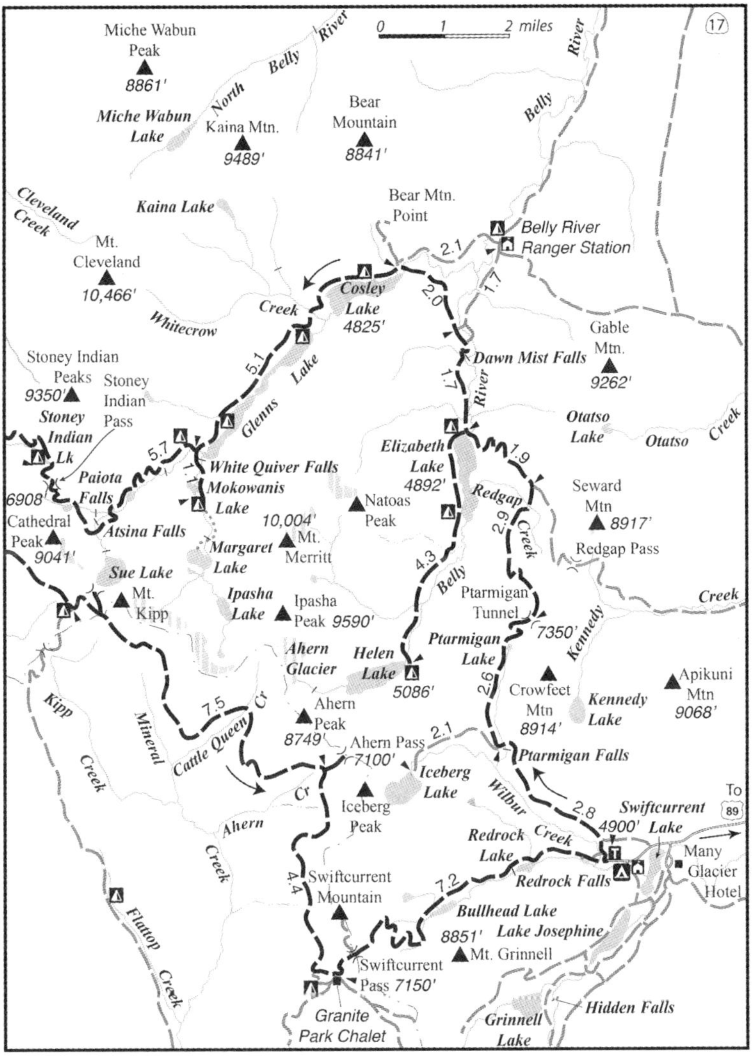

Ptarmigan–Glenns Lake–Highline Loop (East)

The trail now climbs gradually through a forest comprised primarily of lodgepole pines and quaking aspens with a few Douglas firs. The terrain soon opens up on a steep and somewhat brushy slope offering superb views in all directions. This open slope is home to a great variety of wildflowers such as cinquefoil, bear grass, pearly everlasting, and paintbrush. As you make your way up the slope, you'll gather increasingly dramatic views of the tall cliffs and deeply serrated ridge ringing the cirque of Iceberg Lake to the west-northwest.

At a little under 2 miles you reenter the welcome shade of forest and then gradually ascend to pretty Ptarmigan Falls. The trail crosses the cascading creek on a bridge just above the falls and less than 0.1 mile later comes to a junction. The trail to the left goes 2.1 miles to dramatic Iceberg Lake—a great side trip if you have the time—but you might have to reluctantly skip this trail, as you're still a long way to the first legal campsites on this loop.

Turn right, following signs to Ptarmigan Lake and Tunnel, leaving the majority of the day hikers behind. For the next 1.6 miles the trail makes a generally steady, moderately steep climb up the canyon of mostly unseen Ptarmigan Creek. Initially the way is in forest, followed by a traverse across open slopes with good views until reaching the cirque holding relatively small but deep and beautiful Ptarmigan Lake. From here, the trail climbs the steep talus slope north of the lake in two long switchbacks to Ptarmigan Tunnel. Always shady and cool inside, providing a nice break on a hot day, the 200-foot-long tunnel cuts through the top of the steep and rocky Ptarmigan Wall. At the north end of the tunnel is a fantastic view down to Elizabeth Lake, the Belly River Valley, and the surrounding tall peaks.

Beyond the tunnel, the trail, which is lined with a stone wall on the downhill side, cuts to the right and crosses a cliff face often blocked by snow through July. After leaving the cliff and curving to the north, the trail gradually descends another talus slope, this one a striking red color. On the way down you'll revel in some of the finest scenery in Glacier National Park, especially the outstanding view to the southwest of Helen Lake and west to Mount Merritt and Old Sun Glacier. The glorious scenery and stunning views keep coming until you finally return to the cover of forest, cross the first reliable water since Ptarmigan Lake at Redgap Creek, and then come to a junction with the trail to Redgap Pass.

Keep straight on the Ptarmigan Trail and over the next 1.9 miles, descend ten lazy switchbacks to a swinging bridge over Belly River, just below where that stream flows out of Elizabeth Lake. About 100 yards beyond this bridge is the inviting campground at the foot of Elizabeth Lake near a junction.

Side Trip to Helen Lake

The main loop trail goes right at this junction, but for a wonderful side trip, turn left and follow an up-and-down route along the west side of large Elizabeth Lake. This section of trail affords fine views across the water to Gable and Seward Mountains. After 1.6 miles, you reach the end of the lake near a comfortable campsite. With good fortune, you may see a pair of rare trumpeter swans swimming at this end of the lake. From this camp, the gentle trail continues south following the willow-choked valley of the upper Belly River. Like so many trails in Glacier National Park, this path is often overgrown with brush, so expect to get wet with dew on summer mornings. At about 2.7 miles from Elizabeth Lake, you cross a creek on a plank bridge just before Helen Lake. This large and extremely dramatic lake is backed by the towering cliffs of Ahern Peak, a spectacular scene by any standard, especially breathtaking early in the morning when the peak is reflected in the still waters. The low point in the ridge to the left (south) of Ahern Peak is Ahern Pass, a dramatic location that you will visit later in this trip. There is a designated hiker's camp at Helen Lake.

Back at the junction at the north end of Elizabeth Lake, go north, following signs to Belly River Ranger Station, and walk a mostly flat trail for 0.2 mile to a log bridge over an unnamed side creek. Easy hiking then leads to a point about 1.4 miles below Elizabeth Lake, where you pass a rocky viewpoint directly above Dawn Mist Falls, a broad curtain of water plunging into a deep defile. From here, two quick downhill switchbacks lead to a junction with a side trail on the right that in 140 yards reaches a dramatic and photogenic spot just below Dawn Mist Falls.

The main trail goes straight; soon passing a junction with a side trail that goes right to a horse ford, and then finally reaching a junction just

Dawn Mist Falls

above a swinging footbridge over Belly River. Here you have a choice: The trail to the right has the advantage of heading past the Belly River Ranger Station and traveling through open country with better views; the left-hand trail is a cut-off route, 1.8 miles shorter and shadier, but it does necessitate a (usually) not-too-difficult ford of the Mokowanis River at the end.

If you opt for the cut-off route (as most hikers do), then go straight at the junction, and walk through viewless but attractive forest. The trail is mostly either level or uphill for the first 0.8 mile, then goes up and down for 1.2 miles to a ford of Mokowanis River right at the outlet of very scenic Cosley Lake. There is a cable across the stream to hang onto during the ford, though by midsummer this really isn't necessary, as the slow-moving water is only a bit over knee deep. Only 50 yards beyond the ford is a junction with Stoney Indian Pass Trail. This is where you reunite with the longer alternate route that went past Belly River Ranger Station.

Turn left (west) and walk along a partly forested hillside above the north shore of Cosley Lake. After 0.6 mile a signed spur trail goes left to Cosley Lake Camp. Unless you're staying at this attractive campground, keep straight on the main trail and continue hiking west. As you approach the far end of Cosley Lake, be sure to look behind for a brief view of block-shaped Chief Mountain in the eastern distance. Once past Cosley Lake, ascend slightly through a forest of true firs rapidly dying from a beetle infestation, then cross a log bridge over Whitecrow Creek and come to a fork in the trail. The trail to the left soon leads to the often windy but popular campground at the foot of long and beautiful Glenns Lake.

The main trail goes right at the fork and spends the next couple of miles going up and down in the forest above (and out of sight of) Glenns Lake. The forest floor here is covered with a thick growth of thimbleberries, which offer up tart but tasty raspberry-like fruit in mid-August. Just after you cross a bridge over a clear little creek is the campground at the head of Glenns Lake. Even if you aren't staying here, be sure to make a short detour to the water for excellent views to the southwest of the tall spire of Pyramid Peak.

The trail keeps heading up the valley, generally remaining in forest until you come to a junction with the Mokowanis Lake Trail. With extra time, this trail makes an excellent side trip, climbing slightly for about 1 mile to pretty Mokowanis Lake. For even grander scenery, continue past the lake and campground on a sketchy cairned boot path up a rocky gully and past a waterfall to spectacular Margaret Lake, which sits beneath the impressive cliffs of Mount Kipp and Mount Merritt. Nearby Ipasha Lake is another extremely scenic goal.

The Stoney Indian Pass Trail goes straight at the Mokowanis Lake junction and a little over 0.1 mile later reaches viewless but conveniently located Mokowanis Junction Camp. The trail now begins a steady but initially gradual ascent. You soon leave the forest for open, brushy slopes with nice views of a long, tiered, cascading waterfall. This slope is exposed to the sun and can be quite hot, but offers good views back down to Glenns Lake. A series of twelve switchbacks leads to the top of the falls and a pretty little basin holding an unnamed green-tinged lake.

Several tall waterfalls thunder off the cliffs of Cathedral Peak into this scenic basin. The two tallest and most prominent ones are Atsina Falls to the south and Paiota Falls to the north. The trail travels around the right (north) side of the small lake, crosses the inlet creek on a seasonal bridge, and then ascends fourteen switchbacks to the top of the two tall and very beautiful waterfalls. Once on top, you ford the cold creek feeding Atsina Falls and then gradually climb a lovely wildflower-covered terrace to an easy rock-hop crossing of Paiota Falls' creek. Just above this crossing is a shallow but stunningly beautiful little pond with exceptionally photogenic views of the tall tower of Wahcheechee Mountain. A final nine-switchback climb takes you up a partly forested slope to dramatic Stoney Indian Pass, where the impressive views are hard to beat.

The trail drops down the other side of Stoney Indian Pass, utilizing thirteen switchbacks to rapidly drop 600 feet on the way to deep Stoney Indian Lake. The trail goes around the northeast shore to a designated campground near the outlet, one of the more dramatic backcountry campsites in the park, well worth the effort to get a camping permit for. Although beautiful, the camps are fairly exposed and the small trees provide little shade.

The trail continues downhill at a reasonable grade from Stoney Indian Lake on two dozen irregularly spaced switchbacks (see map of Ptarmigan–Glenns Lake–Highline Loop [West]). Part of the descent is beside cascading Pass Creek, but most of the way is on a slope covered with plenty of annoying brush that crowds the trail. At 2.6 miles from the lake is a junction with Waterton Valley Trail.

The return route of the loop goes left—if time is limited, follow that trail. However, if you have a few extra days, schedule time for a magnificent multiday side trip to spectacular Boulder Pass.

Side Trip to Boulder Pass

For Boulder Pass, turn right (north) on the Waterton Valley Trail and follow this brushy route, which even though it's heading *down* the valley seems to perversely spend most of the time going uphill. After 0.9 mile a lightly used trail goes left toward Porcupine Lookout, but stay straight and hike another 1.6 miles to a junction immediately before you reach Camp Creek. The trail to the left goes just under 0.3 mile to Kootenai Lakes Camp, located beside a large, shallow, marshy lake. Even if you aren't camping here, the journey to this lake can be quite worthwhile for spotting moose.

The Waterton Valley Trail goes right at the Kootenai Lakes turnoff, crosses Camp Creek on a log bridge, then continues north on a gentle, woodsy course, passing a few marshy meadows along the way. You cross Cleveland Creek on another log bridge, and then the trail widens and turns to a gravel surface on the way around the right side of a National Park Service building. A little past this building, you reach a junction with the Goat Haunt Overlook Trail heading sharply right.

Keep straight and almost immediately come to a junction amid the cluster of modern buildings around the Goat Haunt Ranger Station, customs office, and boat dock, which are located at the southern tip of very large and long Waterton Lake. Your signed route to Boulder Pass turns sharply left at this junction. ***Tip:*** *There is a convenient trash receptacle near this junction, which allows you to dump the excess weight of your garbage.*

Turn left onto what is signed as the Waterton Lake Trail and travel 0.3 mile to a junction with the Rainbow Falls Trail. Although only 0.7 mile to this low falls, the cascade, which resembles an oversized fish ladder, really doesn't compare in scenic grandeur to the many other waterfalls along this trip. Therefore, keep right, cross a swinging bridge over the Waterton River (one hiker at a time) and come to a spur trail that goes right to well-located, but often-buggy, Waterton River Camp.

Head straight on the main trail, and 0.1 mile later climb two very short switchbacks to reach another junction. You turn left here on Boulder Pass Trail and settle in for some climbing, as the next mile or so is all uphill. Eventually the trail levels out somewhat, where you travel around the corner of a side ridge and enter the valley of Olson Creek. From here, the trail has only intermittent uphill segments until dropping a bit to the shore of scenic Lake Janet. The trail follows the north side of this slightly turquoise-colored lake on the way to Lake Janet Camp, just past the west end of the lake on the inlet stream.

Still heading west, the Boulder Pass Trail leads you on a 2-mile, mostly level segment with just some gentle uphill along the way. The route is viewless and heavily forested, but nicely shaded. Eventually you catch occasional glimpses of greenish Lake Francis on the left before reaching a spur trail to Lake Francis Camp, above the lake's west end. Highlighting a stay at this camp are nice views of an incredibly tall veil-like waterfall that drops off the towering cliffs of The Sentinel to the south. About 0.3 mile past this turnoff is Hawksbill Camp, a brushy site with very little shade, less appealing than most other backcountry camps in the park.

Above Hawksbill Camp the forest opens up as you walk across a mostly flat and very brushy basin featuring a small, deep, and very scenic unnamed lake. The views across this lake to the tall dark cliffs and snowfields of Thunderbird Mountain and the long, sliding cascade of Thunderbird Falls are excellent.

From this unnamed lake the climbing increases, as you trudge up a mostly shadeless slope at a moderately steep grade. The views are grand, but the ascent may feel sweaty and tiring. After thirteen scattered switchbacks, you top out at a junction at wide and grassy Brown Pass on the Continental Divide. The sight of many dead small trees, the result of frequent avalanches, enhances the open feel of this place.

If staying at Brown Pass Camp, go straight at the junction and walk another 0.3 mile to the camp. Although extremely scenic and perfectly located for a base camp for exploring Boulder Pass, this camp is infamously mosquito infested. In addition, after late July when the small snowmelt creek dries up, you'll have to walk almost

0.3 mile beyond the camp to get water from a trickling creek (bring a collapsible bucket or similar water container if you are scheduled to stay here).

Back at Brown Pass, take the Boulder Pass Trail and make a gradual uphill traverse across the mostly open slopes above the pass. As you hike, you'll have stupendous views looking south to towering Thunderbird Mountain and down a very deep canyon to long and sinuous Bowman Lake. Where you round a ridge, the views become even grander to the west of the imposing ramparts of Mount Custer, Boulder Peak, and several unnamed summits. You will also see several long, streaking waterfalls and look down into the impressive basin of Hole in the Wall. To call this terrain "mountainous" seems ridiculously inadequate, as the area is vertical in the extreme, with cliffs thousands of feet high, deeply plunging canyons, towering waterfalls, and soaring peaks.

The trail now contours along a steep hillside with continuous jaw-dropping views, leading to the junction with a 0.4-mile side trail angling left (downhill) to outstandingly beautiful Hole in the Wall Camp, arguably the most spectacular camp in the Glacier backcountry. Snagging a permit to stay here is difficult, but well worth the effort. Grizzly bears are common here, so be extra cautious with your food and make plenty of noise while hiking.

The main trail keeps right at the Hole in the Wall junction and begins gradually climbing again, making a long loop around the open and increasingly alpine slopes above Hole in the Wall. You'll pass fields of wildflowers and hop over several small creeks along the way, which add to the already world-class scenery. You might also have to negotiate a few icy snowfields, so use extreme caution, especially early in the day when the ice is still hard. Most of the few trees growing at this altitude are alpine larches, an unusual tree found only in Canada and a few places in the mountains of the northwestern United States. In the autumn, the light green needles of this scraggly looking conifer turn bright gold and fall off, making larches the only conifers to act like deciduous trees. As you continue climbing, even the hardy larches eventually are left behind, leaving you in a land of grasses, tiny wildflowers, and snowfields.

The tread may disappear in the rocky terrain, forcing you to follow cairns leading up to a flat little upper basin with small snowmelt ponds handsomely reflecting Boulder Peak. The peeping brown birds with the constantly dipping tails are water pipits, a tough little bird that chooses to nest in this inhospitable region. The skinny permanent snowfield at the base of Boulder Peak is all that remains of Boulder Glacier. In historic times, this glacier covered the entire slope below the peak and all the way over to where the trail is located.

A final short uphill over rocks and snow takes you through Boulder Pass. Immediately ahead to the north-northwest is the tall, blocky summit of Gardner Point. If you drop down the other side of the pass a bit, you can also see the tall spire of Kinnerly Peak to the west. This outstandingly beautiful area is why many make this long side trip, so savor the scenery for as long as time allows. A climb to the top of a rocky old terminal moraine on the north side of the pass leads to even higher views. Once you've had your fill, reluctantly turn around and make the long trek back via Brown Pass and Goat Haunt to the main loop at the junction with the trail coming down from Stoney Indian Lake.

Go south, following signs to Fifty Mountain Camp and Granite Chalet, and walk just under 0.1 mile to a log bridge over Pass Creek and a Park Service patrol cabin immediately on the other side of the crossing.

An uphill climb begins in earnest soon after this cabin, as you ascend two switchbacks and begin a long uphill traverse. As usual, improving views come with the added elevation with increasingly excellent vistas up and down the Waterton River Valley and across the canyon to Kootenai Peak. Later in the climb, you'll be able to see glacier-clad Vulture Peak to the southwest. After about 2.5 miles, climb above the trees and enter wildflower-covered meadows. A few more switchbacks finally lead to a level area and a spectacular alpine terrace carpeted with wildflowers and featuring outstanding views, especially of Cathedral Peak (see map of Ptarmigan–Glenns Lake–Highline Loop [East]) and the jagged ridge to the left. Enjoy almost a mile of this hiking heaven before reaching a junction with the Flattop Mountain Trail and outstandingly scenic Fifty Mountain Camp. The little creek nearby may dry up by late summer, but water is always reasonably close by and the minimal extra work required is only a minor inconvenience. ***Warning:*** *Marmots are abundant around*

Fifty Mountain Camp, and they are notorious for chewing anything and everything in search of salt (pack straps, the handles of walking sticks, boots, etc.). Be sure to hang or guard your gear carefully. ***Tip:*** *The camp is right at the edge of a large and fairly recent forest fire scar—charred snags that offer no shade surround some of the camps. Try to arrive fairly early in the afternoon to secure one of the more desirable campsites.*

The Highline Trail goes southeast from Fifty Mountain Camp, ascending talus and scree slopes on the southwest side of rugged Mount Kipp. After gaining about 400 feet in 0.6 mile, you come to a junction. The 0.3-mile spur trail to the left goes to a low point in the divide directly above large Sue Lake. As the lake is 800 feet straight down, the view is a bit dizzying but nonetheless spectacular. The lake often has floating icebergs well into August.

The Highline Trail goes straight at the Sue Lake junction, generally on a long, gradual downhill for the next couple of miles. Part of that distance is in a burn zone from an old forest fire with continuously fine views. The downhill ends where the trail jogs to the east and rounds the slopes above the basin holding Cattle Queen Creek.

The trail makes a steep ascent away from Cattle Queen Creek to the top of a view-packed ridge. From there, make another eastward detour contouring to a junction. Don't miss the side trip from here that climbs about 0.4 mile to Ahern Pass. The view from here up to Ahern Glacier and down to Helen and Elizabeth Lakes (remember these from earlier in the trip?) is stupendous.

Back on the aptly named Highline Trail, you make your way around another basin, where a steep and icy snowfield often blocks the route well into August (be sure to ask about the conditions of this section when you pick up your permit). Another short uphill takes you around a ridge where you can look south to the squat lookout building atop Swiftcurrent Mountain. At the top of the next side ridge is a junction. The trail going straight ahead takes you to Granite Park Chalet, which you can see about 0.25 mile ahead. At this historic stone chalet, you can pay for a comfortable bed (with reservations made *many* months in advance—888-345-2649 or online at *graniteparkchalet.com*); buy coffee, candy, and other items at a small concession stand; and, of course, enjoy an absolutely marvelous view. Hikers planning to stay at Granite Park Camp should go right at the ridgetop junction, switchback down past a patrol cabin, and come to a junction with the short spur trail to the campground. The trail going straight at this junction loops back up to the chalet.

To finish the loop, make your way to a signed junction just under 0.1 mile northeast of Granite Park Chalet. Go east (uphill) on the trail toward Swiftcurrent Pass, climb two switchbacks, and come to a junction. The trail to the left climbs open and rocky slopes for 1.2 miles to the lookout building atop Swiftcurrent Mountain. The view is stupendous, but remember leaving your heavy pack unattended back at the junction is illegal (doing so attracts bears and other creatures, and you could even be fined and/or given a ticket).

The main trail goes right at the junction and almost immediately takes you through Swiftcurrent Pass, where a tall stone cairn marks the Continental Divide. As you drop over the east side of the pass, you'll have fine views down to large and distant Lake Sherburne. Continuing downhill, a whole string of closer but smaller lakes are seen in the basin far below.

The trail drops briefly through a stunted subalpine-fir forest and then begins a long downhill. Most of the way is across cliffs or extremely steep slopes, traveling past several impressive rocky overlooks. The views looking down to several shimmering lakes, up to sky-scraping peaks, and over to Swiftcurrent Glacier and a number of streaking waterfalls are amazing. After negotiating several long sweeping switchbacks, you twice cross plank bridges across Swiftcurrent Creek and soon come to the shores of beautiful Bullhead Lake. The now gentle up-and-down trail goes around the left (north) side of Bullhead Lake, crossing a side creek on a swinging bridge along the way, and then wanders through willow groves, brushy meadows, and open forest. For part of the way you walk beside rushing Swiftcurrent Creek enjoying the sounds of falling water and nice views. About 1.5 miles below Bullhead Lake is a junction with an unsigned but obvious trail heading sharply right. This 80-yard side trail leads to a somewhat disappointing viewpoint just below fairly short Redrock Falls. Although large boulders block most of the view, the minimal effort involved makes a side trip still worthwhile. Just below Redrock Falls is scenic and fairly large Redrock Lake, from where you have an excellent vista back across the water to Mount Grinnell.

Another mile or so of mostly gentle downhill leads to a junction with a very short and lightly used side trail on the right dropping to tiny Fishercap Lake. Keep right on the wide and heavily used trail, usually choked with scads of day hikers, and keep right again where a horse trail forks left about 50 yards farther. About 0.2 mile later is the junction just northwest of the large parking lot where you began the hike. Go right to the Swiftcurrent Picnic Area lot, and reach the end of your magnificent Glacier Park odyssey.

Possible Itinerary

	Camps and Side Trips	Miles	Elevation Gain
Day 1	Swiftcurrent TH to Elizabeth Lake	10.2	+2,500/−2,500
Day 2	Side trip to Helen Lake	8.6	+400/−400
	Cosley Lake	4.3	+400/−450
Day 3	Stoney Indian Lake	10.2	+2,200/−700
	Side trip to Mokowanis Lake	2.2	+100/−100
Day 4	Lake Janet	11.5	+1,100/−2,500
Day 5	Hole in the Wall	7.3	+1,600/−200
Day 6	Side trip to Boulder Pass	8.2	+1,100/−1,100
	Lake Francis	4.5	+100/−1,200
Day 7	Kootenai Lakes	9.5	+400/−1,250
Day 8	Fifty Mountain Camp	8.4	+2,500/−200
Day 9	Granite Park Camp	11.9	+2,250/−2,450
	Side trip to Sue Lake Overlook	0.6	+250/−250
	Side trip to Ahern Pass	0.8	+400/−400
Day 10	Out to Swiftcurrent TH	7.4	+900/−2,500

Giving Back

Glacier National Park Conservancy: www.glacierconservancy.org

Grizzlies–Teddy Bears They're Not

Although two-legged types are relative rare in most of Montana's backcountry (except during hunting season), four-legged critters are incredibly abundant. Montana is one of only three states in the country (along with Alaska and Wyoming) where the total number of deer, elk, bighorn sheep, and other assorted large mammals outnumbers the human population. Anyone who spends much time exploring this state will readily believe that statistic as wildlife is seemingly everywhere.

Most of the time seeing animals in the wild is a pure joy. Grizzly bears, with their sometimes deserved reputation for fearsomeness, may be the exception. And more of them call Montana home than anywhere else in the lower forty-eight states. In some of the state's mountain ranges these mighty bruins are rare or even absent, but generally they are common enough for hikers to be on the alert and to take reasonable precautions. This necessary attitude is reinforced almost every year by local newspapers carrying stories about an unfortunate soul who gets mauled or killed by a "grizz" somewhere in the state. Such misfortunes are statistically quite rare—*far* more people get injured in car accidents while driving to trailheads, in hunting accidents, from hypothermia, from drowning, and a host of other causes than from bear maulings—but attacks occur often enough to keep the possibility perpetually in the back of one's mind.

When hiking in grizzly country hikers should always carry bear spray, have it readily available, and be familiar with its use. Be very careful about keeping food, garbage, hand lotions, and other odorous items well away from camp. Know how to identify bears and quickly recognize signs of bear activity. Backpackers must be amenable to unashamedly camp or hike elsewhere when necessary. On the trail, avoid startling unsuspecting bears by regularly making noise so they will hear hikers coming, thereby avoiding a potentially dangerous encounter. However, such measures don't always work.

Over the years I have faced full-on grizzly bear charges twice: once in Canada and a second time in Yellowstone. Both were unsettling experiences and not ones I wish to repeat. A different encounter holds the place as perhaps the most exciting and disturbing incident, which demonstrates the wisdom of preparedness and taking reasonable precautions.

Late one summer I was in the middle of a solo backpacking trip in a wilderness area with a healthy grizzly bear population. From a base camp near a clear creek in a lovely mountain basin, I went on a day hike to explore the area's impressive cliffs and tall peaks. Among other precautions, two items hung prominently from the belt of my small fanny pack: a canister of bear spray and an aluminum soda can filled with pebbles. The former requires little explanation, while the latter serves as a noisemaker on the trail. When shaken, which happened every 50 to 100 yards, the can makes a useful unnatural sound effectively alerting any bruin to the approach of this skinny and nonthreatening human.

By late morning, on the way down a forest trail paralleling a small creek, I heard an unusual sound: a fairly high-pitched grunting and moaning noise that was clearly coming from a large, distressed animal. My first thought was of the stray cattle I had seen, and perhaps one of them had somehow gotten injured. Still rattling my soda can, I rounded a corner and the mystery of the noise was rapidly and frighteningly solved. The tableau I witnessed involved a cow elk, downed near the small creek about 35 or 40 yards below my location. She wasn't dead, but she was understandably distressed, because feeding on this still-living elk was the huge and truly magnificent mass of rippling muscles and glistening fur on a sow grizzly bear. Happily feeding along with mama bear were two equally spectacular yearling cubs. None of the participants in this little drama had heard or anticipated my arrival due to the background noise of the creek, not to mention the continuous loud wailing of the doomed elk.

Unfortunately, the lack of attention coming my way lasted only a few brief moments, as very soon momma bear locked eyes on me and quickly lost interest in her meal. None of the participants in this scene seemed very happy about the turn of events. The elk kept wailing in pain and distress. The startled cubs let out loud alarm grunts, abandoning their protein feast and scampering up the hillside on the other side of the creek. Second only to me, momma bear seemed the most upset, loudly huffing, looking me straight in the eye, and then taking two rapid steps uphill in my direction.

Despite being reasonably knowledgeable and cautious, I faced a situation that included several elements of a bear encounter that every expert says to avoid. I was hiking alone—strike one. In front of me, and way too close, was a grizzly bear startled by my sudden appearance—strike two. The bear was a healthy sow with nearby cubs to protect—strike three. And she was protecting a food source from possible competition—strike four.

To improve my odds of not being called "out," I was frantically pulling out my can of bear spray, releasing the safety with my thumb, and accurately aiming in the right direction. Fortunately, I never had to use the spray, but had the bear continued with her charge I am reasonably certain it *probably* would have been in time and done the trick. In any event, the bear halted her charge, stopped short, uttered a loud growl, glanced around to make sure her cubs were safely away, and then ran up the hillside after them. Subsequently, stoked with adrenaline, I managed to complete the last 7 miles of my day hike in what must have been record time.

Although a fear of grizzly bears is certainly not an adequate reason to avoid hiking in spectacular places such as Glacier or Yellowstone, being prepared and knowing what you're doing are still very wise. Before a trip, be sure to practice using bear spray to gain confidence in its use. While hiking, remain alert for possibly dangerous situations, such as when a creek is masking the sounds of your approach. And, most of all, know what *not* to do. For example, in my situation, foolishly running from the mama bear almost certainly would have triggered her prey drive to kick in and chase me. Additionally, running away would have made getting out the bear spray and aiming in the right direction effectively impossible. With a little knowledge and practice, your trip to the northern Rockies will be both safer and probably a lot more fun. After all, safely seeing a grizzly bear in the wild is a remarkable and exhilarating experience. One of the reasons most of us visit the backcountry is to enjoy the sight of such magnificent animals in their native habitat. Hopefully, your bear will be walking peacefully through a meadow on the other side of a canyon. But just in case he or she is a bit too close, a little knowledge, luck, and, of course, bear spray, go a long way toward preventing an untimely end.—**Doug**

Glacier National Park

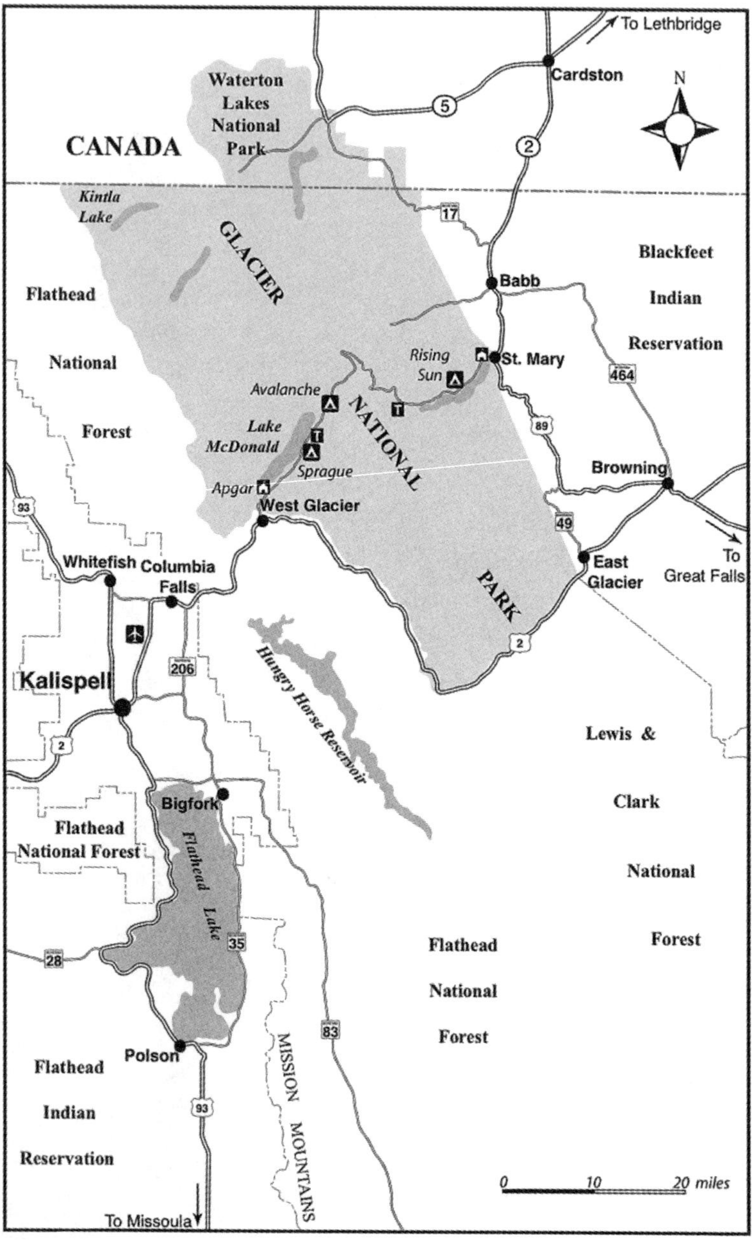

Gunsight Pass Traverse Location Map

TRIP 2
Gunsight Pass Traverse

This across-the-divide traverse unquestionably ranks at or near the top of the list for classic hikes in Glacier National Park. Gift wrapped in one stunning package, this trip includes towering waterfalls, sublime mountain scenery, spectacular lakes, large glaciers, plenty of wildlife, abundant wildflowers, and view-packed ridges and passes—all the characteristics that makes Glacier so special in one magnificent and relatively short hike. The bare bones of the trip could be done in a single very long day, but that would require walking very fast and skipping some tremendous side trips that really should not be missed. I recommend a minimum of three days to adequately explore the area. Be sure to make reservations well in advance, since this trip is deservedly popular.

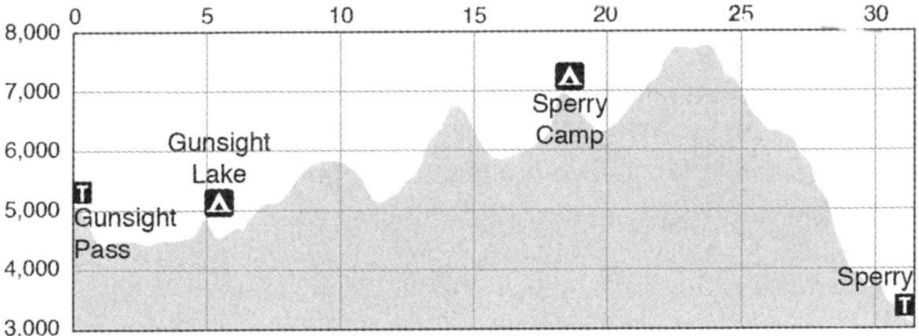

Gunsight Pass Traverse Profile

Days: 3–4

Distance: 32.3 miles (including the best side trips)

Type: Shuttle (relatively easy with the park's free shuttle buses)

Scenery: 10

Solitude: 3

Technical Difficulty: 4

Physical Difficulty: 7

Elevation Gain/Loss: +6,200'/–8,300' (including side trips)

Season: Late July to mid-October

Best: August and early September

Map: Trails Illustrated: *Glacier-Waterton Lakes National Parks*

Resources: *Glacier-Waterton International Peace Park*, by Vicky Spring

Contact: Glacier National Park
PO Box 128
West Glacier, MT 59936
406-888-7800

Permits: All advanced reservations for backpacking in Glacier National Park are made online at www.pay.gov. Starting in 2019, all reservations submitted on March 15 (opening day) will be processed in random order in a "modified lottery" system. Processing reservations received on March 16 or later is done on a first-come, first-served basis, so you should apply as soon as possible to increase your odds of acceptance. Beginning at 8 AM on March 15 (March 1 for large groups of 9–12), requests can be made up to seven days before the day of departure. A charge of $40 (credit card or PayPal) per reservation is levied for each application, $30 of which is refundable if your request cannot be filled. Applicants will be notified by email, which may take up to a month due to the typical high volume of requests. For more information, consult the park's website.

Without a reserved permit you must get in line *very early* (usually by 5 AM or so of the day *before* your trip is to begin) and pray for a first-come, first-served permit. Even for the earliest risers, however, the odds aren't good, so be very flexible about where you want to go, where you want to camp, how many miles you are willing to travel per day, and how many days you can stay for your trip.

Regulations: Along park trails, camping is only allowed at designated campsites. Group size is limited to a maximum of twelve persons.

Visitors are required to properly store all food and other items away from bears *at all times*, even if you are only gone for a few minutes.

Nearest Campground: Sprague Creek Campground—1 mile from exit trailhead

Nearest Airport: Glacier Park International Airport, near Kalispell (GPI or KFCA)—35 miles

Nearest Outdoor Retailer: Rocky Mountain Outfitter—57 miles
135 Main Street
Kalispell, MT 59901
406-752-2446

Outfitter: Glacier Guides and Montana Rafting Company
11970 Highway 2 East
PO Box 330
West Glacier, MT 59936
800-521-7238
www.glacierguides.com

Transportation Logistics: The park operates a free shuttle service over Going to the Sun Road ideally suited for backpackers.

Backcountry Logistics: (GB, Sn, W) Glacier National Park is grizzly bear country. Although rare, attacks do occur and people occasionally get killed. Properly store all food and other odorous items away from the bruins and well away from your tent. All official campsites have bear poles or wires for hanging your food and designated cooking areas—use them! Although not prohibited, solo travel is not recommended. Make noise while you hike, so bears are not surprised by your arrival (a potentially dangerous situation). *Never* approach a bear, especially not a sow with cubs. Stay away from any carcasses you encounter, as bears often feed on these and aggressively protect them from intruders. Always check with park rangers about recent bear activity and any closures due to bear encounters. Finally, you should carry bear spray, know how and when to use it, and keep it readily available.

Lingering snowfields often cover the trail on steep, north-facing slopes well into late July or even early August. These can be dangerously icy, and, as a result, parts of this trail may be hazardous before late summer.

Attractions and Amenities: For tourist-oriented items (T-shirts, snacks, drinks, etc.) the nearest services are at Apgar Village in the park at the southwest end of Lake McDonald. The nearest motels, restaurants, and similar services are in the small tourist-oriented community of West Glacier. Along US Highway 2 on the way to West Glacier from Kalispell, stopping at the **Huckleberry Patch** outside of the town of Hungry Horse is well worth the time. This cannery for wild huckleberries has a gift shop and everything you could want in the way of huckleberry treats (ice cream, pies, cookies, etc.). For a better-than-average pizza place after your trip, try **Glacier Grill and Pizza** in the town of Coram right along Highway 2.

Directions to Trailhead: The easiest way to handle the transportation is to leave a vehicle at the exit Sperry trailhead and then take the free park shuttle bus to the starting Gunsight Pass trailhead. From West Glacier, turn east off US Highway 2 into Glacier National Park, drive 2 miles to a four-way junction, then turn right on Going-to-the-Sun Road and proceed 9 miles to the Sperry trailhead directly opposite the turnoff to Lake McDonald Lodge. Be sure to arrive early in the morning, since finding a parking spot here can be very difficult. Walk a few yards to the bus stop and board one of the frequent park shuttle buses that will take you all the way to Logan Pass. From there, transfer to an east side shuttle bus and ride to the stop for Jackson Glacier Overlook / Gunsight Pass trailhead.

Glacier National Park without Glaciers?

Ancient glaciers, on a scale many thousands of times larger than any in Montana today, were responsible for carving the spectacular canyons, cirques, ridgelines, and other impressive features of what is now, appropriately named, Glacier National Park. Those glaciers receded around 12,000 years ago with the end of the last great Ice Age. Evidence indicates that much smaller alpine glaciers probably started forming here around 7,000 years ago, undergoing periodic advances and retreats depending on snowfall amounts and temperatures. These glaciers reached their maximum extent around AD 1850, just a little over a century and a half ago, following a 450-year period known as the Little Ice Age. At that time the area that would become Glacier National Park had about 150 glaciers of 25 acres or more. Today there are only twenty-five glaciers left in the park, and those that remain are receding at historically rapid rates. A simple comparison of old photographs to what is seen today shows dramatic decreases in the size of virtually all glaciers in the park. The computer models don't agree, but some indicate that *all* of the glaciers will be gone within a few decades. The two big questions that come to mind are: Why? and So what?

The "why" question is complicated by everything from scientific unknowns to, of all things, politics. In one respect, the answer is simple. The long-term climate has changed since the Little Ice Age. Put simply, the winter snowfall has not been adequate to keep up with summer melting, so the glaciers are getting smaller. The best available data indicate that the mean annual temperature in the area around Glacier National Park has increased by about 2.4 °F (1.33 °C) since 1900, which is almost twice the average increase in temperatures worldwide. At the same time, though the average annual precipitation in the area has increased by about 10 percent, a larger percentage of that precipitation is falling as rain rather than as snow, so the snowpack has not been adequate to compensate for the melting during the warmer summer months. What is going on at Glacier is symptomatic of what is happening worldwide, as virtually all alpine glaciers on the planet have been decreasing in recent decades.

The answer to the larger "why" question is enmeshed in the whole "global warming" or "climate change" debate and the long-term impact of human activity on the climate. Most scientists agree that while the initial retreat of glaciers starting around 1860 was the result of natural climate variation, the more recent temperature increases and their impact on glaciers are at least partly the result of human activity.

But that still leaves the question of So what? After all, Glacier National Park will remain stunningly beautiful whether there are any actual glaciers here or not. Although true, this is a question that goes well beyond simple aesthetics. Glaciers play a role here that is more important than simply looking good in photographs. For example, the park's glaciers act as a water "bank" providing a steady source of meltwater to the area's streams in late summer once the winter's snowpack is gone. Without the glaciers, the water flow, especially in late summer, will be significantly reduced and water temperatures will be higher, potentially leading to the extinction of temperature-sensitive aquatic plants and animals. This, in turn, disrupts the entire aquatic food chain and the numerous land-based critters upon which they rely. Bull trout are an example of an already threatened species whose habitat would be dramatically altered if the glaciers went away.

As a showpiece for the impacts of climate change, and because of the importance of ice to the place's character, Glacier National Park is serving as an open-air scientific laboratory for the study of glaciers and their possible disappearance. Since 1991, the Northern Rocky Mountain Science Center and the United States Geologic Survey have been conducting research, monitoring glacial retreat, and trying to determine not only the effects of climate change on the park's glaciers, but also the possible effects of warming temperatures on forest fires, mountain pine beetle infestations, regional water supplies, and local wildlife. Detailed studies continue at Sperry Glacier and other places to determine the links between local climate and glacial retreat.

As you hike the trails in this grandest of all the American West's mountain parks, you will probably notice that the preserve's relatively few remaining glaciers are clearly in retreat. They are rapidly pulling back from the rocky moraines that abutted the ice just a few years ago, and are leaving ever-smaller patches of ice on the hillsides in late summer. Harder to notice are the long-term impacts of this much-less-icy environment on the region's diverse flora and fauna. Hikers in the not-too-distant future may well experience an even more noticeably different place. Perhaps this will be a park, while still dramatically scenic, whose namesake glaciers are a thing of the past.

Trip Description: From the east end of the parking area (see map of Gunsight Pass Traverse [East]) the trail descends about 20 yards to a junction, where you go left and rapidly lose elevation through a relatively lush coniferous forest of firs and pines. At just under 1.3 miles, you'll see pretty little Deadwood Falls on the right, dropping through a twisting slot canyon of red-tinged rock. Shortly beyond this falls is a junction.

Go right and cross a swinging bridge over Reynolds Creek to a junction with the spur trail to Reynolds Creek Camp on your left. Keep straight, and begin a gentle climb with plenty of small ups and downs that continues all the way to Gunsight Lake. The trail is brushy on the way through forest and around the northeast side of a large marshy area and shimmering Mirror Pond. This wet meadow along the upper reaches of the Saint Mary River provides excellent views of Fusillade Mountain, Mount Jackson, and other nearby peaks. This is also a good place to look for moose, which often hang out in this soggy environment.

Side Trip to Florence Falls

At 4 miles you come to a junction with the side trail to Florence Falls. The 0.6-mile one-way trail is brushy but the views of the high, veil-like falls at trail's end is well worth the extra walk.

The main trail goes straight at the Florence Falls junction and immediately crosses a log bridge over an unnamed creek. The trail then travels gently through forest before traversing a mostly open hillside. This open slope offers superb views to the south of Blackfoot Mountain and large Blackfoot Glacier. At a little over 6 miles, the grade levels out as you complete the last 0.2-mile to Gunsight Lake. Fed by tall, streaking waterfalls, this large lake is wildly scenic, with excellent views across the water to the west of the snowfields and small glaciers on rugged Gunsight Mountain. A comfortable and very scenic designated camp near the eastern shore provides an ideal overnight stop for your first night on the trail.

From the campground turnoff, the trail takes you to a swinging bridge over the lake's outlet and reaches a junction immediately on the other side.

Side Trip to Jackson Glacier Viewpoint

The Jackson Glacier Trail goes left at the bridge junction and makes a steep ascent of a brushy hillside. At the top of this climb, the trail goes up and down across an open hillside from which there are excellent views looking south toward Blackfoot and Jackson Glaciers. This open slope is also home to an abundance of huckleberry bushes, which attract large numbers of grizzly bears during the August ripening time—make plenty of noise and have the bear spray handy. Defined tread peters out in this open country at about 1.8 miles from Gunsight Lake, but making your way over the open terrain to Jackson Glacier and beyond is not difficult. When the time comes, retrace your steps to the junction.

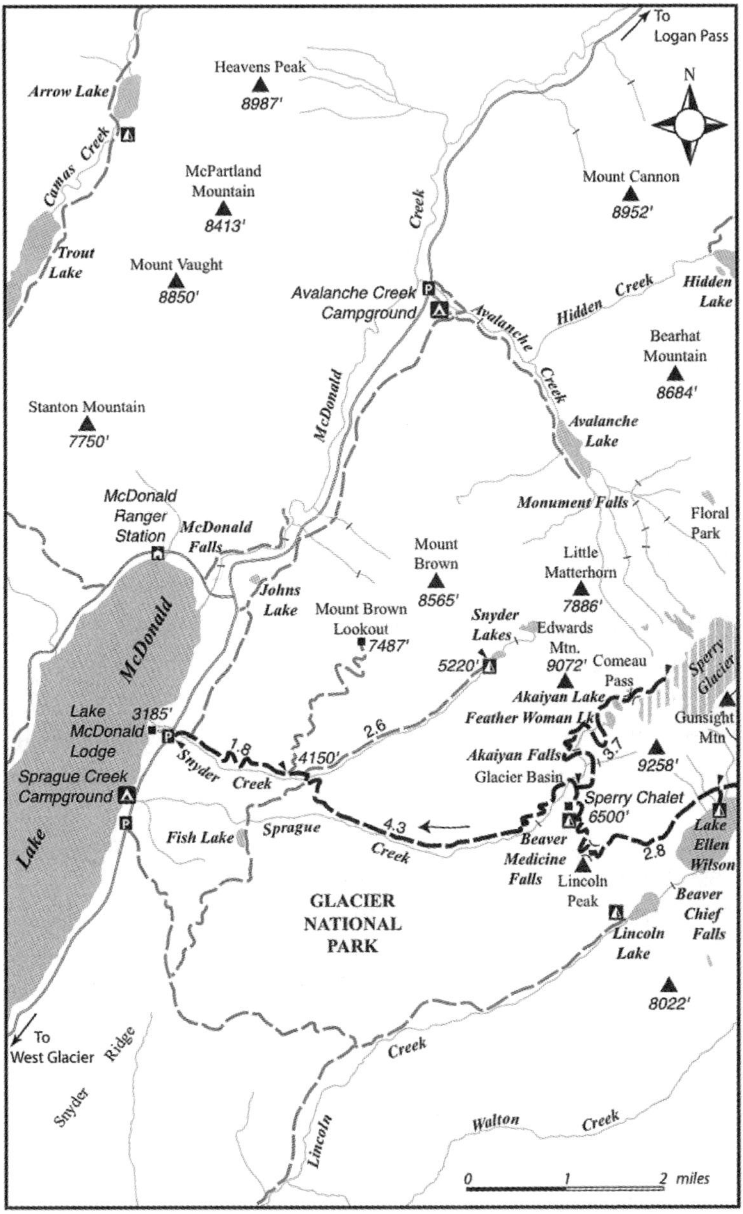

Gunsight Pass Traverse (West)

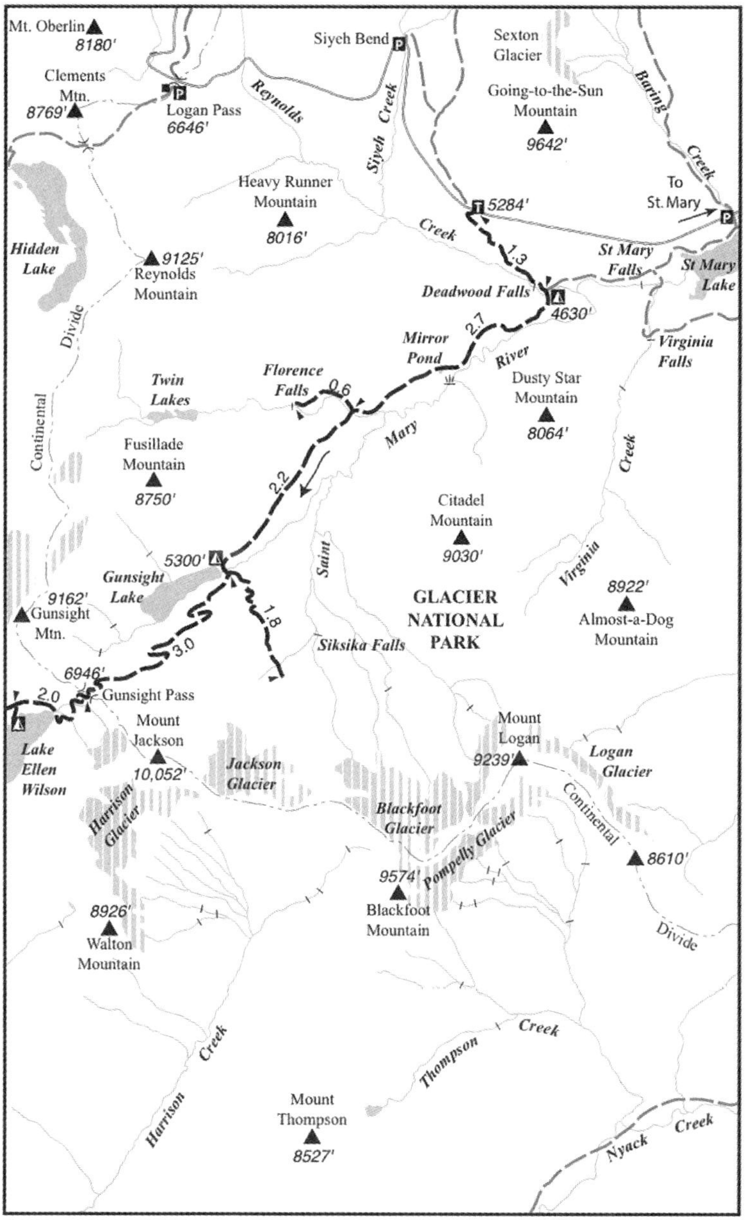

Gunsight Pass Traverse (East)

From the junction beside Gunsight Lake, take the right fork and begin the long, steady climb to Gunsight Pass. The trail ascends a brushy hillside past a series of stunning viewpoints looking north to Gunsight Lake and Mountain. A pair of switchbacks leads to a section of trail blasted out of a north-facing cliff face, which often holds dangerously steep and icy snowfields until early August (when you pick up your permit, ask about current conditions). Six irregularly spaced switchbacks wind up increasingly scenic slopes all the way to Gunsight Pass, where you'll find a small stone shelter and superb views to the west down to sprawling Lake Ellen Wilson. A small herd of surprisingly tame mountain goats often hangs out around Gunsight Pass. The goats are usually easily photographed, but avoid getting too close, as these muscular animals with sharp horns may behave unpredictably.

The trail descends a series of short switchbacks not quite all the way down to Lake Ellen Wilson, then loops to the north and gradually climbs across the hillside well above the shore of this very deep lake (see map of Gunsight Pass Traverse [West]). A signed spur trail drops a few hundred feet to a designated campsite on the lake's shore. Grizzly bears are frequently seen near the lake and on the slopes above.

The main trail remains well above the lake, crossing a mostly open hillside with jaw-dropping views of the lake and tall Mount Jackson. After passing a final lake viewpoint, make an up-and-down traverse on a rocky shelf, from where you have excellent views of Beaver Chief Falls. Even though you never get very close, this 1,300-foot monster waterfall ranks as one of the highest in the American Rockies and is quite a sight. At the end of the rocky traverse, the trail ascends three switchbacks to a high saddle on the shoulder of Lincoln Peak.

For the next mile the route leads down a series of switchbacks with nice views to the west of Lake McDonald and north to the looming mass of Edwards Mountain. At the bottom of the switchbacks is a signed junction with the side trail to the Sperry backpacker's camp. A small pond nearby provides campers with water and excellent views across the water to Edwards Mountain. Just 0.25 mile past this camp is the site of Sperry Chalet, a historic log-and-stone structure. This entire area was devastated by large fires in 2017, including, sadly, burning down the lovely old chalet. Plans call for the facility to be rebuilt in its original style by 2021 or so, but for now all you see are blackened snags nearby and the otherwise unchanged nice views of the surrounding mountains.

The trail loops around the right side of the chalet location before descending for about 0.2 mile to a junction.

Side Trip to Sperry Glacier

The 3.7-mile one-way trail to Sperry Glacier is the final not-to-be-missed side trip along this route. Turn right at the junction below Sperry Chalet and make an uphill traverse on a talus slope above Glacier Basin. The trail passes beneath two tall and wispy waterfalls (Akaiyan and Feather Woman), then switchbacks uphill past Feather Woman and Akaiyau Lakes to tiny Gem Lake at Comeau Pass. The path then goes slightly downhill to reach Observation Point, which sits just above the rocky basin and small lakes near the lower end of large Sperry Glacier, offering outstanding views of the relatively rapidly melting glacier and over to the steep northwest face of Gunsight Mountain.

To complete the traverse, turn west at the junction following the Sperry Trail on a descent through Glacier Basin to a bridge over small Sprague Creek. Still traveling through burned areas, the trail then loses elevation on the way to a smaller lower basin before descending six switchbacks to an open slope with a good view of tall Beaver Medicine Falls. From there, the trail heads along the north slope of the deep canyon carved by Sprague Creek. After about a mile, follow the trail bending away from the creek and traverse over to a junction beside Snyder Creek.

Go right, cross the creek on a bridge, and then climb briefly to a second junction, this time with the trail to Snyder Lakes. Keep left, and walk a little under 0.1 mile to another junction, this time with the trail to Mount Brown Lookout.

Continue straight ahead from the junction, and for the last 1.8 miles walk downhill through partially burned forest, passing one particularly nice viewpoint of huge Lake McDonald along the way. At the bottom of the descent, go straight at a junction with Johns Lake Trail and then pass a pair of side trails to a horse-outfitting facility before ending at the Sperry trailhead.

Possible Itinerary

	Camps and Side Trips	Miles	Elevation Gain
Day 1	Gunsight Pass TH to Gunsight Lake	6.2	+700/−700
	Side trip to Florence Falls	1.2	+150/−150
Day 2	*Side trip to Jackson Glacier*	3.6	+900/−900
	Sperry Camp	7.6	+2,700/−1,350
Day 3	*Side trip to Sperry Glacier*	7.4	+1,700/−1,700
	Out to Sperry TH	6.3	+50/−3,500

Giving Back

Glacier National Park Conservancy: WWW.GLACIERCONSERVANCY.ORG

The Mountain Goat (Oreamnos Americanus)

I love pretty much any wildlife (except mosquitoes), but a long-standing affinity for the taller and more rugged landforms of our continent goes a long way toward explaining why my favorite animal is the North American mountain goat. This hardy white-furred creature is found almost exclusively in the highest and most remote reaches of our western mountains. If you're in their preferred habitat and carefully scan a crag or inaccessible cliff, that small moving "snowfield" is, more often than not, a mountain goat gamboling across some ridiculously steep rock face using remarkable dexterity and cushiony hooves to travel in places where other animals fear to tread. Surviving on alpine grasses, sedges and lichens, and with little fear of predators (mountain lions, wolves, and bears generally lack the ability to reach the places where the goats live), these denizens of the heights live out their lives in a landscape filled with lofty peaks and desolate crags. Anywhere a mountain goat chooses to live is usually the type of landscape and scenery that appeals to mountain-loving backpackers.

Mountain goats are the semiofficial symbol of Glacier National Park. The park is near the heart of the species' range, and the preserve's famously steep

Hikers and Mountain Goats at Gunsight Pass

and rugged terrain offers ideal habitat. Seeing the animals while backpacking on the park's wilderness trails and even at popular roadside locations such as Logan Pass is quite common.

One of Glacier's best areas for spotting mountain goats is along the Gunsight Pass Traverse. Rare is the hiker who fails to encounter at least a few of the animals perched on rocks overlooking the trail, or poking their shaggy heads around corners to check you out. They have even been known to wander into campsites at night hoping to chew on sweaty pack straps or boots in search of salt.

One summer while I happily trudged my way up the trail from Gunsight Lake, the magnificent scenery filling the sky in all directions was, as usual, a delight. I was fortunate enough to have seen deer, moose, a golden eagle, and two grizzly bears so far on my hike, but couldn't help feel disappointment at failing to spy any mountain goats. So, as I rounded the final corner to the pass, a broad smile came to my face upon the sight of a small herd of these nimble ungulates hanging around the stone shelter at the divide. They weren't the only animals in residence, as there were also several people nearby eating lunch or exploring the surroundings. The two species seemed to be perfectly content with one another, as they all walked around and mingled like old pals at a high school reunion.

As I approached the pass, two goats posed on a rock just a couple or yards above the trail. Elsewhere, an old billy simply lay smack down in the middle of the path, forcing me to carefully scramble around the rocks above while he casually studied my behavior. I didn't want to get too close, because even though these particular animals were clearly habituated to people, mountain goats can still be dangerous. They are wild, powerfully built, and in possession of sharp, intimidating horns. In 2010, an exceptionally aggressive mountain goat in Washington's Olympic National Park attacked and killed a hiker. Reportedly, this large billy stood over the hiker's body for more than an hour, barring access to other hikers and denying help to the victim. So, cautiously skirting around the animals, I found a rock to sit on, happily ate lunch, took plenty of photos of the scenery (and especially of the goats), and generally had a great time. After an hour or so of this mountain revelry, reshouldering my pack and finally getting on my way were a bit bittersweet, but I was never more delighted in my preferred landscape and choice of outdoor activity.–**Doug**

Crazy Mountains
Custer Gallatin National Forest

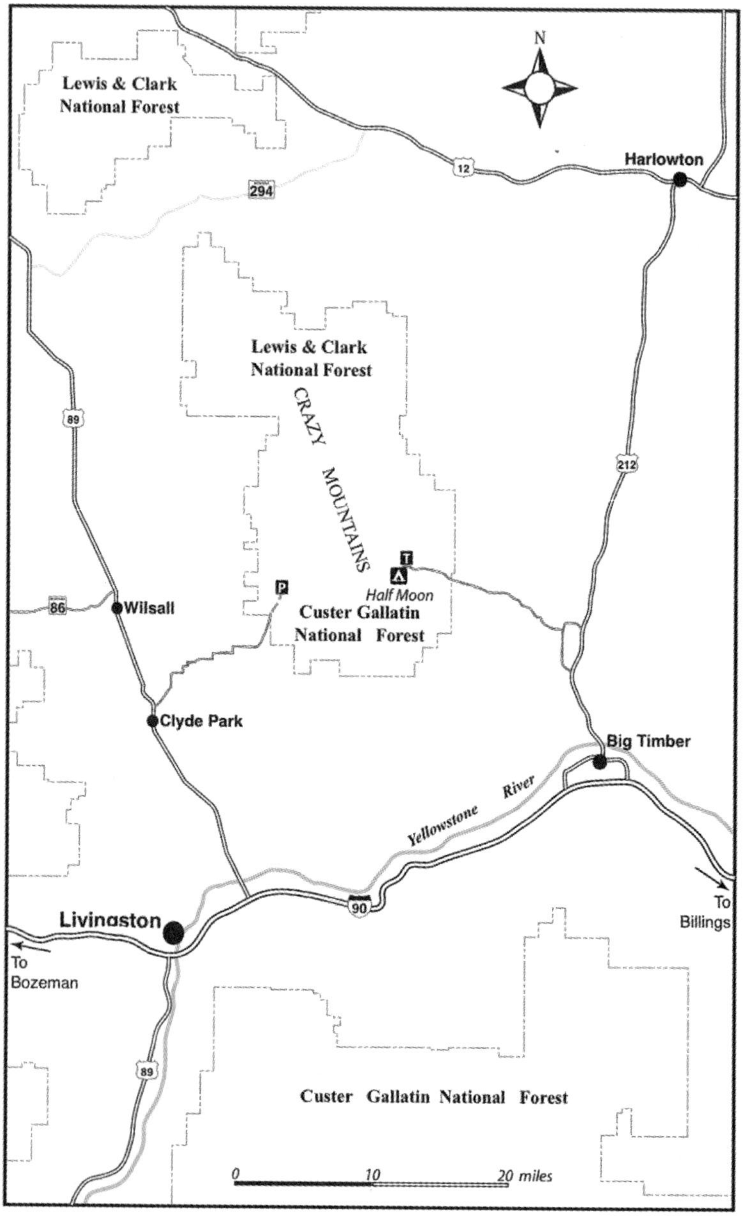

Crazy Mountains Traverse Location Map

TRIP 3

Crazy Mountains Traverse

Far trails await me; valleys vast and still,
Vistas undreamed of, canon-guarded streams,
Lowland and range, fair meadow, flower-girt hill,
Forests enchanted, filled with magic dreams.

—HENRY HERBERT KNIBBS, WRITER AND COWBOY POET

Rising precipitously out of the rolling plains of eastern Montana, the Crazy Mountains are an anomalous cluster of dramatic peaks that, despite their unexpected location, offer all the pleasures of hiking in the high mountains. When you drive from the east across the vast flat expanses of the Dakotas and eastern Montana, these towering granite peaks are your first introduction to "real" mountains. And real mountains they certainly are, because even though surrounded by grasslands, this island range offers abundant mountain delights, including vast expanses of dense coniferous forests, expansive mountain meadows carpeted with wildflowers, icy lakes tucked away in dramatic cirques, summits topping 11,000 feet, and even a couple of tiny remnant glaciers. Not surprisingly, the scenery is tremendous—so good that these mountains were prominently featured as backdrops to such popular movies as *The Horse Whisperer* and *A River Runs Through It.* So don't make the mistake of driving past these first mountains on the assumption that more and better ones are yet to come. The Crazies are equal

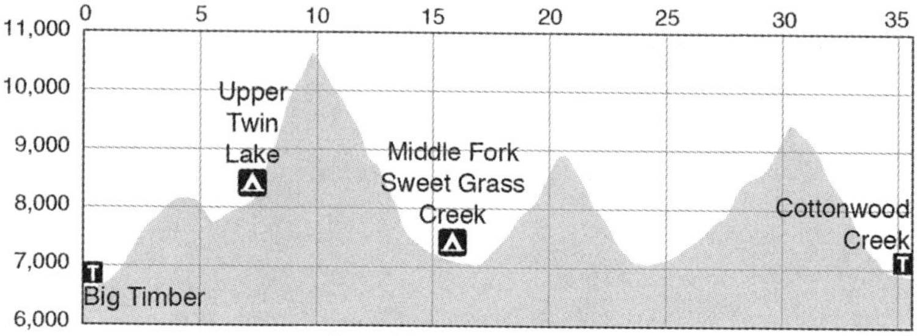

Crazy Mountains Traverse Profile

to anything you'll encounter later in your travels, and their lightly used trails merit at least a few days (or weeks) of exploring.

The only significant downside of hiking here is the checkerboard ownership of private and public lands, the result of railroad land grants in the nineteenth century. Generally, the public is allowed unfettered access to hike the official trails, but camping is sometimes problematic, as you technically need landowner permission to set up a tent on tracts of private land. Check the map carefully to ensure that where you want to spend the night is a legal location.

Days: 3–5

Distance: 35.7 miles (including best side trips)

Type: Shuttle

Scenery: 8

Solitude: 7

Technical Difficulty: 6

Physical Difficulty: 7

Elevation Gain/Loss: +9,850'/–9,500' (including best side trips)

Season: July to October

Best: Mid-July through early August

Map: Beartooth Publishing: *Crazy Mountains*

Resources: *Railroaded*, by Richard White

Contact: Custer Gallatin National Forest
Yellowstone Ranger District
5242 Highway 89 South
Livingston, MT 59047
406-222-1892

Permits: No permits are required.

Regulations: Campfires not allowed within 0.25 mile of Blue Lake and Twin Lakes. Camping on private land along the route is only allowed by permission of the landowner.

Nearest Campground: Half Moon Campground—0.3 mile

Nearest Airport: Bozeman Yellowstone International Airport (BZN)—95 miles (from the starting trailhead)
Billings Logan International Airport (BIL)—109 miles

Nearest Outdoor Retailer: Bob Wards Sporting Goods—35 miles
3011 Max Avenue
Bozeman, MT 59715
406-586-4381

Northern Lights Trading Company—35 miles
83 Rowland Road
Bozeman, MT 59718
406-586-6029

REI—36 miles
2220 Tschache Street
Bozeman, MT 59718
406-587-1938

Outfitters: None

Transportation Logistics: There are no public transportation options, so you must have your own vehicles. Access to the western (exit) trailhead requires particularly careful driving on a rough road.

Attractions and Amenities: Home of Montana State University, Bozeman is a fair-size city by Montana standards, where travelers will find all of the basic necessities. On the campus of MSU is the superb **Museum of the Rockies**, which includes everything from world-class dinosaur exhibits (one of the largest collections of dinosaur fossils in the world—including a T. rex), to fascinating history displays, and even a planetarium laser show. Regularly appearing on various top-ten lists of great outdoor towns, Bozeman caters to a wide variety of recreationists. Along with the outdoor retailers mentioned above, craft breweries and bistros are plentiful. A half hour to the east on I-90, the smaller town of Livingston also accommodates tourists and outfits the outdoor crowd. During summer, this little burg offers a variety of art- and music-oriented festivals.

Big Timber is a small city with an economy oriented toward local ranchers, with very little for the typical tourist. You will find a limited assortment of motels and restaurants with adequate facilities and food, but there's nothing that really stands out above the mundane.

To visit an active prairie dog town, stop at the **Greycliff Prairie Dog Town State Park** right along Interstate 90 just 10 miles east of Big Timber. The "dogs" here are abundant, easy to see, and fun to watch.

Backcountry Logistics: (GB, BB, A, St, L) Black bears are common and a few wandering grizzly bears have been reported in these mountains, so camp and act accordingly. There are a couple of creek fords that must be negotiated, but, while cold, they are rarely more than knee deep.

Directions to Trailhead: From Bozeman, drive 31 miles east on Interstate 90 to exit 340 a few miles east of Livingston.

To leave a car at the exit trailhead, go 15.5 miles north on US Highway 89 to a junction just north of the small town of Clyde Park. Go right on gravel Cottonwood Bench Road, proceed 3 miles, and then go right at a junction, remaining on Cottonwood Bench Road. After another 3.6 miles, turn left onto Upper Cottonwood Road and keep right 0.5 mile later to stay on the main road. This road gradually gets rougher, but is still passable by passenger cars. After 4.7 miles, you bear right at a fork, following signs to Cottonwood Creek and drive another 3.3 miles to a gate at the end of the road. These last 2 miles are very rocky and rough, so drive carefully.

To reach the starting trailhead, return to Interstate 90 and drive 27 miles east to exit 367 for Big Timber. Take the access road into and through town until you're heading north on US Highway 191. At 11.5 miles from Big Timber turn left (west) on gravel Wormser Loop Road (also known as County Road 25), following signs to Big Timber Canyon. Drive 2 miles then turn right onto a road that eventually becomes Forest Road 197. This road is rutted and rather rough but is maintained for passenger cars. At one point you'll cross private land near a ranch where you'll have to get out to open a gate (be sure to close it behind you). At 13.5 miles from the last junction is the signed trailhead on the right just before the road curves to the left and enters Half Moon Campground.

The Curious Case of Checkerboard Ownership in the West

When hiking in the Crazy Mountains, one can't help but notice the confusing and odd pattern of land ownership found here. Why design a system of mismatched alternating sections of ownership rather than having logically adjoining blocks of property? Such a hodgepodge pattern forces hikers to constantly go in and out of public land and continuously check their maps to determine whether or not camping at a particular spot is indeed legal. The problem is common in the American West, and actually has an interesting history.

On July 1, 1862, President Abraham Lincoln signed into law the Pacific Railroad Act. During this period, Lincoln and the rest of the government had more pressing business on their minds—the Civil War. Keeping the country from being torn apart was occupying most of their time and attention.

By 1862 the vast majority of Americans believed the country needed a railroad linking the heavily settled lands of the east with the distant states and territories of the west for a variety of factors. Just getting to California was incredibly difficult, taking five or six months of grueling and extremely dangerous travel, either over land or by sailing around the tip of South America. A legitimate concern during the war was keeping California and the rest of the West loyal to the Union. Gold had recently been discovered in California only a little over a decade before, and a means to allow easier migration to the mines was needed; the railroad would provide the means to cheaply and quickly ship much-needed supplies to the mines (and farms) in the West, and transport the minerals and other western products back to eastern markets. Also, getting supplies to troops in the West to discourage other countries from taking advantage of the Civil War by invading these areas was a military necessity.

A major problem with building a transcontinental railroad was that the federal government lacked the resources to spare on such an enormous project, as both a sizable amount of money and available manpower were being funneled into the war effort. Constructing a transcontinental railroad would probably be the largest, most complicated, and most expensive engineering project since erection of the Great Wall of China. In the middle of a war, the government simply did not possess the cash or the willingness to go into enormous debt to cover the cost. And private industry didn't have the money either. However, the one resource the government did have was seemingly limitless amounts of undeveloped land, which had been acquired through the Louisiana Purchase from France and the conquest of Mexico after the Mexican American War.

This confluence of circumstances led to the idea that the government would partially back bonds for the railroad companies and would also cede them land, which allowed them to sell these bonds and the land to help finance the project. In a series of laws and agreements covering numerous railroad lines stretching from 1850 to 1871, the government ended up giving some 175 million acres of land to the railroads, which equals an area larger than the state of Texas, or over 10 percent of the landmass of the United States!

Incredibly complicated legislation resulted in a series of laws with countless changes along the way. The land transfer generally provided the railroad a right of way of 200 feet on either side of the line. In addition, they received 10 or more square miles of federal land for every mile of rail built. However, the land wasn't given in conveniently contiguous blocks, but rather in alternating one-square-mile sections up to 20 miles on either side of the track. The federal government retained ownership of the other alternating sections. As the lines were built, the hope was that both the railroad and the interspersed government lands would increase in value. Although the desired outcome occurred as advertised, the unintended result was a "checkerboard" pattern of ownership across huge swaths of the American West.

The railroads long ago sold off most of their land to individuals or other corporations, managing to accrue billions of dollars of profits in the process. Meanwhile, the messy land ownership patterns remain with us today, easily seen in places such as Montana's Crazy Mountains. The checkerboard ownership of land makes management of publicly owned parcels extremely difficult, diminishes property values for the private landowners due to the disconnected nature of their holdings, creates significant difficulties for wildlife when interlocking fences block logical migration corridors, and makes preservation efforts extremely difficult when faced with a range of landowners each with competing interests. The only realistic way to rectify these problems is through outright purchase of important parcels or through complicated land exchanges.

With the benefit of hindsight, looking back and saying this whole scheme was corporate largesse on an unprecedented scale and decrying the foolishness of the lawmakers for giving away so much to private industry is easy. Moderns may see this as a "sweetheart" deal of ridiculous proportions. However, such a viewpoint isn't quite fair, as in the 1860s the obstacles to building a transcontinental railroad were so enormous, most people didn't even consider the idea possible. No such railroad had ever been attempted anywhere else in the world. Native Americans still lived throughout the American West and they were understandably angry with travelers traipsing through their traditional lands, let alone constructing a railroad. Engineers would have to overcome the difficulties of building a rail line over the precipitous Rocky and Sierra Nevada Mountain ranges, as well as across vast stretches of barren desert without available food, water, and materials. And even if these obstacles could be overcome, the project would be enormously expensive and would take many years to complete before investors could even begin to hope to make a profit.

Without modern mechanized equipment, all of the enormous amounts of labor—spanning major rivers with bridges of unprecedented length, digging tunnels thousands of feet long through solid granite, cutting through mountain passes, and filling huge chasms with rock—all had to be done by hand. Workers would have to chip away with picks and shovels, moving millions of tons of rock with nothing but wheelbarrows and horse-drawn carts.

Finally, it is important to remember that all of this land the railroad companies were being given was virtually worthless at the time. As one writer points out, if property taxes had existed then, accountants would probably have been forced to record most of the land as a liability since it would have cost the companies more than it was worth. The land would only potentially gain in value *if* the railroad could actually be built.

Despite the government-backed bonds, the patriotic fervor to build the rail line, and the enormous, and unprecedented land giveaways, virtually no investors at the time considered the project a good deal. The stock deemed as too risky, history shows that attempting to sell any of it to new investors in order to raise capital was nearly impossible.

Last but not least, as we look back and conveniently judge the supposed folly of these elected officials, keep in mind that the scheme worked. Without the government having to take on enormous amounts of debt, the railroads were built. The nation's unity was assured. And the building of the rail lines became one of the most important factors in turning the United States into the economic powerhouse of the twentieth century.

Trip Description: Following the route of a rocky old road that is now just a wide trail, the route heads west and gently ascends a partly forested hillside above rushing Big Timber Creek (see map of Crazy Mountains Traverse [East]). The dramatic-looking walls on either side of the canyon rise as much as 4,000 feet. Reach a junction at 0.5 mile with the 0.1-mile one-way path veering left (downhill) and leading to Upper Big Timber Falls. This short side trip is well worth the effort, resulting in a nice view of the twisting falls plummeting down a rocky chute in an impressive display of hydropower.

The main trail goes straight at the Upper Big Timber Falls junction and maintains a steady uphill grade beside Big Timber Creek's series of loud cascades and small waterfalls. Near the 1-mile point, you cross the creek on a large bridge, and then walk another mile to another bridged crossing of the boisterous stream. Meadow openings offer nice views of tall Crazy Peak to the south shortly before you reach a signed junction at 2.9 miles.

Side Trip to Blue Lake

To visit the lovely Blue Lake basin, bear left at the junction, soon cross a wooden bridge over Big Timber Creek, and then climb eight irregularly spaced switchbacks across a mostly forested slope. At the top of these switchbacks, the trail passes between a pair of shallow ponds before heading south-southwest over mostly level terrain to some nice campsites between adjoining Granite and Blue Lakes. Even though campfires are prohibited within 0.25 mile of either lake, axe-wielding lawbreakers in search of firewood have trashed the most popular campsites near Blue Lake. Also, the map indicates that the camps at the south end of Granite Lake are on private land and therefore should not be used. Both lakes have fine scenery highlighted by towering Crazy Peak to the southeast.

Adventurous souls can set up a base camp at Blue Lake for further explorations. An easy and obvious social trail heads a short distance northeast to Thunder Lake and Thunder Rapids. For a more challenging trip, make the rewarding off-trail scrambles up to very scenic Druckmiller and Pear Lakes, or all the way to the summit of Crazy Peak.

The traverse route goes straight at the Blue Lake junction, almost immediately passes a small campsite on the left, and then resumes climbing on the old rocky roadbed. After about 0.5 mile, you finally leave the old road for a more pleasant foot trail and climb through forest to Lower Twin Lake. This beautiful lake has a marshy shoreline with poor camping prospects, but with tremendous views across the water to a row of jagged brownish-gray peaks to the west. Morning reflections in the lake's calm waters are especially photogenic.

The trail passes a couple of good campsites along the creek above the lower lake before you reach the shore of Upper Twin Lake. Upper Twin is arguably more scenic than Lower Twin Lake, situated even closer to the row of jagged peaks. Camping is also better here, as the shore is less marshy; these sites are fairly popular, so don't expect solitude. As at Blue Lake, campfires are not allowed within 0.25 mile of either of the Twin Lakes.

Along the northwest shore of Upper Twin Lake, the trail switchbacks away from the water and begins climbing. You'll gain 2,000 feet in the next 1.9 miles, so be prepared for a steep and tiring ascent. There are nearly 100 minor turns and switchbacks in the first 1.5 miles, and the tread is often muddy and/or rocky. After leaving the lake, the forest shade becomes rare but an abundance of views and alpine wildflowers affords fine scenery. Heading for an obvious pass in the ridge to the northwest is not possible due to impassable cliffs, forcing the trail to follow a route climbing almost 500 feet higher to travel over the divide. Once you reach the high point, the tremendous view includes countless tall cliffs, deep canyons, and high peaks in all directions. A reasonably simple scramble route leaves the trail here and takes you northeast for 0.9 mile to the summit of Conical Peak. From this even higher grandstand, the views extend far out over the vast prairies of Montana to the north, east, and west.

The trail now descends more than two-dozen switchbacks (see map of Crazy Mountains Traverse [West]), losing 1,250 feet on the way to starkly beautiful Glacier Lake. This chilly pool is tucked beneath tall peaks and typically has icebergs floating on the surface into late July or

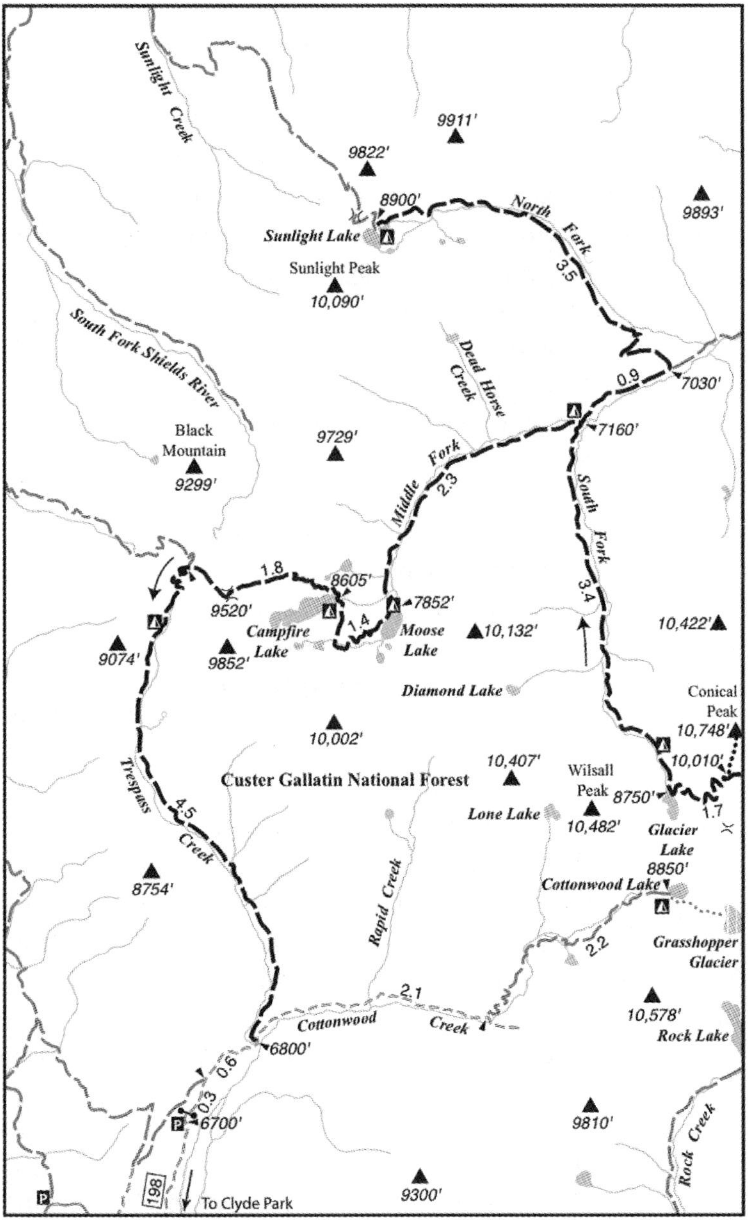

Crazy Mountains Traverse West

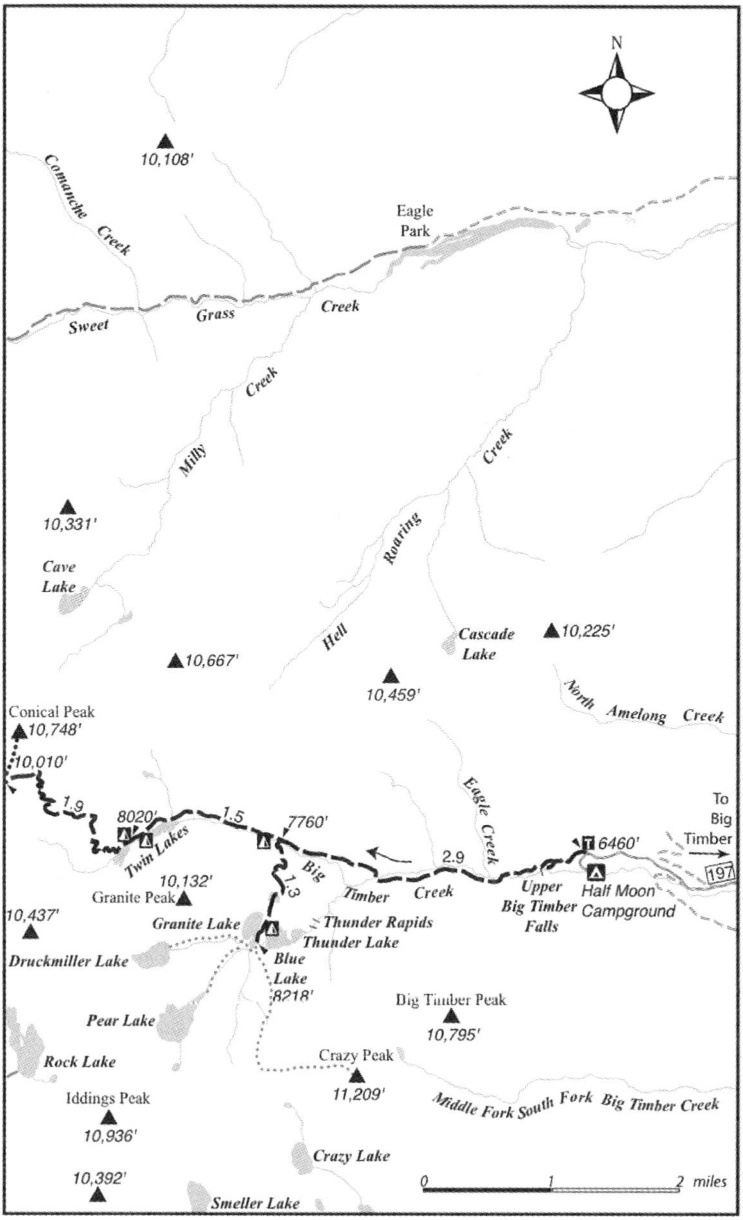

Crazy Mountains Traverse East

Gazing down South Fork Sweet Grass Canyon

even August. Swimming is not recommended, but neither is camping since the surrounding terrain is both rocky and fragile and the nights are usually quite cold.

For a better overnight option, take the South Fork Sweet Grass Trail, which follows the tumbling headwaters of its namesake stream down to a wonderfully scenic campsite in a meadow about 0.5 mile below Glacier Lake. From there, descend back into forest and past several small waterfalls for another mile to an easy, shin-deep ford of very cold South Fork Sweet Grass Creek. The often-faint trail is quite gentle over the next couple of miles, heading mostly downhill in forest and meadows with fine views, never far from the joyful stream. At the end of this section is a junction near the confluence of South and Middle Forks Sweet Grass Creek, with several fair campsites in the immediate area.

Side Trip to Sunlight Lake

If you have an extra day, set up a base camp near this junction and take the highly rewarding side trip up to Sunlight Lake. Continue hiking on the gently descending tread of South Fork Sweet Grass Creek Trail for another 0.9 mile to a possibly unsigned junction. At this point, turn left and ascend a hillside via three switchbacks before entering the canyon of North Fork Sweet Grass Creek. The often-faint route then travels up along the creek for about 1.5 miles, crosses its flow, and then makes a final, sometimes-steep climb to the basin holding the lake. This outstandingly scenic lake usually has ice floating on the surface through late July, while 10,090-foot Sunlight Peak rises impressively above the southwest shore. Camping is marginal, as the entire area is quite exposed, which makes visiting the lake as a day hike the better option. Mountain goats can often be seen on the cliffs above the lake. Anglers can fish for cutthroat, brook, and rainbow trout.

To continue the Crazy Mountains traverse, return to the junction at the confluence of Middle and South Forks Sweet Grass Creek, and head up the canyon of the Middle Fork, following signs to Moose and Campfire Lakes. This good trail makes a moderately graded climb through the relatively dense forest beside Middle Fork Sweet Grass Creek. About 1.5 miles up this trail you make an easy ankle-to-calf deep ford of the creek, then continue another 0.5 mile to tranquil Moose Lake. This beautiful lake rests in a deep hole at the base of snow-streaked cliffs. However, since the excellent campsites here are located on private land, you'll need permission to use them.

The trail ascends almost 800 feet up the hillside west of Moose Lake via twenty-one switchbacks. At the top, you hop over a creek and then travel up and down for about 0.3 mile to reach spectacular Campfire Lake. This long, irregularly shaped, and attractive lake has outstanding views of the surrounding rugged peaks, good (if overused) campsites, and lots of large rainbow trout. Idyllic places such as this explain why people come from all over the country to backpack in the mountains of Montana.

The trail winds uphill away from Campfire Lake and then follows a few switchbacks and a long uphill traverse to a high pass. From here, not only can you look down to where you came from, but west to the Bridger Mountains and beyond. Additionally, the pass is a good place to scan the hillsides for mountain goats.

The trail descends from the pass at a moderate grade using a traverse and a series of short switchbacks to reach an obvious but unsigned ridge crest junction. Turn sharply left on a trail that is unfortunately open to motorcycles, as you continue downhill on eleven switchbacks to the meadow-filled basin at the headwaters of Trespass Creek, where you will find some nice and very scenic campsites. From this high basin the trail follows a long, mostly gentle downhill route along Trespass Creek, first in meadows and then in viewless but attractive forests. Rock-hop the creek a little below the upper basin, and then follow the east bank of this cheerful little stream.

At 4.5 miles from the ridgetop junction is a signed junction with a jeep road just a few yards before a bridge over Trespass Creek. A fine but strenuous side trip turns left and follows a rather long and sometimes tough 4.3-mile climb to very scenic Cottonwood Lake set beneath a serrated ridge (good campsites).

To exit the hike, go right at the junction with the jeep road, cross the bridge, and then walk along the gated road through shady forest. After 0.6 mile, keep left on the jeep road where a trail forks to the right, then continue 0.3 mile to the Cottonwood Creek trailhead.

Possible Itinerary

	Camps and Side Trips	Miles	Elevation Gain
DAY 1	Big Timber TH to Upper Twin Lake	4.4	+1,700/−150
	Side trip to Upper Big Timber Falls	0.2	+50/−50
	Side trip to Blue Lake	2.6	+600/−600
DAY 2	Middle Fork Sweet Grass Creek	7.0	+2,150/−3,000
	Side trip to Conical Peak	1.8	+750/−750
DAY 3	Day hike to Sunlight Lake	8.8	+2,050/−2,050
DAY 4	Out to Cottonwood Creek TH	10.9	+2,550/−2,900

Giving Back

Montana Wilderness Association: WWW.WILDMONTANA.ORG

Madison Range
Lee Metcalf Wilderness (Spanish Peaks Unit), Custer Gallatin National Forest

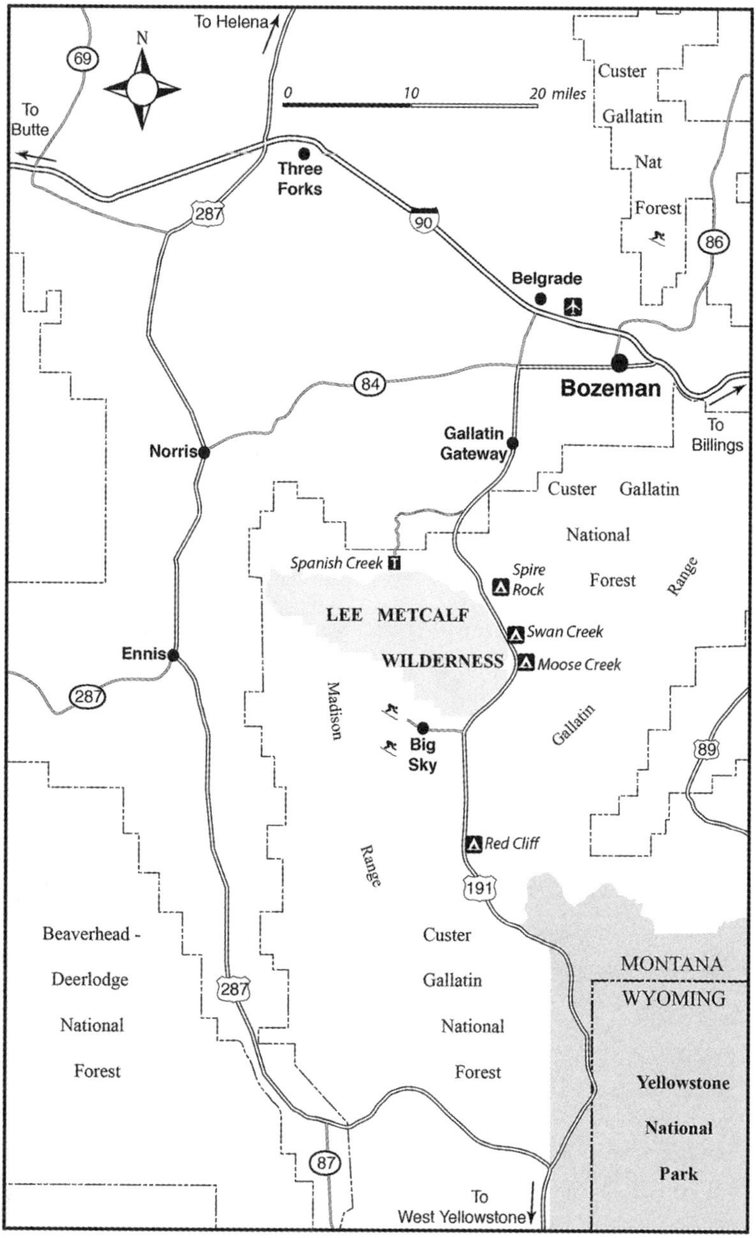

Spanish Peaks Loop Location Map

TRIP 4

Spanish Peaks Loop

> Conversation enriches the understanding, but solitude is the school of genius.
>
> —EDWARD GIBBON, FROM *DECLINE AND FALL OF THE ROMAN EMPIRE*

Although backpackers from the rest of the country usually come to Montana to hike the world-famous trails of Glacier National Park, locals often prefer one of the dozens of other beautiful mountain ranges that pepper the western half of this huge state. One of the more popular destinations for such savvy locals is the Spanish Peaks, and with good reason. At their best, the Spanish Peaks are extremely dramatic looking, with rugged and very high peaks rising precipitously above sparkling mountain lakes, along with high ridgetop meadows offering views seemingly extending forever. However, such rugged terrain makes for steep trails, so enjoying the many charms of this compact range requires considerable physical effort. The loop described below explores much of the Spanish Peaks' best scenery but also includes some less rugged and much less crowded terrain, thus allowing you to experience the full spectrum of delights this mountain wilderness has to offer. For hikers prepared to work for their scenery—and what great scenery to work for—this is definitely a "life list" hike. If you have less time, taking one of two shorter versions—either a loop in the more remote western part

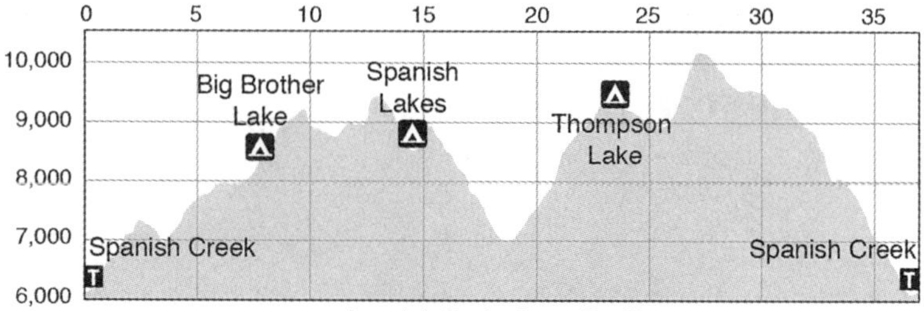

Spanish Peaks Loop Profile

of the wilderness, or a more spectacular (and crowded) loop through the eastern part of the range—is quite easy. The full trip is well worth the time, so the best plan is to schedule an extra couple of vacation days for the entire experience. You won't be disappointed.

Days: 4–6

Distance: 36.6 miles (with shorter options)

Type: Loop

Scenery: 8

Solitude: 5

Technical Difficulty: 6

Physical Difficulty: 7

Elevation Gain/Loss: +9,350'/–9,350'

Season: July to October

Best: Mid-July through early August

Map: USFS: *Lee Metcalf Wilderness*

Resources: None

Contact: Custer Gallatin National Forest
Bozeman Ranger District
3710 Fallon Street, Suite C
Bozeman, MT 59718
406-522-2520

Permits: No permits are required.

Regulations: Group size is limited to a maximum of fifteen persons. Camping is prohibited within 200 feet of any trail or water. Visitors are required to properly store all food and other items away from bears at all times.

Transportation Logistics: There are no public transportation options, so you must have your own vehicle. Convincing a cab driver to take you to the trailhead from the Bozeman airport might be possible (only about

30 miles), but getting one to come back and pick you up at the end might be more difficult.

Nearest Campground: There are several well-developed campgrounds off US 191 along the Gallatin River not far above where the Spanish Creek Road departs from that highway.

Nearest Airport: Bozeman Yellowstone International Airport (BZN)—30 miles

Nearest Outdoor Retailers: Bob Wards Sporting Goods—35 miles
3011 Max Avenue
Bozeman, MT 59715
406-586-4381

Northern Lights Trading Company—35 miles
83 Rowland Road
Bozeman, MT 59718
406-586-6029

REI—36 miles
2220 Tschache Street
Bozeman, MT 59718
406-587-1938

Outfitters: None

Attractions and Amenities: Bozeman is a thriving, outdoor-oriented city with all the usual shopping, motels, restaurants, and related services.

To the south is the busy resort community of **Big Sky**. Although best known for winter skiing, this bustling place has activities and high-end shopping throughout the year. If you want to check out the local natural attractions, two superior hikes from Big Sky are to **Beehive Basin** and **Ousel Falls**.

The surrounding area is home to a wide range of attractions, with the obvious top of any list being **Yellowstone National Park**, less than 50 miles south of the Spanish Peaks. About 30 miles west of Bozeman is the fascinating **Madison Buffalo Jump State Historic Site**. For perhaps 2,000 years, Native Americans used this location to herd large numbers of bison off a cliff as a convenient means of hunting. On the campus of Montana State University in Bozeman is the superb **Museum of the Rockies**, which includes everything from world-class dinosaur exhibits (one of the largest collections of dinosaur fossils in the world—including a T. rex), to fascinating history displays, and even a planetarium laser show. Regularly appearing on various top-ten lists of great outdoor towns, Bozeman caters to a wide variety of recreationists.

Along with the outdoor retailers mentioned above, craft breweries and bistros are plentiful.

Backcountry Logistics: (GB, BB, W, A, Sn, L) Black bears are common and a small but growing population of grizzly bears live in the area, so camp and act accordingly. There is a 5.6-mile waterless section as you make the long climb over Beacon Point between Thompson and Arrow Lakes. In addition, by late summer the water level in Arrow Lake often drops so much it becomes an unreliable source. In this case, you face an extremely long and waterless almost 12 miles before reaching the crossing of Little Hell Roaring Creek near the trailhead. As a result, a late summer trip is not advisable.

Directions to Trailhead: From Bozeman, drive 19 miles south on US 191 to a signed junction. Go right onto Spanish Creek Road (aka Forest Road 982) and stay on this good gravel road, which turns to pavement after 6 miles, to the large trailhead parking area, 9.5 miles from US 191.

The Political Environmentalist: Lee Metcalf (1911–1978)

The environmental movement is very good about celebrating the founding giants who eloquently brought forward the idea of resource conservation and who made this concept an important part of the national and international discussion. Quite correctly, countless books and articles have been written, and many awards given to the likes of Aldo Leopold, Bob Marshall, John Muir, Rachel Carson, and Henry David Thoreau. Less celebrated, but no less important, are the visionaries from the world of politics who took up the environmental banner and did the hard work of writing and guiding environmental legislation through the complicated political process to actually become law. Without the work of such men as Theodore Roosevelt or Stuart Udall, laws setting aside countless national parks and wildlife refuges, protecting endangered species, and combating pollution would have never become reality. One standout politician who deserves credit for much of the legislation protecting Montana's natural resources is Lee Metcalf.

Metcalf was born and raised in the small town of Stevensville, in the Bitterroot Valley of far western Montana. Although he was never a hunter, angler, or outdoor enthusiast, growing up in this beautiful valley without having a close relationship with nature would be next to impossible.

After completing his college education, Metcalf practiced law for a few months in Stevensville but soon turned to public service, running for and winning a state legislative seat in 1936. He served in the U.S. Army during World War II, but returned to Montana and won election to the Montana State Supreme Court in 1946.

In 1952 Metcalf won a close election for a seat in the United States House of Representatives. Although now remembered as a strong preservationist, at the time Metcalf believed in and ran on a platform of the full development of Montana's natural resources. This specifically included the construction of numerous dams to harness the rivers of Montana for cheap power and irrigation, the building of thousands of miles of roads on national forests to provide better access for loggers and recreationists, and significantly increasing the cutting of national forests to feed lumber mills and the jobs they produced. Although he was not actively hostile to the idea of land preservation, he believed in the active management and development of Montana's vast natural resources. Interestingly, he often supported environmental causes in other parts of the country, such as opposing dams in Colorado and Utah's Dinosaur National Monument. At the same time he actively pushed for similar wilderness-killing hydroelectric projects in his home state.

Over time Metcalf's opinions evolved on how best to manage the public lands of Montana, primarily due to the concerns eloquently expressed by large numbers of his constituents in a series of public meetings about logging and other proposed developments. He was strongly influenced by the testimony of backcountry outfitters, anglers, residents concerned about overlogging their local forests, and those who valued primitive recreation. Despite the fact that his changing priorities cost him support with loggers, ranchers, and other major resource users, Metcalf's electoral support grew, and he won nearly 70 percent of the vote when running for reelection to the House in 1958. This gave Metcalf more confidence to act on his evolving environmental agenda with less fear of losing an election.

Metcalf actively opposed bills he saw as special-interest giveaways that would have permanently vested private ranchers' grazing rights to use public lands. Fully a decade before Rachel Carson's seminal book *Silent Spring*, Metcalf, hearing disturbing reports from his constituents, called attention to the problem of overusing pesticides, herbicides, and other chemicals that he termed "economic poisons." In fact, Metcalf was personally responsible for getting a law passed to scientifically study the issue; the resulting devastating report formed much of the basis for Carson's famous book.

In 1960 Metcalf left the House and was elected to the Senate, where conservation issues became an increasingly important part of his agenda. He co-sponsored nationally important legislation such as the Clean Air Act, the Clean Water Act, the Endangered Species Act, and the Wild and Scenic Rivers Act, all of which passed during his time in the Senate. He signed on as a co-sponsor to the 1964 Wilderness Bill, which set aside large areas of Montana—such as the Bob Marshall, Anaconda-Pintler, Cabinet Mountains, and Selway-Bitterroot Wilderness Areas.

His first major battle over new wilderness in his home state came with the proposed Scapegoat Wilderness adjoining the Bob Marshall country in north-central Montana. Heavily influenced by public meetings in support of a large wilderness and by a report from one of his aides after a reconnaissance trip deep into the proposed preserve, Metcalf eventually supported a much larger wilderness than he had originally considered. With the senator's indispensable help, the Scapegoat became the first national forest wilderness to be protected as the result of an initiative by local citizens.

From the late 1960s through the 1970s, Lee Metcalf's record on behalf of wild lands is without parallel. He worked to pass the National Forest Management Act, dramatically reforming timber-harvesting practices on National Forest lands. He was almost single-handedly responsible for passing bills to protect the Great Bear, Absaroka-Beartooth, and Welcome Creek Wilderness Areas of Montana. For the last on that list, his blunt statement at a congressional hearing, "I've been there and it should be protected," carried the day. He also helped to protect Idaho's Upper Selway River country, just across the border from his home in the Bitterroot Valley. He greatly assisted in passing legislation to regulate strip mining and to designate new national parks in Alaska. He got through the controversial Montana Wilderness Study Act protecting numerous roadless areas around the state while their wilderness potential was more carefully examined. Finally, he worked tirelessly to set aside an enormous 175-mile section of the upper Missouri River in Montana, a beautiful and unique free-flowing stretch of that famous river, ironically where he had previously called for dams to be built. Many of these accomplishments came as Metcalf's health was failing during his final term in the Senate, or passed as part of his legacy shortly after his death on January 12, 1978.

In 1983 the Montana congressional delegation pushed through a bill protecting over 250,000 acres in four separate areas in the Madison Range of south-central Montana. This outstanding wilderness includes Bear Trap Canyon along the Madison River, the tall and scenic Taylor Peaks just west of Yellowstone National Park, and the dramatic Spanish Peaks area south of Bozeman. In a fitting tribute to the politician who did more than any other man to actually enact legislation protecting the wildlands of Montana, this preserve was named the Lee Metcalf Wilderness. The hardworking and skillful politician from Stevensville would have been honored.

Trip Description: Several trails depart from this popular trailhead. You begin on the Spanish Creek Trail (see map of Spanish Peaks Loop [East]), which starts from the northwest corner of the parking lot. This heavily used path leads quickly to a bridge over South Fork Spanish Creek and immediately reaches a junction on the far side.

Option for Eastern Loop

If you're taking the shorter loop option through the eastern half of the wilderness, turn left here. This trail goes up the gentle canyon of South Fork Spanish Creek, traveling in forest and a few small meadows for 4.4 miles to a junction with a trail that goes to the right on its way up to the Spanish Lakes (a tough, but worthwhile side trip). Here you go left toward Mirror Lake and follow the description for the last half of the full trip in the text below.

To do the full loop as recommended, turn right on Cherry Creek Trail and gradually ascend to the north across a partly forested and partly grass- and sagebrush-covered slope. Not far into this climb you enter private land, where signs direct you not to venture off the official trail. After 0.7 mile, switchback to the left, then continue slowly climbing up the spine of a minor ridge. After just 0.2 mile you leave the

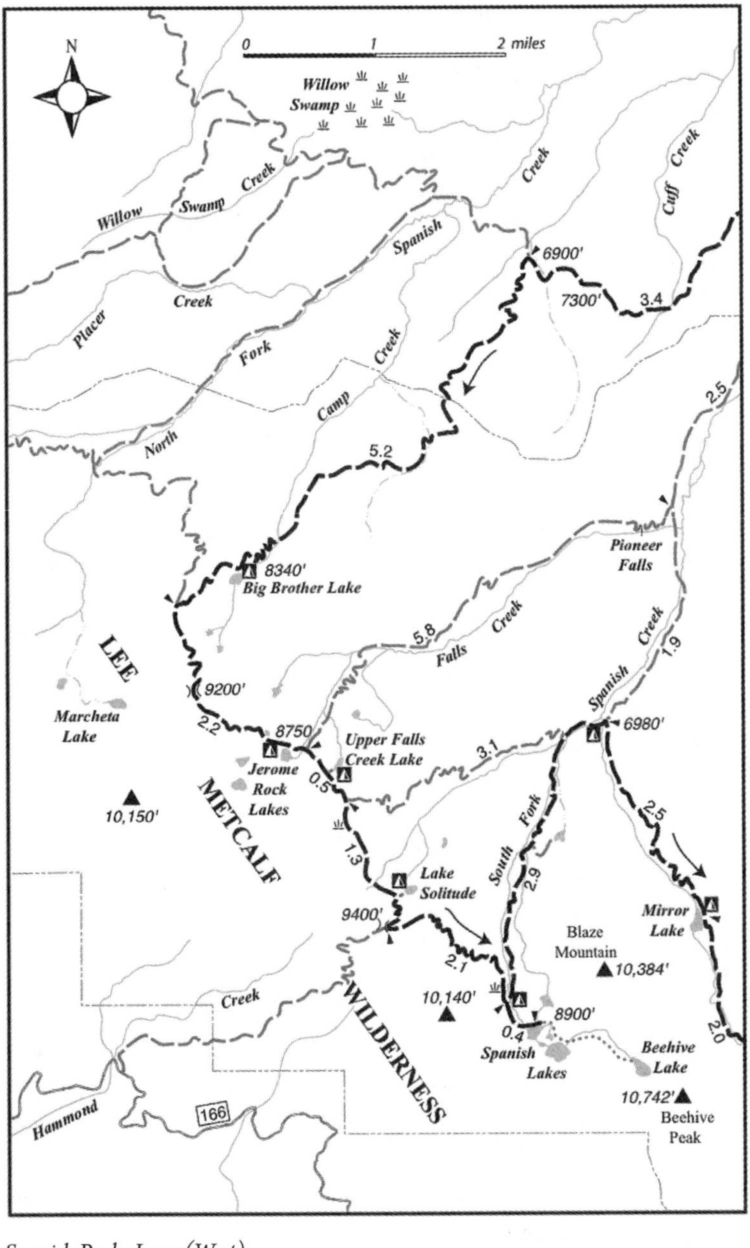

Spanish Peaks Loop (West)

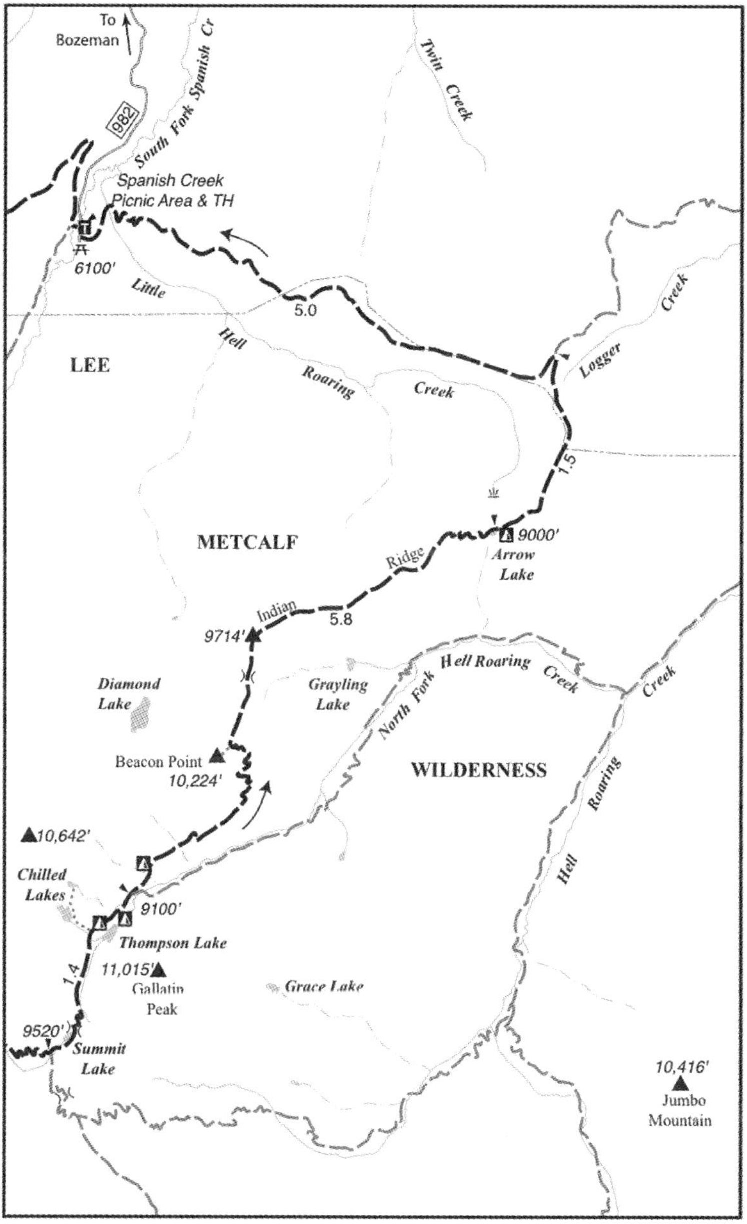

Spanish Peaks Loop (East)

ridge and briefly reenter public land before beginning a 1.4-mile stretch on another section of private land (the same stay-on-the-trail rules apply). This up-and-down segment travels mostly through a young second-growth forest regrowing after harvest. More attractive than this managed forest are splashing Cuff Creek (see map of Spanish Peaks Loop [West]), which you hop over along the way, and some pretty, wildflower-covered meadows with pleasant views of the valleys and forested hills to the north. After reentering Forest Service land, the trail goes mostly downhill for about 0.4 mile to a signed junction.

At the junction, turn sharply left on the trail to Big Brother Lake and immediately resume climbing. The path winds up through a mostly lodgepole-pine forest for the next few miles. The relatively monotonous scenery in this section is broken only rarely by small creeks or meadows. Eventually, at around 7.1 miles, you rock-hop Camp Creek, then wind uphill across a rocky and partly forested slope. About 0.7 mile above the crossing of Camp Creek, you pass Big Brother Lake on the left. A little hard to see from the trail, this pretty lake is worth the 100-yard side trip to enjoy the nice meadow- and forest-rimmed setting, or possibly camp at the fine sites near the lake's outlet at the northeast end.

The trail quickly climbs away from Big Brother Lake up to a small dry meadow carpeted with buttercups, bistorts, elephant heads, and other mid-July wildflowers. About 0.1 mile above this meadow is a similar but smaller meadow where a large cairn is the sole identification of an important junction. You will see a line of cairns marking a trail on the right (a little uphill), but you turn left on an initially very faint path that becomes more distinct after about 50 yards. Head south-southeast for the next mile, following cairns and indistinct portions of tread on a circuitous but scenic route across rocky areas, wet subalpine meadows, and high-elevation forest. Reach the ridge top about 100 feet above an obvious pass.

The trail now descends through a very attractive subalpine landscape at the headwaters of Falls Creek, from where you have nice views of the rugged Spanish Peaks to the east. The trail travels through marshy areas and past an unnamed pond, then drops to a possible campsite near the lowest Jerome Rock Lake. An upper basin to the southwest holds a cluster of more scenic and less crowded lakes, which are certainly worth the time for the off-trail exploration.

The main trail continues downhill 0.1 mile from the lowest Jerome Rock Lake to a signed junction. (For a really short loop, you could turn left and return to the trailhead in about 8.3 miles.) Most of the best scenery is yet to come, so continue straight at the junction and travel 0.3 mile mostly uphill to Upper Falls Creek Lake. A short side trail goes left to the lake, which has some good campsites. A bit more uphill takes you over a ridge and then 50 yards down the other side to a junction with High Lakes Trail. Keep right on the Lake Solitude Trail and descend to a lovely, but oftentimes mosquito-infested meadow. The next 0.7 mile is an up-and-down romp through wet meadows and open forests to a meadow a little above the small basin holding Lake Solitude, which is well worth the short side trip for good fishing and campsites.

The main trail turns right in the meadow above Lake Solitude and very steeply gains about 500 feet in the next half mile to a junction on a windswept ridgetop. The views from here, especially to the south and southwest, are tremendous (easily the best so far on the trip). The main attraction is the tall, unmistakable pyramid of Lone Mountain and the area around Big Sky resort.

Turn left at the junction, crossing an open slope with fine views to the north of the Bozeman area. Where you round a ridge, you're suddenly faced with an outstanding bird's-eye view of the dramatic crags forming the heart of the Spanish Peaks. Of the many rugged peaks in sight, Blaze Mountain, featuring a distinctive long snowfield on the west face, is the only named summit. But just because people have not seen fit to give names to most of these mountains is no reflection on their grandeur. In addition to the peaks, you can see several of the lakes in the Spanish Lakes group clustered in a basin to the southeast. This view alone would make this trip worthwhile.

The trail steeply descends from the high ridge rapidly switchbacking downhill. At the bottom of the switchbacks you go up and down across meadows and rocky areas, then around the end of a rocky promontory before you start climbing again. Shortly past a series of scenic little marshy ponds is a signed junction with some comfortable campsites nearby.

Side Trip to Spanish Lakes

For a nearly mandatory side trip to the Spanish Lakes, take the trail to the right, which in 0.4 mile climbs gradually to the lowest of the Spanish Lakes. This deep, extremely scenic lake is virtually surrounded by tall, jagged peaks. The rocky terrain limits camping, and some sites are closed for rehabilitation. Hardy hikers can explore the rough terrain above the lake to the other Spanish Lakes and even up to stark but dramatic Beehive Lake. After your visit to Spanish Lakes, return to the junction 0.4 mile below the lowest lake.

From the junction, bear right and follow the heavily used Spanish Lakes Trail, soon crossing the outlet from the lakes (expect wet feet unless you can find a convenient log), and then make a steady but moderately graded descent. About 1.4 miles down this trail, shortly after you hop over a tributary creek, reach an unsigned junction with a trail heading sharply back to the right and which is not shown on the official maps. Go straight (downhill), remaining on the main trail and continue mostly downhill to a calf- to knee-deep ford of the creek. About 0.3 mile farther, hop over a tributary creek and immediately reach a junction with the High Lakes Trail (you passed the upper end of this trail earlier in the trip).

You keep right and travel gradually downhill 0.3 mile to a bridged creek crossing. There are two spacious campsites between this crossing and a log crossing of another creek just 0.1 mile away. Less than 100 yards after this second creek crossing is a junction with the South Fork Spanish Creek Trail.

Eastern and Western Loop Options

By turning left at the South Fork Spanish Creek Trail junction, you can complete the shorter, western-only version of this loop on an easy 4.4-mile descent to the trailhead. This is also where those doing only the eastern half of the loop join the main route.

Blaze Mountain over Mirror Lake

To complete the full loop, following signs to Mirror Lake you turn right at the junction and begin a gradual climb through the forest. The trail follows numerous switchbacks and crosses several avalanche chutes on a steady ascent. In a little over 2.5 miles, you reach Mirror Lake, a gorgeous mountain gem tucked neatly beneath enormous snow-streaked peaks and ridges on three sides. Fine campsites, especially above the northeast shore, allow you to appreciate the charms of this lake at leisure.

All too soon, the trail pulls away from Mirror Lake and switchbacks up to a wildly scenic upper basin, where you twice must ford or make a long hop across a splashing creek. The trail then leaves this basin and switchbacks thirteen times in a steady ascent to the next junction (see map of Crazy Mountains Traverse [East]). The Bear Basin Trail goes right, but you turn left on the Indian Ridge Trail and climb for another 0.2 mile to rock- and meadow-rimmed Summit Lake. This above-timberline lake is extremely scenic, but the lakeshore is too fragile and exposed for camping.

Just a few yards past Summit Lake, you top a pass and gain fine views looking down the canyon of North Fork Hell Roaring Creek, which is your next goal. Follow the trail on a descent through either rocky switchbacks or over steep snowfields that often remain until late July. At the bottom of this short, steep section, you gradually lose elevation through meadows and past a small pond before reaching Thompson Lake. There are several good camps amid the trees a little above this very scenic lake.

The trail stays above Thompson Lake heading around the northwest shore. ***Tip:*** *For those up for a bit of relatively easy uphill scrambling, the Chilled Lakes make a fine goal. Follow game trails and rough boot paths that climb to a narrow basin about 350 feet up the rocky slope northwest of Thompson Lake.*

About 0.3 mile below Thompson Lake is a fork in the trail. Bear left, still on Indian Ridge Trail, and soon come to a small but comfortable campsite next to a small creek. ***Tip:*** *Be sure to fill your water bottles here, as there is often no water (except from snowfields) for the next 5.6 miles (11.8 miles if Arrow Lake is unusable).*

For almost a mile after crossing the little creek, the trail goes lazily up and down past a string of lovely meadows and then begins a long and tiring climb. Your goal is Beacon Point, almost 1,400 feet above. The route employs a least twenty-six switchbacks, depending on how you count all the twists and turns, and every one of them is necessary to avoid being too steep. Fortunately, the views improve with every step, especially to the south of extremely rugged Gallatin Peak and to the north of long Indian Ridge. The forest cover thins as you gain elevation so that near the top the only remaining trees are some stunted whitebark pines, and even these finally disappear as you top out at about 10,150 feet, just below the summit of Beacon Point. The short and easy side trip to the top affords you a wonderful view encompassing mountains and valleys in all directions. ***Warning:*** *The winds often howl atop Indian Ridge, and it's no place to be in a thunderstorm—schedule your trip to be past Beacon Point and the next few miles of Indian Ridge before about 2 PM.*

The sometimes-sketchy trail now follows cairns along the top of the ridge north from Beacon Point, rapidly descending to a saddle. Although small lakes in the basins to either side look enticing, the trail sticks with the ridge, regaining 250 feet of the elevation you just lost on the way to a huge cairn atop a treeless 9,714-foot knoll.

The view-packed ridge now turns northeast and the trail follows suit, going up and down for the next 1.7 miles near the top of the divide. You go in and out of windswept forests of whitebark pines along the way, but they rarely obscure the extensive vistas. Finally, the trail drops sharply down from the ridge in a series of mostly short switchbacks to small Arrow Lake. In early summer this oversized pond is clear and inviting with good campsites above the northwest shore. However, by late summer the water level drops so much (without a permanent inlet) that obtaining decent water can be challenging. Nonetheless, this is the only trailside water for the 11.8 miles between the small creeks past Thompson Lake and the crossing of Little Hell Roaring Creek near the trailhead. If water in Arrow Lake is unusable, the only realistic option is to go cross-country to the north-northwest, dropping through forest for about 0.4 mile and losing some 350 feet to a small, wet meadow at the head of Little Hell Roaring Creek. Water should be available here, though there is no decent place to camp.

Beyond Arrow Lake, the trail is waterless but fun, heading gently up and down through open forest and some blowdown for just less than 1.5 miles on the way to a signed junction. You turn sharply left on Little Hell Roaring Trail and make a short downhill traverse across the north side of a knoll. From here there are fine views to the north of the Bozeman area. The trail now follows an undulating east-west-oriented ridge, generally going downhill but with a few very minor uphills along the way, traveling over or around high points in the ridge. The terrain is about an even mix of forest and open slopes, the latter offering outstanding vistas, especially to the south and southwest of the Spanish Peaks. As you lose elevation, the open slopes are increasingly covered with sagebrush, juniper, and wildflowers, such as yarrow, buckwheat, monument plant, larkspur, harebell, lupine, and geranium. The last 2.5 miles are all downhill, as several switchbacks lead to a log crossing of Little Hell Roaring Creek (water!) and, 0.3 mile later, back to the trailhead.

Possible Itinerary

	Camps and Side Trips	Miles	Elevation Gain
Day 1	Spanish Creek TH to Big Brother Lake	7.8	+2,850/−600
Day 2	Camps below Spanish Lakes	6.9	+2,100/−1,750
	Side trip to Spanish Lakes	0.8	+150/−150
Day 3	Thompson Lake	8.6	+2,650/−2,250
Day 4	Out to Spanish Creek TH	12.5	+1,600/−4,600

Giving Back

Montana Wilderness Association: www.wildmontana.org

Beartooth Mountains
Absaroka-Beartooth Wilderness,
Custer Gallatin National Forest

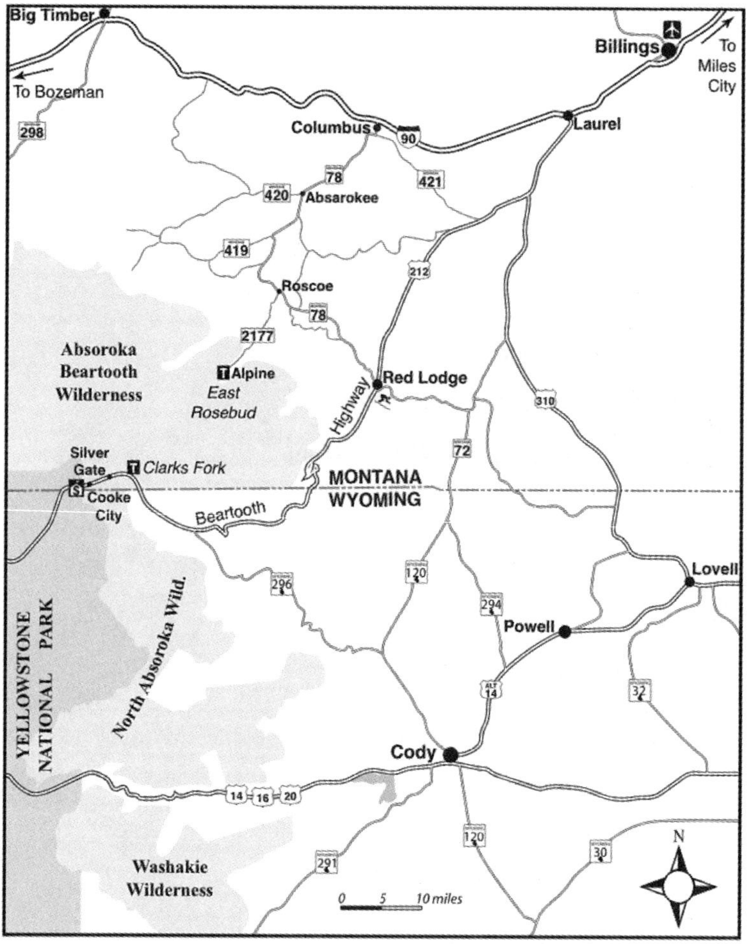

The Beaten Path Location Map

TRIP 5

The Beaten Path

> I'm in love with Montana. For other states I have admiration, respect, recognition, even some affection. But with Montana it is love. And it's difficult to analyze love when you're in it.
>
> —JOHN STEINBECK, *TRAVELS WITH CHARLEY*

Derived from the Spanish word for "mountain," Montana is home to seventy-seven named mountain ranges and some of North America's most stunningly picturesque mountain scenery. Although the Beartooth Mountain range, located in south central Montana, is less well known among the general public than neighboring Yellowstone National Park, or more distant Glacier National Park, knowledgeable outdoor enthusiasts consider this area to harbor some of the most dramatic alpine topography in the state. Without question, the Beartooths hold Montana's highest summit, 12,799-foot Granite Peak, tallest of the twenty 12,000-foot peaks in the range. The Beartooths also contain one of the largest contiguous landmasses in the United States over 10,000 feet. Composed primarily of Precambrian granite, the range is characterized by rugged peaks clad with glaciers and snowfields and high, open plateaus dotted with an abundance of sparkling lakes. Named for the distinctively sharp peak resembling the namesake mammal's tooth, the Beartooth Mountains offer some of the West's most sublime and rugged mountain scenery.

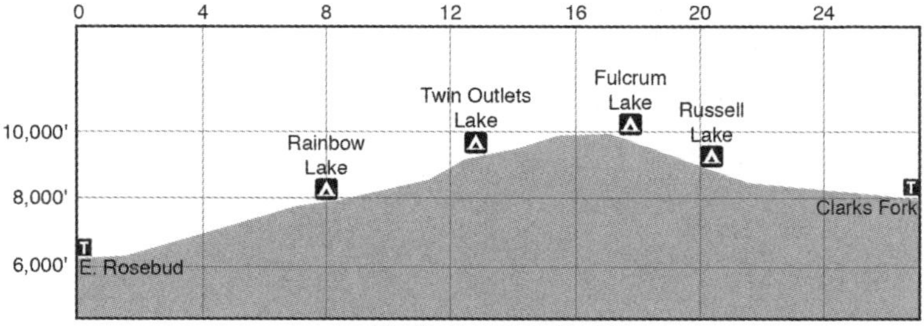

The Beaten Path Profile

The Beaten Path (so named for the trail's frequency of use—at least by Montana standards) is a 26-mile, point-to-point journey from East Rosebud Lake, near the tourist town of Red Lodge, to the outskirts of Cooke City, a small gateway town near the northeastern entrance of Yellowstone National Park. Traversing the incredibly scenic Beartooth Plateau, hikers travel through a part of the 943,626-acre Absaroka-Beartooth Wilderness, hiking beneath some of the range's tallest peaks and past some of its prettiest lakes. Along with the numerous lakes, an amazing number of roaring waterfalls and tumbling cascades are encountered on the way through the deep canyon of East Rosebud Creek.

While many in-shape and acclimatized hikers could do the entire 26-mile route in a couple of days, the staggering beauty of this area demands much more attention, particularly when the vast area of backcountry beyond what is accessible by trail is considered. So many lakes and tarns dot the backcountry that an entire month could easily be spent wandering cross-country over the Beartooth Plateau without seeing the same place twice. Mountaineers will find plenty of challenging climbing away from the trail as well. Anglers should be quite satisfied with the abundant trout fishing opportunities in both lakes and streams, as well as with the size of the individual fish and the size of the catch.

Days: 3–6

Distance: 27 miles

Type: Shuttle

Scenery: 9

Solitude: 8

Technical Difficulty: 5

Physical Difficulty: 5

Elevation Gain/Loss: +5,235'/–3,600'

Season: Mid-July to late September

Best: Late July to early August

Maps: USGS: *Alpine, Castle Mountain, Fossil Lake*; USFS: *Absaroka Beartooth Wilderness*

Resources: None

Contacts: Custer Gallatin National Forest
Beartooth Ranger District
HC 49, Box 3420
Red Lodge, MT 59068
406-446-2103
www.fs.fed.us/r1/custer

Gardiner Ranger District
PO Box 5
Gardiner, MT 59030
406-848-7375
www.fs.fed.us/r1/gallatin

Permits: Not required.

Regulations: Maximum group size: fifteen. Campfires prohibited within 200 feet of lakes and 100 feet of streams. No campfires between Twin Outlets Lake and Fossil Lake.

Nearest Campgrounds: Start: East Rosebud—1/2 mile from East Rosebud trailhead
End: Chief Joseph—1/2 mile from Clarks Fork trailhead

Nearest Airport: Billings Logan International Airport (BIL)—122 miles

Nearest Outdoor Retailer:
Sylvan Peak—35 miles
9 S. Broadway
Red Lodge, MT 59068
406-446-1770 or 800-249-2568

Outfitters: Limited—check with Custer National Forest for currently licensed outfitters.

Transportation Logistics: First the bad news: Since the Beaten Path lies far away from anything close to any form of mass transit a metropolitan area might provide, backpackers have no other option than to leave a vehicle at the ending trailhead and then drive back to the starting trailhead. Plan on a 2.5- to 3-hour drive between the Clarks Fork and East Rosebud trailheads. The good news is that most of the drive is on the Beartooth Highway, one of the most scenic roads in the entire country.

Backcountry Logistics: (A, BB, GB, L, Sn, W) The weather can be fickle at times at this high of an altitude this far north in the Rocky Mountains. Backpackers should be prepared to handle inclement weather, including severe thunderstorms, bringing with them the possibility of high winds and hail, as well as the occasional snowstorm. This is also bear country, with both black and grizzly bears present, so take the proper precautions.

Many parties reverse the direction of the following description, opting to start at Clarks Fork trailhead and end at East Rosebud. Doing so reverses the elevation change such that backpackers gain only 3,800 feet instead of 6,500 feet. While hiking in this direction may require less effort, the scenic rewards are better experienced in the direction described herein.

Trail runners occasionally run the entire 26-mile route in a single day, which is nowhere near the proper amount of time to fully enjoy this beautiful area.

Amenities and Attractions: Over the years, **Red Lodge** has become a chic mountain community with a main drag (Broadway) full of trendy shops, eateries, and bars. Upscale dining at **Bridge Creek Backcountry Kitchen and Wine Bar** is elegant but pricey, which is also the case in the dining room at the **Pollard** hotel. **Red Lodge Pizza Co.** is the spot to enjoy more common fare, while **Red Box Car Drive-in** serves old-fashioned hamburgers, fries, and shakes in a way that puts the fast-food chains to shame. Lodging runs the gamut from basic independent and chain motels to fancy bed-and-breakfast establishments. **Rock Creek Resort** is touted as *the* place to stay in Red Lodge for both locals and tourists. If you plan to fish while hiking the Beaten Path, you should pick up a Montana license at the **True Value** hardware store at the corner of 11th and Oakes.

Near the Clarks Fork trailhead, the Yellowstone gateway towns of **Cooke City** and **Silver Gate** offer modest accommodations and cafés. As long as you don't expect chocolate mints on your pillow or haute cuisine on your plate, these two small wide spots in the road can provide a decent night's sleep and a full belly. In Silver Gate, **Pine Edge Cabins** and **Silver Gate Cabins** offer rustic but reasonably priced log cabins. Across the street, **Log Cabin Café** is a fine place to grab a pre- or post-trip meal. Although Cooke City offers more lodging options, none stand out beyond a merely adequate rating. **Beartooth Café** and **Bistro** are perhaps the best restaurants in town. Along with the usual tourist trinkets, anglers can obtain tackle and Wyoming and Yellowstone (but not Montana) fishing licenses at **Cooke City Store**.

Connecting Red Lodge and Cooke City–Silver Gate is the **Beartooth Highway**, arguably one of the most scenic drives in America. The highway climbs up a steep grade from Red Lodge through the deep cleft of scenic Rock Creek Canyon, where occasional pullouts offer incomparable vistas of the canyon and surrounding mountains. After zigzagging up the east wall of the canyon, motorists emerge onto dramatic alpine tundra, with sweeping views of the spectacularly beautiful, glacier-carved, lake-dotted terrain of the Beartooth Plateau. Motorists reach the high point of the journey at 10,947-foot Beartooth Pass and then continue through gorgeous alpine parkland sprinkled with more picturesque lakes. Just beyond Beartooth Lake, keen eyes may spy lovely Beartooth Falls south of the highway. Although driving the Beartooth Highway between Red Lodge and Cooke City can be done in 2-plus hours, stops at the numerous overlooks, picnic areas, and campgrounds en route can justifiably extend the time considerably. Eventually the road drops below timberline, once again traveling through the drainage of Clarks Fork Yellowstone River, reentering Montana before arriving at Cooke City and then Silver Gate near the northeast entrance to Yellowstone National Park.

Coming all this way to a remote section of Montana without stopping over at nearby **Yellowstone National Park** seems almost criminal. However, those desiring to stay overnight anywhere inside the park should make plans well ahead of time, as reservations for lodging fill up extremely quickly. Campgrounds inside the park are also in high demand during the summer tourist season.

Trailhead Directions: From the Billings area, head west on Interstate 90 about 11 miles to the small community of Laurel (Exit 367) at a junction with US Highway 212. Leave the freeway here, and proceed south on 212 to the quaint town of Red Lodge (services, ranger station). From Red Lodge, follow the Beartooth Highway toward Cooke City, eventually crossing the border into Wyoming. The turnoff for the well-signed Clarks Fork trailhead and interpretive area is 1.4 miles past where the road reenters Montana, 1.2 miles before Colter Pass and 3.25 miles before Cooke City (services). The trailhead has a large parking area, picnic facilities, and vault toilets. The entrance to Chief Joseph campground (fee, six sites, drinking water, vault toilets, fire rings, picnic tables) is just a short distance farther up the road on the right. Colter and Soda Butte are larger and more developed Forest Service campgrounds farther up the road toward Cooke City.

After leaving a vehicle at Clarks Fork trailhead, retrace your route to Red Lodge and then turn northwest at the junction with State Highway 78. Follow 78 approximately 20 miles to the very tiny community of Roscoe and then turn southwest onto East Rosebud Road, marked by a small sign that's easily missed. Proceed on sometimes paved and sometimes dirt road along East Rosebud Creek for 14.5 miles to the trailhead on the east side of East Rosebud Lake. The trailhead has a large parking area with vault toilet and a water pump nearby. East Rosebud Campground is 0.5 mile northeast of the trailhead (fee, fourteen tent-only sites, drinking water, vault toilets, fire rings, picnic tables). Jimmy Joe is a primitive, no-fee campground 4.5 miles back down the East Rosebud Road.

General Phillip H. Sheridan and the Beartooth Highway

When the general public discovers the true nature of its heroes, we oftentimes find them to be much like ourselves—flawed beyond an entirely comfortable level. Such is the case with General Sheridan, a notable hero of the Civil and Indian Wars and a staunch defender of Yellowstone against commercial interests. Unfortunately, while commanding the Army of the Potomac, Sheridan was responsible for carrying out a scorched-earth policy in Shenandoah Valley that residents would heretofore refer to as "The Burning," a precursor to the more infamous "Sherman's March to the Sea." Although he continuously denied the allegation, the phrase "the only good Indian is a dead Indian" was attributed to Sheridan, who publicly expressed no remorse for the killing of women and children when an attack on an Indian Village was deemed necessary. Despite such shortcomings, General Sheridan played a critical part in the exploration of the Beartooth Mountains and the preservation of Yellowstone.

Cooke City was originally founded as Shoo-fly, a settlement quickly springing up in the New World Mining District after the discovery of gold in 1870. The town was soon renamed for Jay Cooke Jr., an influential mining investor, who planned on building a rail line from Gardiner over the top of Yellowstone and down to the mines in Cooke City. Fortunately, Congress ultimately put an end to Cooke's railroad plans, which eventually derailed his finances as well. Without a feasible rail line connecting Cooke City to Gardner, Billings, an eventual stop on the Northern Pacific Railroad, served as the principal resupply point for the numerous mines sprinkled throughout the Beartooth Mountains. As a direct route across the Beartooth Plateau was deemed unfeasible, travel between Billings and Cooke City was accomplished by a difficult and much longer journey along Clarks Fork Yellowstone River, which meets the main stem of the Yellowstone River near Laurel, immediately west of Billings.

Following an inspection tour of Yellowstone in August of 1872, General Sheridan and a party of 120 men and over 300 animals set out from Cooke City, guided by George Greer, a local hunter familiar with the area. Sheridan's expedition crossed over Beartooth Pass and then descended Rock Creek, basically following the present-day route of the Beartooth Highway, and then continued on to Billings. Sheridan's success proved that a more direct route across the Beartooth Mountains to Cooke City was indeed feasible.

Although a wagon road was proposed along this route soon after the success of Sheridan's expedition was known, the construction of a highway suitable for the modern automobile had to wait until the 1930s. Funding was appropriated in 1931, and construction, which was limited to the snow-free months on the calendar, took about four years to complete. The nearly

70-mile-long road opened to traffic in 1936 and was designated a federal scenic byway in 1989. Considered an engineering marvel even by today's standards, the Beartooth Highway remains the most picturesque entry into Yellowstone National Park.

Trip Description: The northern half of East Rosebud Lake (see map of Beaten Path [East]) is encircled by private property dotted with summer homes that form the small community of Alpine, the last signs of civilization backpackers will see on their 26-mile journey along the Beaten Path. A fire raced through the area in the recent past, leaving behind the charred remnants of a sparse forest all the way up the canyon past Elk Lake, which slightly diminishes the otherwise attractive scenery. Beyond the trailhead sign, which lists a number of destinations and corresponding mileages, the trail follows above the east shore of East Rosebud Lake through thick shrubs and grasses, and widely spaced, small conifers—all results of nature's post-fire recovery. Initially, the trail offers fine views of 10,990-foot Shepherd Mountain hovering over the west side of the canyon. Cross the signed Absaroka-Beartooth Wilderness past the far end of the lake, and proceed on gently graded tread to where the trail draws alongside East Rosebud Creek. Farther up the canyon, the first of many fine cascades and waterfalls to come spills down a steep cleft between two humps of rock. On the approach to this lovely cascade, the trail starts to climb more steeply, still through mostly open terrain. Cross over a trio of vibrant side streams, via a stout wood bridge, a boulder hop, and a pair of culverts, on the way into an intact grove of forest just before Elk Lake.

A short stroll through the trees leads to the northeast shore of the 7-acre, 6,782-foot lake. Although late starters could find passable but overused campsites near the inlet or along the east shore, much better campsites await farther up the trail near Rainbow Lake. Anglers can ply the waters in search of cutthroats and a smaller population of rainbows, though fishing pressure this close to the trailhead is understandably high.

As the next lake of any substance, Rimrock Lake, lies another 3 miles up the trail, almost all the day hikers will be left behind as you head away from Elk Lake and continue up the canyon on a moderate climb alongside roaring and tumbling East Rosebud Creek. The last of the evidence from the fire is left behind, where the grade increases and the forest thickens momentarily on the way to a set of switchbacks leading up the east wall of the narrowing canyon. Out in the open again, the trail passes through a boulder field with good views of the roaring creek, which twists and cascades downstream between steep rock walls, culminating in a very picturesque waterfall spilling into a deep green pool. More switchbacks climb above the falls and back under forest cover briefly before you break out into the open again above scenic Rimrock Lake. A short, steep drop winds down to a sturdy wood bridge spanning the outlet just below where it emerges from the long, green lake.

The 25-foot-deep lake is sandwiched between the walls of the canyon, vaguely reminiscent of a Norwegian fjord. Such steep topography severely limits potential campsites, and most backpackers seeking a good night's sleep tend to press on another mile or so to better sites around Rainbow Lake. Fishing is good for rainbow trout, with a smaller amount of golden trout present as well.

The trail traverses above the west shore of Rimrock Lake for three quarters of its length before zigzagging up flower-filled slopes in order to pass over a rock outcrop that prevents the continuation of a shoreline route. Where the path momentarily veers into a side canyon, hikers are treated to a fantastic view of cascading Whirlpool Creek across the valley, which appears to tumble down from the very rim of the canyon directly southwest of 12,401-foot Castle Rock Mountain. Once the hiker is above the rock outcrop, some of that hard-earned elevation is sacrificed on a descent toward the north shore of Rainbow Lake. Along the way, you cross a couple of streams on earthen bridges, climb through shady forest, and pass a small pond and meadow before coming above the lake's outlet. The trail stays high above the surface of the lake, slicing across the steep hillside with good views of the glacier-tinted lake and the surrounding mountains. Eventually the trail drops down to heavily forested, flat terrain beyond the west shore.

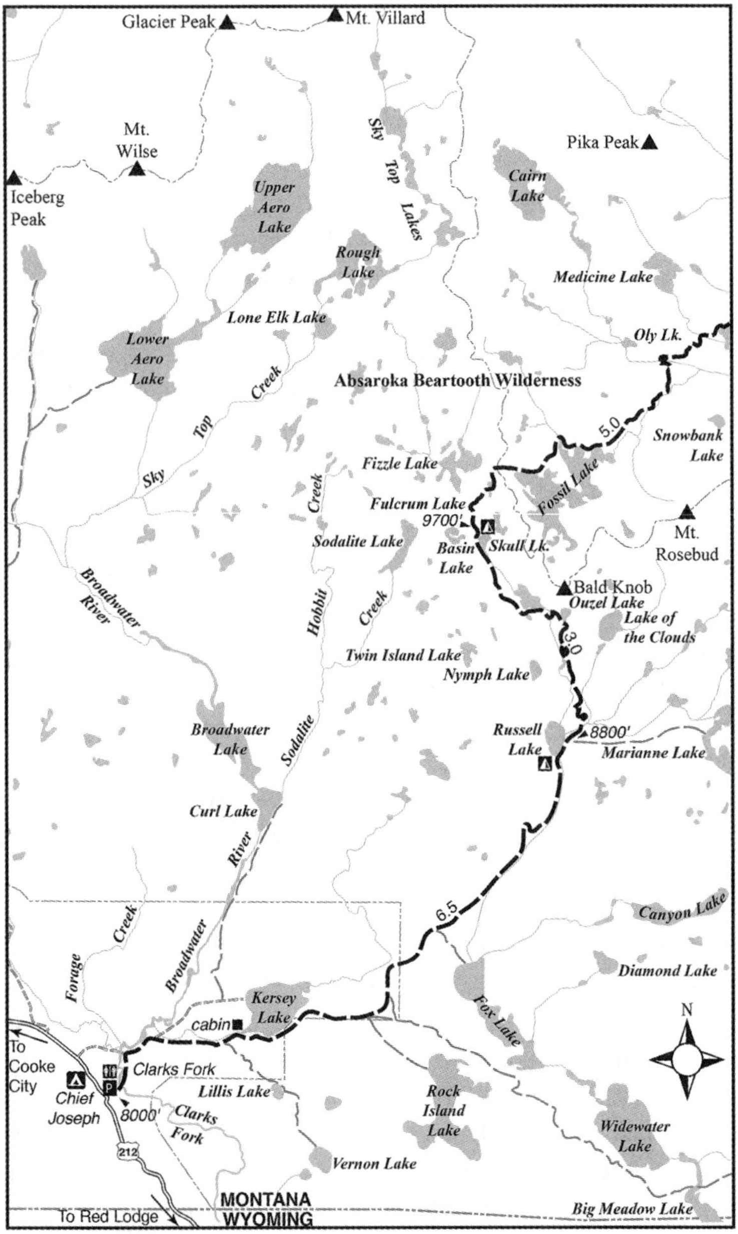

The Beaten Path (West)

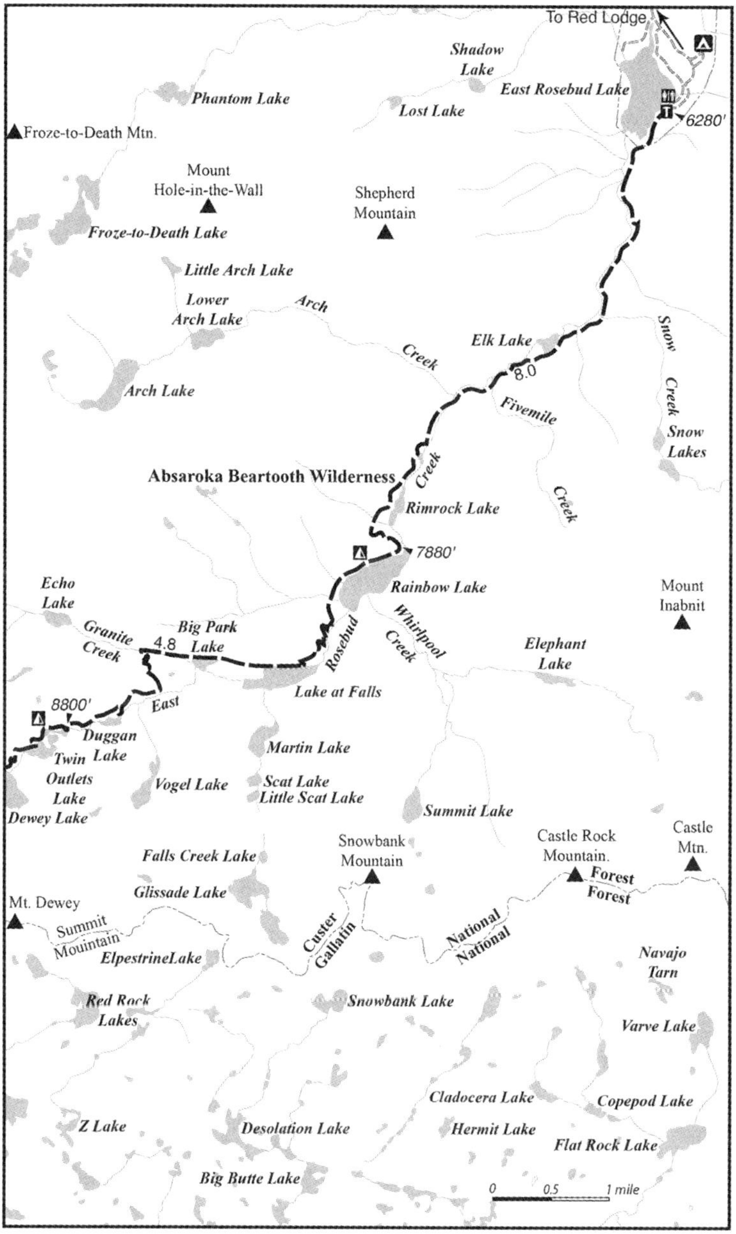

The Beaten Path (East)

A large number of campsites are tucked beneath conifers on the west side of large Rainbow Lake. While numerous parties may be camped here, the area is big enough to usually disperse the crowds. However, due to the lake's popularity, you may have to search far and wide for enough firewood to build a campfire. At 7,770 feet, the 180-foot-deep lake should provide anglers with good fishing for fair-sized rainbow and golden trout, though shoreline access is a tad difficult in spots due to the steep topography at the far end and heavy brush at the near end.

Away from Rainbow Lake, the trail passes through a flower-filled meadow and then dense forest on the way to a set of switchbacks leading up toward Lake at Falls. The terrain opens again farther up the draw between the two lakes, with fine views behind of Rainbow Lake and ahead toward a pair of scenic falls tumbling down from Martin Lake into aptly named Lake at Falls. After a short jaunt through a stand of trees, the trail cuts across the steep slope above the north side of the lake. Similar to some of the previous lakes, steep topography limits campsites to a small area above the northwest shore, where use trails drop down the hillside from the main trail to a few passable sites. The nearly 50-acre, 50-foot-deep lake harbors a good population of cutthroats, some goldens, and an increasing number of hybrids.

A mild climb leads away from Lake at Falls until the grade levels out along the north shore of forest-rimmed, shallow (3 feet deep) Big Park Lake, at 7.8 acres the smallest of the named lakes up to this point. Plenty of potential campsites can be found west of the lake. Anglers can fish for goldens, cutthroats, and hybrids in the lake and nearby streams. Gently graded trail continues through light timber and lush trailside vegetation for another half mile to a bridged crossing of churning Granite Creek.

Beyond Granite Creek, the trail turns south and starts climbing more steeply again with the aid of some switchbacks that lead out of Granite Creek canyon and eventually back alongside East Rosebud Creek. Along the way, the grade momentarily eases on a small bench with a correspondingly small pond, before the climbing resumes. Back in the main part of East Rosebud Creek canyon, a stretch of open terrain provides hikers with a fine view of another picturesque waterfall

Hikers above Rainbow Lake

on the stream draining Vogel Lake. Heading back under forest cover for a bit, the trail climbs around a corner and then emerges to a stunning view of Duggan Lake, where the whitewater torrent of strikingly picturesque Impasse Falls crashes into the far end of the lake in dramatic fashion. The trail starts out close to the northeast shore of the lake and then climbs high above Duggan Lake in order to surmount Impasse Falls, providing excellent views along the way from both perspectives of below and above the falls.

While camping with such an incredible view of the falls would seem to be highly desirable, the steep topography around Duggan Lake severely limits potential campsites. Fishing in the 4.4-acre, 10-foot-deep lake should be good for both cutthroats and goldens. Whether or not you can find a decent campsite, the beautiful scenery around the lake is worthy of a lingering rest stop. The canyon of Falls Creek provides an excellent cross-country option for those with plenty of stamina and the appropriate off-trail skills.

Leaving the beautiful surroundings of Duggan Lake and Impasse Falls behind, the trail closely follows cascading East Rosebud Creek for a while before angling away via switchbacks on the journey to Twin Outlets Lake. The ascent leads to a view of yet another scenic waterfall, where the creek is funneled down a steep rock chute. From there, work your way around some cliffs and come out above the fall to immediately reach the northwest shore of the smaller lobe of Twin Outlets Lake.

Campsites are a bit more plentiful around the irregular shoreline of 29.5-acre Twin Outlets Lake, and the fishing for goldens, cutthroats, and hybrids in the 50-foot-deep lake should be excellent as well. Lush flower gardens and scattered timber ring the lake, the mostly open terrain of low granite hummocks allowing for fine views of the rugged canyon. As fires are banned above here until the other side of the crest beyond Fossil Lake, this may be your last opportunity to enjoy an evening campfire for a while. The trail wraps around the northwest shoreline, surmounting a low hill to a viewpoint of the upper part of the lake and yet another pretty cascade coursing down the basin's rock headwall.

Away from Twin Outlets Lake, a short descent leads to the bridged crossing of a wood plank bridge spanning a roaring stream from an unnamed tarn to the east of Medicine Lake (see map of The Beaten Path [West]). The trail skirts a flower-covered hillside and then switchbacks up the canyon of East Rosebud Creek to the north shore of lovely Dewey Lake.

At 9,316 feet, 37-acre Dewey Lake sits due north of rugged, 11,436-foot Mt. Dewey, with permanent snowfields gracing the north-facing flanks. Scattered timber and pockets of shrubs line the shoreline below the rocky cliffs above. Nearly level trail leads around to use trails that access campsites at the far side of the lake. Anglers should enjoy good fishing in the 95-foot-deep lake for cutthroat trout.

Beyond Dewey Lake, gently ascending tread leads past a small tarn and then follows the sinuous course of the creek through a small strip of meadow to a boulder hop of the creek draining Medicine Lake. A steeper section of trail winds up from the creek across mostly open, subalpine terrain before the grade eases again near another small tarn. After cresting a rise, a winding descent leads down through forest cover to a wet ford of the creek from fishless Oly Lake. Climbing away from the creek, you pass through lovely, flower-carpeted slopes alongside raucous East Rosebud Creek on a very picturesque stretch of trail. Where the trail moves away from the creek, the grade eases and the terrain opens up to alpine parkland surrounding the irregular shoreline of sprawling, 165-acre Fossil Lake.

The trail skirts some of the northern lobes of the lake before veering slightly into a drainage swale and the crossing of a dancing stream before arcing around to eventually reach the northwestern tip. Nearing 10,000 feet, the barren plateau around Fossil Lake casts an austere ambiance that can seem both beautiful and foreboding. You certainly have the feeling of being at the top of the world in this wide-open setting. The long shoreline offers plenty of opportunities for establishing a base camp from which to make off-trail explorations of the lake itself and the numerous alpine lakes scattered around the immediate vicinity. Fossil Lake is 150 feet deep at the deepest point, with the resident cutthroat trout providing plenty of fishing opportunities for anglers. As the topography offers no place to hide, experiencing an afternoon thunderstorm, which happens with some regularity at this elevation, can be quite exhilarating, if not downright frightening.

Immediately beyond the far side of Fossil Lake, gently rising tread leads to the apex of the trip at the low divide separating the East Rosebud and Clarks Fork drainages, where a large cairn rising above the open topography marks the otherwise indistinct boundary between the Beartooth Ranger District and the Gardiner Ranger District of the Custer Gallatin National Forest. Directly west is Fizzle Lake (also called Windy Lake on some maps), one of the many lakes and tarns dotting the alpine tundra of the Beartooth Plateau. Cross-country enthusiasts with the luxury of extra days will find plenty of rewarding territory worthy of exploration in this part of the Beartooth Plateau.

The trail turns south and passes two lovely tarns on the way into the narrow drainage of a tributary of Russell Creek. Soon the azure-colored waters of Skull Lake spring into view. Just before reaching the lake, the trail crosses the creek to follow the west shore. Neighboring Fulcrum Lake (also called Mermaid Lake on some maps) is just a short off-trail jaunt to the northeast, where anglers can fish for good-size cutthroats. A bench between the two lakes provides a fine campsite with a fantastic view of the surrounding topography. With a little more effort, Basin Lake (Picasso Lake on some maps) is a short, 0.1 mile off-trail ramble to the west of Skull Lake. Fishing for cutthroat trout in these lakes should satisfy even the most discriminating angler.

Heading away from Skull Lake, the trail heads downstream through open, subalpine terrain with a smattering of conifers before ascending high above the next lake in the chain, 38-foot deep Bald Knob Lake, so named for the promontory to the east. Gray cliffs provide a dramatic backdrop to the lake, which boasts a fair-size island near the south shore. Brook trout will tempt anglers here.

Briefly follow the outlet from Bald Knob Lake, cross over a log to the east side, and then hike a short distance past use trails leading to campsites near the southeast shore. Flower-lined tread leads up to a small knoll with some more campsites before dropping down to diminutive, 3.5-acre Ouzel Lake. Picturesque, 23.6-acre Lake of the Clouds is nestled into a basin east of Ouzel Lake, easily reached by a quarter mile of cross-country hiking. Both lakes harbor cutthroat trout.

Wind down alongside the creek away from Ouzel Lake, where the water temporarily takes a subterranean course beneath a substantial boulder field. Fine down-canyon views grace the descent on the way to a crossing of a rock-strewn side creek. Talus slopes eventually give way to a scattered forest broken by small patches of meadow as the descent continues. Where the trail wraps around a promontory, Russell Lake springs into view, followed by switchbacks that lead down to a bridge across the main branch of the creek. Now heading southwest, the trail passes several campsites before reaching the east shore of the 27.5-acre lake.

Residing at an elevation of 8,372 feet, the vegetation surrounding Russell Lake denotes a return to more temperate climes, as lodgepole pines and firs rim the lakeshore. With what some would consider a more hospitable environment, Russell Lake receives a fair amount of use from overnighters—solitude seekers may want to camp at some of the more remote lakes nearby. The junction for the faint trail branching east from the midway point along the east shore of Russell Lake toward 50.8-acre Mariane Lake is easy to miss. Although the first quarter mile of this trail is quite steep, the rest of the 1.4-mile ascent to the 9,542-foot lake is much less severe, providing a fine base camp for off-trail explorations to such gems as Ward Lake, Lake of the Winds, Z Lake, Rock Tree Lake, Triangle Lake, Indian Knife Lake, Picket Lake, and Otter Lake.

Although a final campsite is an option at either Fox or Rock Island lakes via short side trails, most parties elect to hike all the way out the final 6 miles from Russell Lake to the Clarks Fork trailhead. The trail follows cascading Russell Creek away from the lake, soon crossing to the west bank on a stout wood bridge. On dirt and pine needle tread, the descent continues alongside the creek through forest cover briefly interrupted by a stretch of talus. A set of switchbacks leads over a set of cliffs and then down and away from the creek for a bit. Pass through a couple of breaks in the lodgepole-pine forest where small meadows provide some visual interest before the trail draws near to the creek again, which glides peacefully through the trees. After veering away from Russell Creek to swing around the back side of a large rock knob, the trail leads to a signed junction with Fox Lake Trail (the trail shown on the USGS map that follows Russell Creek to Russell Lake has been abandoned).

Side Trip to Fox Lake

Fox Lake is a suitable place for a campsite if you're looking for one more night in the mountains before returning to civilization. The half-mile trail to Fox Lake rises gradually away from the main trail and then plunges steeply to the north shore. Marshy grass bordered by dense forest encircles the north side of the 111.4-acre lake, which inhibits access for anglers plying the waters for the resident brook, rainbow, and Arctic grayling trout. A few campsites are tucked beneath the conifers, but they appear to be heavily used by horse packers. An abundant population of mosquitoes should be expected here until late in the season. Although attractive in its own right, Fox Lake could be viewed as an ugly stepsister in comparison to the stunningly beautiful lakes seen previously along the Beaten Path.

Away from the Fox Lake junction, the main trail proceeds through the forest until emerging at a large meadow. Back under forest cover the signed junction with the Big Moose Lake Trail is reached, leading to 137-acre Rock Island Lake, which offers attributes similar to Fox Lake.

Continuing west on the main trail, you exit the Absaroka-Beartooth Wilderness and stroll across an expansive meadow on a raised boardwalk. Mosquitoes can be a huge nuisance in this area until late season. Beyond the meadow the trail climbs above Kersey Lake through an old burn area and then follows an undulating course to a Y-junction with a lateral that leads to a rental cabin on the west shore of the lake. A short distance farther is another junction, this one with the well-traveled Vernon Lake Trail heading southeast.

Soon the trail merges with a dirt road that provides vehicular access to forest-rimmed Kersey Lake. On the far side of the road, a stretch of the aptly named Broadwater River can be seen through the trees. After following the road for a good distance, the trip resumes more of a wilderness setting back on a section of single-track trail that gently climbs and then descends to a stout bridge across Clarks Fork Yellowstone River. Once across the raging watercourse, follow the interpretive trail a short distance to the large parking area at the Clarks Fork trailhead.

Possible Itinerary

	Camps and Side Trips	Miles	Elevation Gain
Day 1	East Rosebud trailhead to Rainbow Lake	8.0	+2,275/−725
Day 2	Rainbow Lake to Twin Outlets Lake	4.8	+1,675/−250
Day 3	Twin Outlets Lake to Fulcrum Lake	5.0	+875/−500
Day 4	Fulcrum Lake to Russell Lake	3.0	+50/−975
Day 5	Russell Lake to Clarks Fork trailhead	6.5	+350/−1,150

Giving Back

Absaroka Beartooth Wilderness Foundation: www.abwilderness.org

John and Isaac

In our fast-paced society, a simple moment to oneself is a harder and harder luxury to come by these days, let alone the even grander extravagance of a long period of quiet reflection sans distractions. One of the most wonderful aspects of backpacking is the ability to lose yourself in your own thoughts, far away from the excessive stimuli generated from computers, cell phones, TV screens and from the constant drone of IPods, MP3 players, and Muzak. Once a steady rhythm on the trail is obtained, a backpacker is left to his or her own musings, free from the man-made clutter of everyday life. Some hikers can get into such a mindset soon after stepping onto single-track tread, while others need a much longer period in which to decompress before leaving the cares of the world behind. However long that process, a trip into the wilderness is usually both a restorative and refreshing tonic.

One summer, I had the good fortune to take three separate trips into the Rocky Mountains of Montana and Wyoming with three companions from San Diego. Tic and I rendezvoused at Cooke City with Andy, whom I had backpacked with occasionally on trips in the Sierra and Trinity Alps, and John, whom I hadn't met before. We spent a night in a rustic cabin, ate breakfast the next morning in the café across the street, and then waited for my sister-in-law, Claire, and her daughter, Ariel, to shuttle us to the East Rosebud trailhead. After whetting our appetites to be in the mountains with the amazingly scenic drive along the Beartooth Highway, we bade farewell to my greatly appreciated relatives and set out on the trail.

For the next few days, we backpacked up East Rosebud canyon and onto the Beartooth Plateau, enjoying the incomparable scenery and camping each night alongside a beautiful lake. We shared parts of our personal journeys through life along the way, which allowed me the opportunity to get to know a little bit more about John and his particular story. John had grown up in Appalachia as a self-proclaimed hillbilly before eventually heading west to Southern California. Consequently, he grew up in a rural mountain setting, where hunting and fishing in the hills and streams outside his back door was a way of life. Each night around the campfire, John would regale us with interesting stories about growing up poor in the Appalachian Mountains. At one point during his youth he had a woodchuck for a pet—not in a cage in the backyard, but in his house (his story of the woodchuck terrorizing an unsuspecting real estate agent was priceless).

Despite what his upbringing and woodsy ways might imply, John was a very capable and intelligent man. He was an excellent and industrious carpenter, having worked for several years in the trades, building his current home in his spare time. Occupationally, he was an extremely gifted high school teacher, with a deep love for history and the rare capacity to make that subject come alive for teenagers—the type of history teacher every public school student should be afforded but rarely experiences. Perhaps his most appreciated roles are as devoted husband, loving father, and doting grandparent.

While the three of us were generally easygoing and somewhat laid back, John was the type of person who had a hard time sitting still. In addition, he possessed a few qualities that were initially mildly irritating, but over the long haul became somewhat comical, if not totally endearing. His frugality was much more evident during our layover days in the towns of West Yellowstone and Jackson, but even on the trail Andy, his sleeping and cooking partner, would have to suffer through the quirks of John's old equipment and the blandness of his very basic cuisine. In the evening, John loved to build campfires, not your run-of-the-mill campfires, but gigantic bonfires, towering infernos of biblical proportions that would have surely defied God's miraculous intervention and thoroughly consumed Shadrach, Meshach, and Abednego. The few times the rest of us were allowed to build a fire while John was out fishing (his favorite pastime), he would invariably return to camp, make a fleeting, sidelong assessment of our work with a look of disdain, and from out of nowhere toss a gigantic tree trunk or two onto our insufficiently modest blaze. Since we were traveling in black and grizzly bear territory, we carried our food in bear canisters, much to John's consternation, who, in his slight but still distinct twang, continually referred to this cylindrical inconvenience as that "damn bear canister."

Each morning of our trip, we were filled with excitement and anticipation about what the day would bring, at least until our final day in the Beartooths, when we traveled through mostly featureless forest toward our exit point at the Clarks Fork trailhead. Previous days we were very social, with periods of lively conversation along the trail that would reach crescendos during rest stops. But the last day we seemed to put our heads down and grind onward toward the trailhead as mainly solitary beings lost in thought, propelled by the prospects of a hot shower, good food, and proper refreshment. For most of that last day we were spread out along the trail, only occasionally snapping out of our solitary states to briefly regroup at trail junctions. Otherwise, we kept our personal ruminations to ourselves.

Following a long stretch of solitary hiking, Tic, Andy, and I caught up with one another at a trail junction and waited for John to join us. As he approached, we noticed a few tears streaming down his cheeks, prompting Tic to inquire about his well-being. In a slightly shaky voice John replied, "I've been grieving for Isaac. I haven't grieved for Isaac for over twenty years." Tic and Andy were well acquainted with this story, having lived through the ordeal with John and his wife in San Diego, but I was new to this tragedy. However, recounting this event for my benefit at this particular time would not have been appropriate, so we gave John some space to process his feelings, resuming our walk in reverential silence.

Later in the day, I asked Tic about the story of Isaac. John and his wife, Gwen, had lost their infant son to a choking accident. He was on the kitchen floor at his mom's feet while she was preparing a meal, when he picked up a wayward bean and stuck it into his mouth. Before Gwen could react, the bean lodged in Isaac's throat. Paramedics came and transported Isaac to the hospital. Several days later, John and Gwen faced the agonizing decision of having to okay the order to take their brain-dead son off of the respirator in order to allow his passing. That day in the Beartooths would have been Isaac's twenty-fifth birthday.

Alone on the trail, John was given the opportunity to clear his head from the milieu of modern life we all encounter in our everyday existence, and given the permission to experience a holy and tender moment that his mind may have temporarily repressed but his soul desperately needed. Bombarded by busyness and incessant electronic stimuli, we rarely, if ever, are afforded the chance to reflect and ponder the truly important aspects of life while in the "real" world. Here in the mountains, stripped of all the human-made inhibitors, our minds are unencumbered and free to wander to places that are perhaps unreachable when surrounded by the trappings of our daily existence. As with John, backpacking can provide the rest of us with the time and space not only for our feet, but also our minds, to wander freely.—**Mike**

PART 2

Wyoming

Yellowstone National Park

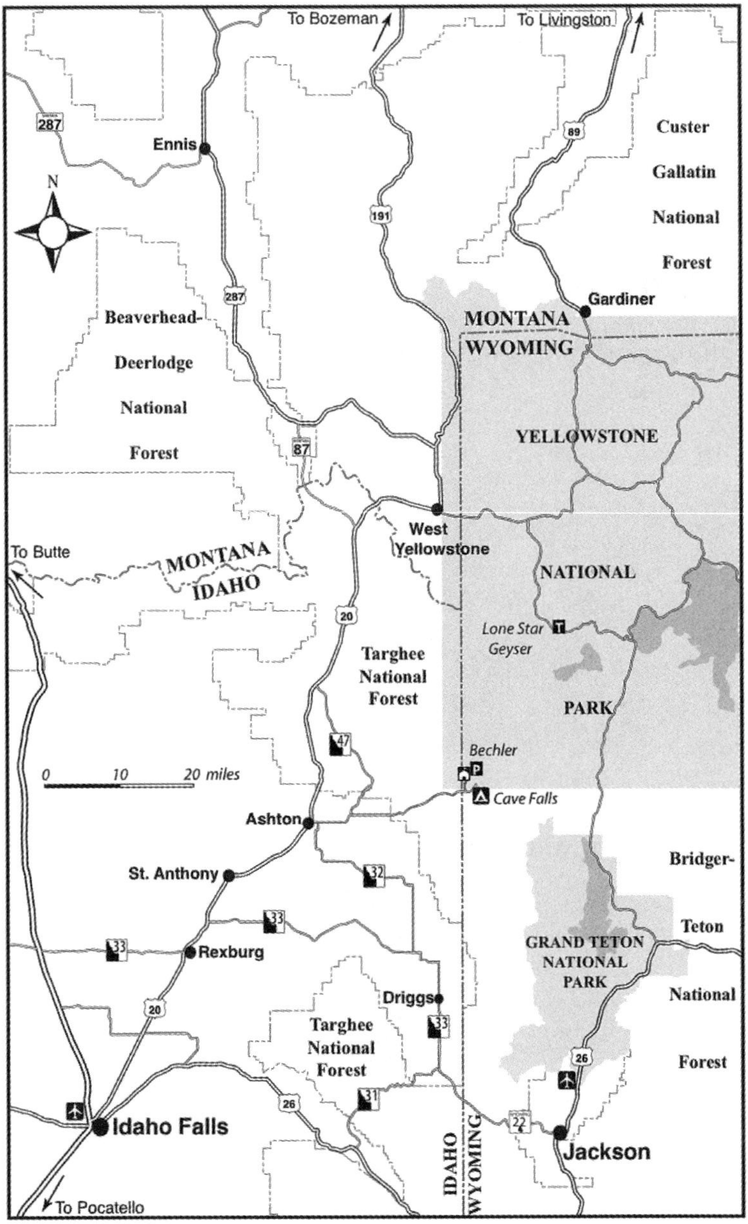

Bechler River Trail Location Map

TRIP 6

Bechler River Trail

> National parks are the best idea we ever had. Absolutely American, absolutely democratic, they reflect us at our best rather than our worst.
>
> —WALLACE STEGNER, AUTHOR AND CONSERVATIONIST

Since this book covers the Rocky Mountain states, it's not surprising that nearly all of the trips described in these pages involve hikes through the spectacular high peaks of this impressive mountainous region. This trip is different. Although you'll be traveling through the fairly high, forested terrain of the Yellowstone Plateau, there are no craggy peaks, cirque lakes, or view-packed ridges. Instead, the highlights of this wonderful excursion are a lush river canyon and lots (and *lots*) of waterfalls. They plunge over high cliffs, they twist down narrow chasms, they drop in broad cascades: in fact, in just about any way imaginable of water combining with gravity, a waterfall exists in this region to make that vision a reality. The hike also includes many of the other treasures of much-heralded Yellowstone National Park, including wildlife in abundance, especially moose, elk, bison, sandhill cranes, black bears, and possibly even a few grizzly bears (so camp and act accordingly). The trail also takes you past a small but interesting sampling of other famous Yellowstone attractions: geysers, glory pools, hot springs, and assorted thermal features. Arguably the best and certainly one of the more popular long hikes in Yellowstone, the Bechler

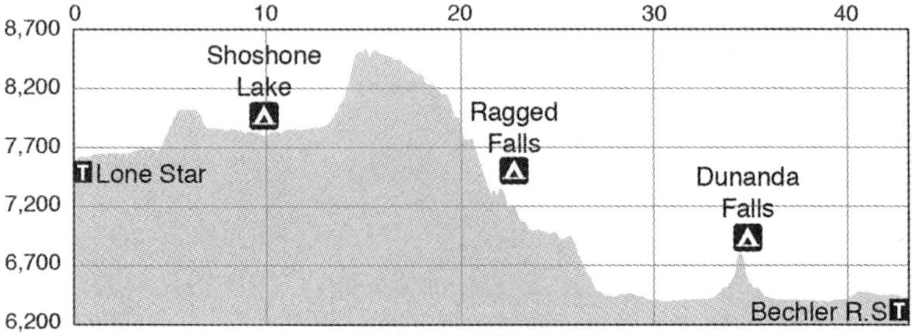

Bechler River Trail Profile

River Trail is well worth every fun mile, even if you don't see any rugged mountains along the way.

Days: 3–5

Distance: 30 miles (shortest possible version), 43 miles (including recommended side trips and variations)

Type: Shuttle

Scenery: 7

Solitude: 3

Technical Difficulty: 6 (due to river fords)

Physical Difficulty: 4

Elevation Gain/Loss: +2,550'/–3,700' (with side trips)

Season: Mid-July to October

Best: Late August through early October

Map: Trails Illustrated: *Old Faithful and SW Yellowstone National Park*

Resources: *Top Trails: Yellowstone & Grand Teton National Parks*, by Andrew Dean Nystrom; *Free Fire*, by C. J. Box; *Yellowstone Trails: A Hiking Guide*, by Mark C. Marschall; *Super Volcano: The Ticking Time Bomb Beneath Yellowstone National Park*, by Greg Breining

Contact: Yellowstone National Park
PO Box 168
Yellowstone National Park, WY 82190-0168
307-344-7381
Backcountry Office: 307-344-2160

Permits: Permits are required and advance reservations are strongly advised, especially during the peak-use months of August and September. Reservations may be made in person, by fax, or by mail (no telephone or e-mail reservations are taken) starting on January 1 for the upcoming calendar year. All reservation requests received by the park by March 31 are processed in random order starting on April 1. A nonrefundable fee of $25 is charged for each reservation. Backcountry Permit Reservation Applications can be downloaded from the park's website. In addition, fees of $3 per person per night ($15 maximum) are charged for overnight camping. An annual camping permit can be purchased for $25 for those planning on multiple overnight trips. For forms and further information, go to the park website. The nearest locations to pick up your (preferably reserved) permit are the Old Faithful Ranger Station backcountry office (located near the post office in the southwest corner of the complex of parking lots and buildings around Old Faithful Geyser) and the Bechler River Ranger Station right at the southern (exit) trailhead.

Regulations: Camping is allowed only at designated campsites. At several campsites, parties are limited to stays of no more than one or two nights. Fires are allowed only at specified camps.

You are required to store all food and other odorous items away from bears *at all times*, even if you are only gone for a few minutes. Anglers must obtain a special Yellowstone fishing license.

Nearest Campground: Cave Falls Campground—3.5 miles from the southern (exit) trailhead. Madison Campground—18 miles from northern (starting) trailhead

Nearest Airport: Idaho Falls Regional Airport (IDA)—77 miles (from the exit trailhead)

Nearest Outdoor Retailer:
3 Peaks Outdoor Sports—78 miles
910 E Lincoln Road
Idaho Falls, ID 83401
208-523-7325

Outfitter:
Wildland Trekking Company
Montana Office
2304 North Seventh Avenue, Unit K
Bozeman, MT 59715
800-715-4453
www.wildlandtrekking.com

Transportation Logistics: A very long and rather tedious car shuttle is required to make this trip. Unfortunately, there are no public transportation options and no conveniently available shuttle companies to service hikers. Thus, you'll need two vehicles and plenty of extra time in your schedule.

Backcountry Logistics: (GB, BB, St) Grizzly bears are relatively rare in this part of Yellowstone, but they do live here and their somewhat smaller black bear cousins are common. Camp and act accordingly.

Before late summer, the meadows at the southern end of this hike are often flooded with as much as one or two feet of water, making hiking then both uncomfortable and unsafe. Well into August, the mosquitoes in this area are extremely abundant (think clouds of the little vampires that seem to block out the sun). There are also several river fords required along this trip, which can be difficult or even dangerous in early summer. All of these factors argue in favor of a late summer or early fall trip. In fact, the park generally will not even take backcountry reservations for the Bechler River area unless your trip is scheduled to start after July 15.

Attractions and Amenities: If you need a motel, a restaurant, or just somewhere to purchase a T-shirt, a guidebook, or a postcard, your best selection is in the tourist-oriented town of West Yellowstone. In Yellowstone National Park itself, the various gift shops are worth looking at for purchasing smaller items, but the accommodations and food service options (although grand and historic such as the magnificent old lodge at Old Faithful) are limited, very expensive, and usually require getting reservations months in advance. Even if you don't stay there, however, take some time to at least tour the **Old Faithful Lodge** for its history and grand architecture.

Needless to say, the attractions (both human-made and especially natural) of Yellowstone National Park and the surrounding area are superb and could (and do) fill volumes. A visitor can easily spend weeks here exploring the many natural wonders and not feel like they have wasted a moment, or even seen everything worth seeing. Still, a (woefully inadequate) listing of a few of the very best attractions that are on, or reasonably close to, the shuttle route for this hike include **Great Fountain Geyser** (find out when it is next scheduled to erupt, and wait for this amazing show to happen); **Midway Geyser Basin**, and especially the amazingly colorful **Grand Prismatic Spring**; **West Thumb Geyser Basin** and **Yellowstone Lake**; **Upper and Lower Yellowstone Falls** in the **Grand Canyon of the Yellowstone**; the hike up **Mount Washburn**, with its great views and high likelihood of seeing bighorn sheep; **Old Faithful** (despite the crowds, no visit to Yellowstone is complete without watching this geyser erupt); **Upper and Lower Mesa Falls** in the Targhee National Forest southwest of the park; and the surprisingly excellent **Grizzly and Wolf Discovery Center** in the town of West Yellowstone, Montana.

Directions to Trailhead: From Idaho Falls, drive 53 miles northeast on US Highway 20 to a junction in the town of Ashton.

To leave a car at the exit trailhead, you turn right (east) onto State Highway 47 and drive 1 mile to a junction. Go straight, still on Highway 47, and proceed 5.2 miles to a junction with Cave Falls Road. Turn right onto this paved road, which eventually turns to good gravel and becomes Forest Road 582. At 16.6 miles from Highway 47, you come to a junction just after a sign identifying the Wyoming state line. You turn left then drive 1.5 miles to the trailhead parking area beside the Bechler River Ranger Station.

To reach the starting trailhead, return to Ashton and go northeast on US 20 for 56 miles to the bustling tourist community of West Yellowstone, Montana. Follow signs through town directing you to Yellowstone National Park (or simply follow the flow of cars, because almost everyone staying in this little city is heading for the park), and come to the entrance station just on the outskirts of town. Proceed east for 14 miles to Madison Junction (there is a campground here), then turn right (south) on the Grand Loop Road, following signs to Old Faithful. Drive 16 miles, passing all kinds of geyser basins and other great attractions along the way, to the turn off for Old Faithful. Continue straight on the Grand Loop Road and drive 2.7 miles to the signed Lone Star Geyser trailhead on the right. This trailhead is immediately past the signed viewpoint turnout for Kepler Cascades.

Yellowstone's Volcanic Temper

Supervolcano! It sounds like a term dreamed up by some unimaginative movie producer to help promote his next disaster epic, with lots of impressive special effects but no believable story. However, it's actually real, and when hiking in Yellowstone you are literally walking right over the top of one.

Yellowstone's volcanic nature has been known for a long time. All those hot springs, geysers, mud pots, and associated thermal features are fueled by a whole lot of heat from down below. What wasn't clear until fairly recently is just how huge a volcano actually lies below.

Not all volcanoes are alike. Most volcanoes are stratovolcanoes, classic cone-shaped peaks built up over time in layers of ash and flows of very thick lava. Occasionally, these volcanoes produce violent eruptions, such as the 1980 blast of Mount St. Helens in Washington State. Shield volcanoes, like those in Hawaii, build large mountains with long, gently sloping sides from rapid flows of very liquid lava. Shield volcanoes rarely produce large, violent explosions.

So-called super volcanoes are a relatively newly discovered phenomenon. Fortunately, they erupt very infrequently, but when they do it can be with an overwhelming force dwarfing the eruptions of "normal" stratovolcanoes. Typically, these huge eruptions blast out everything above them (sometimes entire mountain ranges) and leave behind gaping calderas—massive holes in the ground created by the explosion and subsequent collapse of an enormous magma chamber underneath.

Yellowstone is one of the twenty or so identified "super volcanoes" that have erupted periodically throughout Earth's history. A super volcano eruption is an earth-shattering event, on par with an asteroid impact, or a major nuclear war. Some scientists believe the periodic eruptions of super volcanoes may have been responsible for triggering ice ages. Although the facts are uncertain, there is some evidence to suggest that the last time a supervolcano erupted about 74,000 years ago, as much as 90 percent of the human population on earth was killed. Such eruptions certainly kill huge numbers of animals and may be responsible for mass extinction events, when over half the species of animals on the planet simply disappear in a matter of months. For perspective, the caldera of the last big eruption at Yellowstone, which occurred about 640,000 years ago, measures fully 34 miles wide by 45 miles long and encompasses most of the current national park. The true size of this caldera wasn't realized until satellite photography allowed scientists to grasp its full enormity. The Yellowstone caldera is at least *1,000 times* larger than the crater left behind by even a fairly large eruption of a typical stratovolcano. And the last major eruption at Yellowstone, though enormous, was significantly smaller than the one that took place about 1.5 million years earlier.

The 1980 eruption of Mt. St. Helens is still familiar to many readers. The enormous blast took 1,300 feet off the top of a mountain, completely leveled some 200 square miles of forests, covered eastern Washington in enough ash to turn day into night in cities such as Yakima, and killed fifty-seven people. Although a terrible disaster, humans have experienced much worse volcanic eruptions in recent geologic times. For example, the famous eruption of 1883 on the Indonesian island known as Krakatau (sometimes called Krakatoa) was approximately ten times bigger than that of Mt. St. Helens. Thirteen percent of the globe heard the explosion, which created a tsunami over 100 feet high and killed over 36,000 people. Worse yet was Tamboro, also in Indonesia, the biggest volcanic eruption in recorded human history. In 1815 this mountain erupted with enough force to pull the entire planet into a volcanic "year without summer," when global temperatures plunged five degrees, causing enormous crop failures and widespread starvation. Estimates put the human cost at well over 100,000 lives. As devastating as those events were, they were all *regular* volcanoes. An eruption of the Yellowstone supervolcano is many orders of magnitude larger than any earthquake or volcanic eruption in recorded human history.

The Yellowstone Volcano is fueled by what geologists call a "hot spot," where an enormous plume of magma (super-heated molten rock under the Earth's surface) has remained relatively stationary over millions of years. While the hot spot has stayed in place, the crust of rock above, which is part of the North American Plate, has slowly slid to the southwest at a rate of a little over one inch per year (about as fast as your fingernails grow). As the plate moves, the fixed-in-place Yellowstone hot spot has erupted numerous times. Geologists have pieced together evidence of 142 large, violent eruptions (and an untold number of smaller eruptions) of the Yellowstone Volcano over the last seventeen million years. All of these eruptions have left behind evidence of a string of progressively older volcanic activity as you travel southwest across the lava plains of southern Idaho and into northern Nevada and eastern Oregon.

All this raises the question of just what kinds of impacts can we expect with the next big Yellowstone eruption? Well, unless you happen to be within a hundred miles or so of Yellowstone when it blows, the biggest concern will likely be the enormous amounts of ash and sun-blocking gases emitted by the volcano. Fossil and geologic records reveal that previous big Yellowstone eruptions have buried much of the American West, as well as the Great Plains and Midwest, under as much as two feet of ash. Nothing can be done to stop this material from getting into lungs and killing virtually all life in its wake. All power plants, machinery, electronics, and virtually everything you can imagine would be clogged up and shut down, probably for months or years. The farm fields of the Great Plains, which produce almost half of the world's grain crops, would be useless for several years at a minimum and possibly for a whole generation. Basically, the United States as we know it would simply cease to exist. The significant global cooling from such an event, which will likely last for several years or even decades, would effectively prevent other parts of the world from making up the difference in lost agriculture, resulting in mass starvation across the globe. The numbers are very hard to determine, but some estimates predict the worldwide human death toll could easily reach one billion.

Given the potential impacts, scientists now monitor Yellowstone very closely to try and figure out what may or may not be happening. Since no one has been around during a supervolcano eruption, the signs of an impending event are hard to determine. Earthquakes often precede eruptions of other volcanoes. But Yellowstone already has many earthquakes—on average between 1,000 and 2,000 a year. Although nearly all of these tremors are too small to be noticed by visitors, they are happening and dutifully recorded nonetheless. Sudden swarms of hundreds of earthquakes over just a few days might indicate movement of molten rock, but these aren't uncommon at Yellowstone either. Concern arose between 2004 and 2008 when a large part of the central Yellowstone Park bulged upward, rising a full 8 inches over a fairly short time, which caused noticeable changes in the water level of Yellowstone Lake. This could mean the magma chamber below is pushing toward the surface, but no one knows for sure. Regardless, by the end of 2009 the bulging had slowed considerably and "probably" didn't mean anything ominous anyway.

When Yellowstone will erupt again (and it almost certainly will) is anyone's guess. Let's all hope, at least, that it isn't any time soon.

Lone Star Geyser

Trip Description: Begin by following a partially paved old road, now used as a hiking and mountain biking path, that travels south-southeast through a forest of lodgepole pines and a few Engelmann spruces. The route goes gradually upstream along the Firehole River, crossing its flow after 0.4 mile and always staying near the beautiful crystal-clear waters. At 1.6 miles the Spring Creek Trail goes left, but you stay straight on the bike path. Shortly after this junction, the route pulls away from the river and travels through a mix of forest and pretty meadows. After 0.8 mile from the junction, you come to the abrupt end of the bike path immediately before the thermal area around Lone Star Geyser. This extremely photogenic geyser features a 12-foot-tall cone (one of the tallest such geyser cones in the park) and reliably erupts about every 3 hours. If you have the time, sticking around to see the plume of hot water shooting up to 40 feet high is certainly worthwhile.

The trail goes around the left (east) side of the geyser and then wanders through forest for 0.3 mile to a junction. Turn left and soon pass Camp 0A1 just before a wooden bridge over the Firehole River. Not far on the other side of this bridge is an interesting thermal region featuring numerous bubbling hot springs. Bison are occasionally seen lounging around the meadows and thermal features here, often very close to

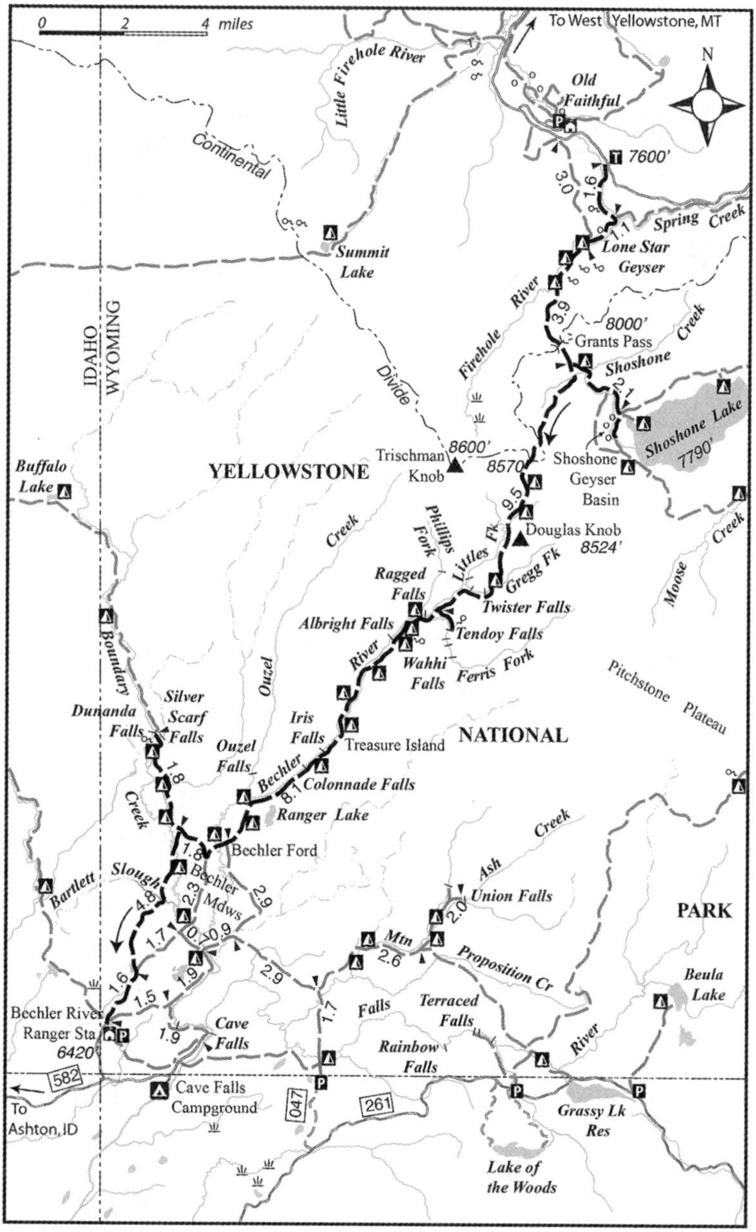

Bechler River Trail

the trail—give these large and potentially dangerous animals a wide berth. The trail then passes Camp 0A2 before heading very gradually uphill through forest and across meadows for another mile to Camp 0A3, an inviting location right along the Firehole River.

After Camp 0A3 the trail stays in the meadow for another 0.2 mile and then climbs through forest, gaining about 300 feet to a crossing of the Continental Divide at low and viewless Grants Pass. The trail then descends about 250 feet from the pass, breaks out into meadows, and then reaches a junction, 6.6 miles from the trailhead.

Side Trip to Shoshone Lake and Geyser Basin

The Bechler River Trail, and the continuation of your trip, goes right at the junction. Before going that way, consider this fun 5.2-mile side trip. The diversion is worth the time to see Shoshone Lake, the largest lake in the lower 48 United States without road access, and the Shoshone Geyser Basin, one of the best backcountry thermal regions in the park. To see both, veer left at the junction, almost immediately pass Camp 8G1, and for the next 2.1 miles follow the lovely grass-lined waters of Shoshone Creek to a prominent junction. Straight ahead you can see the enormous expanse of Shoshone Lake, which stretches for several miles to the east. On your right is the bubbling highlight of this side trip, Shoshone Geyser Basin. To visit this land of strong sulfur smells, intermittently erupting plumes of hot water, mud pots, and glory pools, simply follow the hiker-only trail on the right. After 0.1 mile you keep right at the junction with a side trail to Camp 8R5 on Shoshone Lake, and for the next 0.4 mile wander wide-eyed through the basin's thermal playground. This relatively small basin holds an amazing total of eighty known geysers, one of the highest concentrations in the world. As with any thermal area, never get too close to the hot water or stray onto the dangerously thin and unstable soils around the pools. After spending plenty of time to marvel at these features, return to the junction below Grants Pass.

From the junction below Grants Pass, turn south on the Bechler River Trail, which soon leaves the meadow and for the next 2 miles heads uphill through mostly viewless forest. After gaining about 700 feet, you top out at a second crossing of the Continental Divide, this time at an unnamed pass. The trail dips into the gully of a usually dry tributary of the Firehole River, and then climbs briefly to a third and final crossing of the Continental Divide just a short way before you reach Camp 9D4. About 1.2 miles of very gentle downhill follows to rocky Camp 9D3, which often smells fouled from stock use, and the pretty high-elevation meadow at the headwaters of Littles Fork, where quiet and observant hikers may have a good chance of seeing moose in this wet environment. The small craggy knoll of Douglas Knob rises above the south side of the meadow.

Having now entered the drainage of the Bechler River, you'll be traveling down this gorgeous stream for the rest of the trip. Because of the many waterfalls, this relatively remote southwest corner of the park is often called Cascade Corner. You won't have to wait very long before discovering the aptness of that name.

The trail crosses just west of Douglas Knob and then descends through forest to a crossing of Gregg Fork just a short distance before Camp 9D2. Less than 60 yards below this camp is the canyon's first waterfall, Twister Falls, which can best be viewed from the end of a short and possibly unsigned spur trail. This 55-foot cascading fall is not as impressive as some of those to come, but still worth at least a few minutes of your time to stop and admire.

The main trail continues its gradual descent through increasingly lush canyon forests. The unusually dense greenery here is nourished by the abundant precipitation falling in this the wettest part of Yellowstone National Park. After following the Gregg Fork downstream for about 1.5 miles, you come to an unsigned but obvious fork in the trail.

Side Trip to Tendoy Falls

The unofficial but well-traveled trail to the left goes past a livestock hitch rail and then up the north bank of Ferris Fork for about 0.5 mile. At the end of this very worthwhile side trip is an area of diverse thermal features with colorful hot springs, steam vents, and other fascinating geothermal features clustered in the canyon near Tendoy Falls. The thermal areas in this region are constantly changing. Some of these recent changes have created some new hot springs and pools with dangerously thin soils right along the trail. Be very careful where you step. The really adventurous can continue bushwhacking upstream for another 0.5 mile to beautiful Wahhi Falls and a series of other impressive but seldom-seen waterfalls on the upper reaches of Ferris Fork. After admiring the falls, retrace your steps back to the fork.

The Bechler River Trail goes straight at the unsigned junction with the side trail to Tendoy Falls and switchbacks down to a little bluff. From here you can see the 45-foot drop of Ragged Falls, where the stream's waters split and fall in two parts around a small island. ***Tip:*** *Although there are nice views of this falls from the trail, even better and more photogenic views can be had from the opposite side of the Ferris Fork. Although usually requiring wet feet to get there, the water is actually surprisingly warm, due to the hot springs not far upstream.*

From Ragged Falls, a short stroll leads to a crossing of Gregg Fork and Camp 9D1 almost immediately thereafter. The camp sits on a little bench above Three River Junction, where Ferris Fork, Gregg Fork, and Phillips Fork join to form the main stem of the Bechler River.

Continuing downstream, the trail follows the river for another mile before coming to a patrol cabin and a stock campsite beside a small meadow with several hot springs and other thermal features. Like many others in the park, this thermal area has an abundance of colorful algae growing in the warm waters. Hikers looking for a good overnight spot will be pleased with Camp 9B9, a little over 0.1 mile below this meadow. This scenic spot is positioned right beneath the towering rock cliffs of Batchelder Column and very near the loud cascade of Albright Falls, a wide, sloping cascade that drops fully 260 feet on the Bechler River.

Bechler Canyon remains narrow, lush, and scenic as you continue your steady but not very steep descent for another mile to Camp 9B8. Immediately after the camp is the first significant river crossing. Without a bridge, you must ford the river, as will be the case at all of the river crossings ahead. In early summer, these crossings can be difficult or even dangerous—one of many good reasons to avoid this hike before late summer. By August this first crossing is usually fairly straightforward and typically only a little over knee deep. Look for orange blazes placed to assist hikers in identifying the safest place to wade across.

After the first ford, you follow the west side of the river for another mile, crossing several small, spring-fed side streams and then come to a second ford of the river. This crossing is usually more challenging than the one upstream, with slippery rocks and a water level as much as thigh or even hip deep. If you don't like the look of the ford where the trail crosses, try scouting a bit downstream, where a riffle area indicates a somewhat shallower spot. On the other side is Camp 9B7. Although not as scenic as some of the camps you passed upstream, this is still a very pleasant spot, shaded by forest and right beneath the towering canyon walls.

The trail becomes a bit rockier on the way downstream past a series of beautiful, gently sloping cascades and Treasure Island, a large, forested island in the river. A little less than a mile below the second ford is Iris Falls, where the river drops 40 feet over a wide ledge. On sunny afternoons the mist from this falls produces a wonderful rainbow. Only about 300 yards farther down the trail is Camp 9B5, which is often a bit damp. The camp is otherwise well located, as not only is Iris Falls just upstream, but is also just above thunderous Colonnade Falls, a two-stage drop in the river, the lower part of which is a broad sheet of water tumbling over a basalt cliff into an impressive amphitheater. A 130-yard side trail leads to a dramatic viewpoint of this waterfall and a world-class lunch spot.

Continuing down Bechler Canyon, the trail passes through a forest of large Douglas firs and Engelmann spruces with a dense understory of buffaloberry, horsetails, gooseberry, and mountain ash. The fern-lined path also features lots of wildflowers, including coneflower, monkshood, grass of Parnassus, aster, and birchleaf spirea. In late August you can delight your taste buds with huckleberries and thimbleberries, both of which are also favorites of the local black bears.

The remarkably gentle trail stays close to the river as you pass several boulder areas, where you may be fortunate enough to see, or at least hear, pikas, which look like small guinea pigs and sound like a dog's squeaky toy. About 2 miles downstream from Colonnade Falls, you start to leave the narrow confines of the canyon shortly before reaching very attractive Camp 9B4. From here you can look north to see Ouzel Falls, where Ouzel Creek drops 235 feet over a cliff about 0.5 mile north of the river. Unfortunately, by late summer, which is the only reasonable time to make this hike, this falls diminishes to a rather unimpressive trickle, so the off-trail scramble to the base is probably not worth the sometimes tricky river ford and tiring bushwhack.

The Bechler River Trail leaves its namesake stream shortly after Camp 9B4 and wanders gently through forest for about 0.5 mile to Camp 9B3. Here you reach the northeast extension of the huge grassy expanse of Bechler Meadows. The trail takes you through this generally flat meadow for 0.4 mile before coming to a junction. Go right, soon pass a side trail to Camp 9B2, and almost immediately thereafter reach thigh-deep Bechler Ford. The river here is wide and slow moving with a sandy bottom that provides good footing, making it one of the easier fords on this trip. Keep an eye out for moose and sandhill cranes, both of which are common in this vicinity.

Once on the other side of the river, the trail leads across the waving fields of grass comprising Bechler Meadows. In early summer this area is flooded with up to 2 feet of water but by August the water is usually gone, leaving only some residual mosquitoes (come prepared for bugs) and fine views to the south of the jagged spires of the distant Teton Range. About 0.5 mile from Bechler Ford is a junction and a choice of routes.

The most direct course to complete the hike is to go straight on the Bechler Meadows Trail, which heads south across this huge clearing. Wildlife is often seen in this area, especially sandhill cranes, tall birds with loud, squawking voices that commonly nest in these meadows. After 1.5 miles you reach Camp 9B1 just before a bridge over slow-moving Boundary Creek. The trail then reenters lodgepole pine forest and comes to a junction. Keep straight, and walk through generally viewless and flat forest terrain for 1.7 miles to a junction with Boundary Creek Trail (the end of the longer alternate route described below).

You go left here and finish the trip with a gentle wander through open woods to a junction just 100 yards east of the Bechler River Ranger Station. Keep right, cross a small creek on a bridge, and come to the parking lot and trailhead.

Alternate Trip to Dunanda Falls

For a longer, alternate route that includes another particularly excellent waterfall, I recommend turning sharply right at the junction 0.5 mile past Bechler Ford onto the Bechler Meadows Cutoff Trail. This path takes you through meadows and forests to a junction near the edge of a small meadow. The trail to the left is the route to the exit point at Bechler River Ranger Station. However, before going that way you'll want to visit Dunanda Falls, so turn right and walk 0.35 mile to a knee-deep ford of a branch of Boundary Creek. Just on the other side of this ford is the side trail to Camp 9A2, yet another pleasant spot to spend the night in this corner of Yellowstone National Park. Watch for moose in the meadow and along the creek near this camp.

The trail now goes gradually uphill for about 1 mile through an area that burned in 1995. Many charred snags are still around, but an abundance of plants that experience beneficial habitat after fires—such as bracken ferns, fireweed, sunflowers, and young lodgepole pines—thrive here. After splashing across several small creeks, you reenter unburned forest and come to a crossing of a larger creek on a log. The trail then passes a side trail to popular Camp 9A3 and climbs fairly steeply to a viewpoint of the tall, sliding cascade known as Silver Scarf Falls. A little beyond this falls is a junction.

The Boundary Creek Trail goes steeply uphill to the right. You bear left, however, and in about 200 yards reach the top of Dunanda Falls, a wide sheet of water that plunges 110 feet into a scenic canyon of dark gray rock. There is a very steep scramble route to the base of the falls, worthwhile not only for the excellent photo opportunities but also because just a bit downstream from the falls is a wonderful hot spring. Here you can soak in the warm water while looking up at the falls and the rainbow often present on sunny days—a truly memorable experience!

After retracing your steps 1.8 miles to the junction with the Bechler Meadows Cutoff Trail, you keep right (south) on the Boundary Creek Trail. This remarkably level path takes you through a section of forest and then travels through a particularly wildlife-rich zone between the forest and the willow thickets beside meandering Boundary Creek, where both moose and beaver are usually abundant. Eventually you leave this enchanting habitat and then cross another grassy portion of Bechler Meadows to a calf-deep ford of Boundary Creek and Camp 9A1 on the far side.

The trail continues south for 1 mile past several tree islands amid the grassy expanse of Bechler Meadows to a ford of Bartlett Slough, a muddy-bottomed backwater that is usually around thigh deep. From here you follow a gently rolling course through lodgepole-pine forests and small meadows to a junction with the Bechler Meadows Trail. This is where you reunite with the shorter alternate route described above. Bear slightly right and finish the hike with a gentle 1.6-mile stroll to the Bechler River Ranger Station and trailhead.

Possible Itinerary

	Camps and Side Trips	Miles	Elevation Gain
Day 1	Lone Star TH to Shoshone Lake	8.9	+500/–300
	Side trip to Shoshone Geyser Basin	1.0	+50/–50
Day 2	Camp below Ragged Falls	12.0	+900/–1,800
	Side trip to Tendoy Falls area	1.0	+250/–250
Day 3	Camp below Dunanda Falls	11.3	+400/–800
	Side trip to Dunanda Falls	0.4	+250/–250
Day 4	Out to Bechler Ranger Station TH	8.0	+200/–250

Giving Back

Greater Yellowstone Coalition: www.greateryellowstone.org

Grand Teton National Park

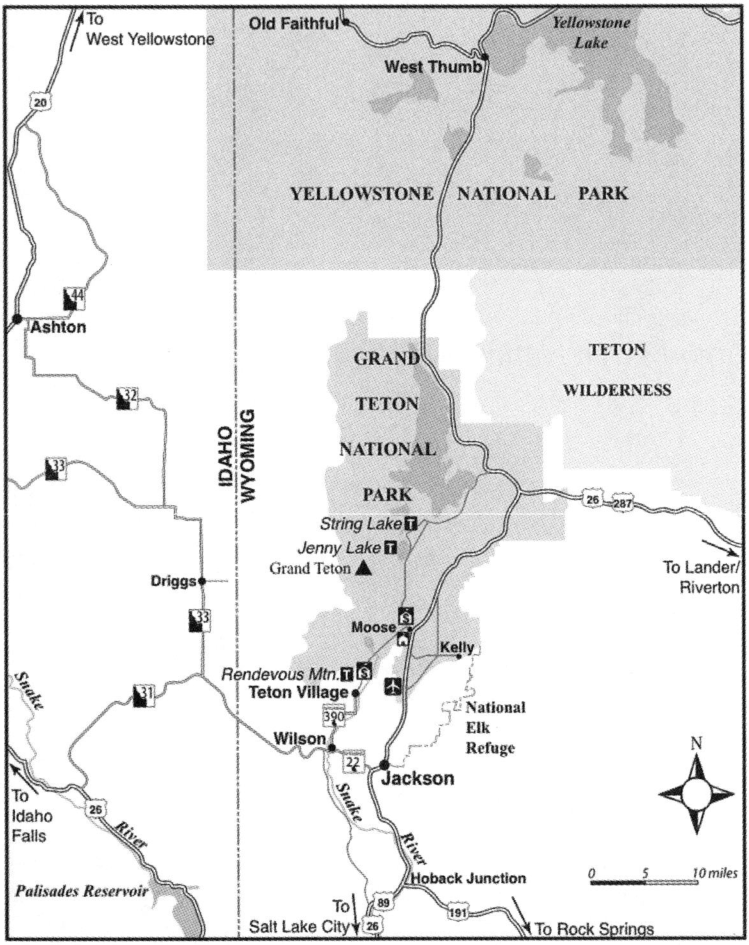

Teton Crest Trail Location Map

TRIP 7

Teton Crest Trail

> The farther one gets into the wilderness, the greater is the attraction of its lonely freedom.
>
> —THEODORE ROOSEVELT

Grand Teton National Park, just inside the western boundary of Wyoming, offers some of the most spectacular mountain scenery in the West, with "Les Trois Tetons" (the three breasts) piercing the Rocky Mountain sky with the same topographic majesty as when lonely French fur trappers first encountered them in the early 1800s. The range rises above the Snake River drainage in singular dominance over the surrounding terrain, creating a photographic profile recognizable throughout the world. The utter beauty of the area combined with well-deserved national park status lures sightseers, photographers, backpackers, and climbers from the four corners of the globe. With over 200 miles of trails, the park offers myriad opportunities for multiday backpacks, but none is more revered than the south-to-north, high traverse of the park on the Teton Crest Trail.

Rarely dipping below 8,000 feet, the majority of the trail travels through beautiful subalpine and alpine terrain, with flower-covered slopes and jagged peaks a nearly constant presence. Outside of the east-west-trending canyons near the exit points, widely scattered stands of forest are all that infrequently inhibit the customary wide-ranging

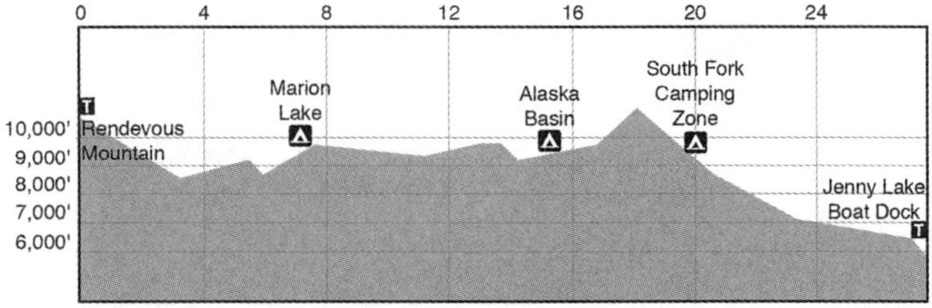

Teton Crest Trail via Cascade Canyon Profile

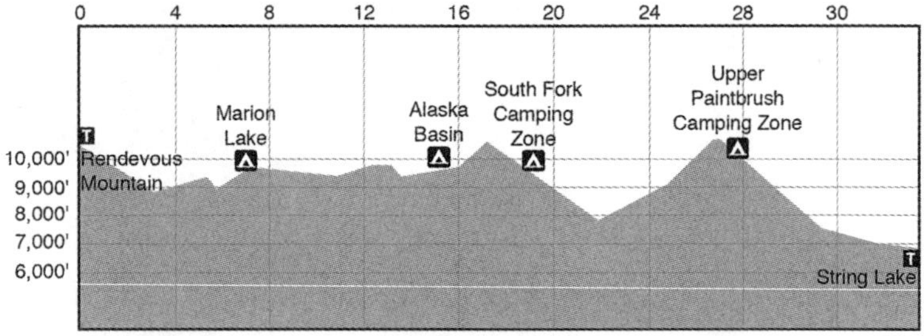

Teton Crest Trail via Paintbrush Canyon Profile

views of the Tetons themselves and the more distant ranges and valleys to the west and east. Near the crest of the range, lakes tend to be limited in number and rather small in stature, but the few encountered along the trail are picturesquely stunning. Both Cascade Canyon and Paintbrush Canyon, the two possible exit routes, are deep holes surrounded by rugged peaks with beautiful cascading streams, providing plenty of scenic diversity for the conclusion of the high traverse along the spine of the Tetons.

The full length of a trip along this spectacular trail spans 40 miles from Highway 22 in the south to the String Lake trailhead in the north. However, many parties elect to shorten the journey and avoid some significant elevation gain by riding the tram from Teton Village to the top of Rendezvous Mountain and then connecting with the Teton Crest Trail near Marion Lake. Exiting the route also has a couple of variations, with options of concluding the trip at Jenny Lake via the Cascade Canyon Trail, or at String Lake via the Paintbrush Canyon Trail. With off-trail areas to explore, peaks to climb, and plenty of reasons for layover days, the mountain splendor found within Grand Teton National Park suggests visitors spend as much time here as they can afford, and then some. Additionally, the nearby town of Jackson offers enough indulgent diversions for at least a day or two of rest and relaxation at the conclusion of the trip.

Days: 4–7

Distance: 27.2 miles via Cascade Canyon Trail (plus side trip to Alaska Basin), 34.9 miles via Paintbrush Canyon Trail (plus side trips to Alaska Basin and Snowdrift Lake)

Type: Shuttle

Scenery: 10

Solitude: 5

Technical Difficulty: 5

Physical Difficulty: 6

Elevation Gain/Loss: +5,225'/–8,850' (Cascade Canyon Exit), +7,275'/–10,300' (Paintbrush Canyon Exit)

Season: Mid-July to mid-September

Best: Late July to mid-August

Maps: USGS: *Teton Village, Mount Bannon, Grand Teton, Mount Moran, Jenny Lake*
Earthwalk Press: *Grand Teton National Park Hiking Map*
National Geographic: *Trails Illustrated Map: Grand Teton National Park*

Resources: *A Climber's Guide to the Teton Range*, by Leigh Ortenburger and Reynold Jackson.

Contacts:
Grand Teton National Park
PO Drawer 170
Moose, WY 83012–0170
307-739-3300
www.nps.gov/grte
www.fs.fed.us/r4/caribou-targhee

Caribou-Targhee National Forest
Headquarters Office
1405 Hollipark Drive
Idaho Falls, ID 83401
208-524-7500

Permits: Permits are required for all overnight stays in the backcountry. Advanced reservations are available for one-third of the permits during the period between the first Wednesday in January and May 15. Applications must be made online through the Recreation.gov website. The nonrefundable fee for advanced reservations is $35. The remaining two-thirds of the permits can be obtained for $25 on a first-come, first-served basis at the Craig Thomas Discovery & Visitor Center, Colter Bay Visitor Center, or Jenny Lake Ranger Station beginning the day before departure. Permits must be picked up before 10 AM on the day of departure. Be forewarned that competition for walk-in permits is extremely stiff. Call 307-739-3309 for more information.

Regulations: Maximum group size: twelve. Camping is limited to designated zones. Groups of 7–12 must camp in designated group campsites. Bear canisters required. No campfires, pets, or firearms.

Nearest Campgrounds: Start: Coal Creek—17 miles, Trail Creek
End: Jenny Lake (tents only)—4 miles

Nearest Airport: Jackson Hole Airport (JAC)—22 miles

Nearest Outdoor Retailers:
Cloudveil—12 miles
120 W. Pearl Avenue
Jackson, WY 83002
307-739-3930

Skinny Skis—12 miles
65 W. Deloney
Jackson, WY 83001
307-733-6094 or 888-733-7205

Teton Mountaineering—12 miles
170 N. Cache Drive
Jackson, WY 83001
307-733-3595

Moosely Seconds Mountaineering—25 miles
100 Dornan Road
Moose, WY 83012
307-739-1801

Outfitters: Consult the park's website for information about concessionaire activities, including guided climbs, backpacks, fishing trips, and float trips.

Transportation Logistics: The Teton Village and Jenny Lake or String Lake trailheads are approximately 40 miles apart by road, which requires about an hour of driving time. In lieu of two vehicles, or a friend who will agree to drop you off and pick you up, shuttle arrangements can be made with Teton Taxi and Backcountry Shuttle (307-733-1506).

Backcountry Logistics: (A, BB, L, Sn, Su, W, XC) The weather can be fickle at times at this high of an altitude this far north in the Rocky Mountains. Backpackers should be prepared to handle inclement weather, including severe thunderstorms, bringing with them the possibility of high winds and hail, as well as the occasional snowstorm. The high passes may be snowbound through mid-July, requiring ice axes to successfully navigate; check with the park service regarding current conditions.

This is also bear country, with both black and grizzly bears present. The NPS requires backpackers to use bear canisters, which are available for rent from the visitor center. The park service also recommends carrying bear spray.

Designated campsites are at a premium during the height of the summer season, especially the few at Marion Lake, where parties customarily hope to make a first-night's camp. Unless you've made advanced reservations, plan on arriving at the Craig Thomas Discovery and Visitor Center in Moose before opening the day before departure to increase your chances of grabbing a preferred campsite with your permit.

Amenities and Attractions: The town of **Jackson** offers the best and worst aspects of a tourist-based community. Rampant commercialism and congestion are two of the more obvious problems readily apparent to discerning visitors. A high cost of living, resulting in few economical housing alternatives for the low-end wage earners who staff the numerous stores, bars, and restaurants provides a challenge for many of the locals. Prior to the Great Recession, the burgeoning second home market saw the explosion of McMansions, producing a suburban sprawl that strained the relatively small amount of private land in the area. Despite these problems, Jackson has been able to hold onto some of the cowboy flavor one associates with Wyoming in general, albeit with perhaps a hint of rhinestones.

Overnight guests will find the price of lodging a bit steep for the level of quality, especially for some of the less elegant properties, but you're definitely paying a premium price for the close proximity to the Tetons. Advanced reservations are usually essential during the busy summer months, which can be made through **Jackson Hole Central Reservations** (888-838-6606, www.jacksonholewy.com).

Although a bit on the campy side, a visit to Jackson is not complete without a drink while sitting in a saddle at the **Million Dollar Cowboy Bar**, located in one of the premium spots around the historic town square. After your drink, and armed with plenty of cash (or a sufficiently high limit on your credit card), you can descend to the **Million**

Dollar Cowboy Steakhouse for traditional steakhouse fare in a casual and rustic setting typical of Jackson's western ambiance. Just far enough from the downtown core to avoid being completely overrun with tourists, **Snake River Brewing Company** is the area's microbrew headquarters, with a pub-style menu boasting, among other dishes, better than average pizzas. Carnivores will find regional fare such as bison, elk, and antelope amid the woodsy decor of the **Gun Barrel Steak & Game House** near the edge of town. Diners have a plethora of other options that run the gamut from barely edible plebian fare to expensive haute cuisine. For the famished, an ample supply of basic and hearty food is available at **Dornan's Chuckwagon** outside of Moose (near the park's visitor center), where you can enjoy rustic outdoor dining at reasonable prices for breakfast, lunch, and dinner, while picturesquely seated at a picnic table in the shadow of the Tetons along the banks of the Snake River. For a truly authentic Wyoming experience, visit the **Stagecoach Bar** In Moose, which has been serving patrons with libations since 1942.

Art enthusiasts shouldn't miss the truly exceptional **National Museum of Wildlife Art** located off US 89/189 just 2 miles north of Jackson. The museum houses an outstanding collection of paintings and sculptures, including numerous recognized masterpieces depicting wildlife. The museum is open from 9 to 5, every day of the year except for a few major holidays.

Trailhead Directions: From the center of Jackson, follow W. Broadway (US 26) to the junction with Wyoming 22 near the west edge of town. Following signs for Teton Village proceed northwest on Highway 22 for 4 miles, and then turn right onto Teton Village Road. After traveling north for 7 miles, turn left at Village Drive and wind around shortly to the large Teton Village parking area. Purchase tickets for the aerial tram, nicknamed "Big Red" at the counter near the base, and follow the posted boarding instructions. The scenic tram ride climbs over 4,000 vertical feet in 9 minutes, almost to the very summit of Rendezvous Mountain and the start of the hike.

End Via Cascade Canyon Trail: Head north out of Jackson on N. Cache Drive (U.S. 26, 89, and 191) into Grand Teton National Park. Reach Moose Junction about 8 miles from the park boundary, turn left onto Teton Park Road, and head across the Snake River on the way to the visitor center turnoff (backcountry permits). Continue another 8 miles on Teton Park Road to South Jenny Lake Junction, turn left, and proceed a short distance to the parking area, which tends to fill up quickly during the height of the summer—plan on an early arrival to secure a space.

End Via Paintbrush Canyon Trail: Follow directions as described above to the South Jenny Lake junction. Rather than turning west at the junction, continue ahead (northbound) on Teton Park Road for another 4 miles to the North Jenny Lake junction, and turn left onto Jenny Lake Road. Proceed on Jenny Lake Road for 2.75 miles to the String Lake turnoff. The trailhead parking area is a short distance west down this road.

Note: *When leaving private vehicles at both trailheads, after dropping off a car at the ending trailhead at either Jenny Lake or String Lake, a more direct route to the starting trailhead than returning to Teton Village via Jackson is possible by traveling the Moose-Wilson Road. From Jenny Lake, head south on Teton Park Road to Moose and then follow the Moose-Wilson Road to the Teton Village turnoff. The road is narrow and has a dirt surface for a stretch, so anticipate slow travel through the park. On the other hand, the marshy areas near the north end of this road are probably the best place in the park for up-close-and-personal observations of moose.*

John D. Rockefeller Jr. and the Creation of Grand Teton National Park

John D. Rockefeller Jr. (1874–1960) was the only son and youngest child of John D. Rockefeller Sr., who amassed the Rockefeller family fortune as founder of Standard Oil. After a short tenure in the family business, Junior furthered his personal riches in Manhattan real estate and banking. He was a man of high ideals, which, coupled with his wealth, led him into the role of philanthropist, eventually giving away over 500 million dollars during his lifetime to a variety of causes.

Advocates for expanding Yellowstone National Park south into Jackson Hole appeared on the political landscape as early as the late 1800s. However, by the time legislation for such inclusion was proposed in Congress in 1918–19, opposition to park status was widespread among a host of diverse interests: local ranchers feared the loss of grazing permits; the Forest Service was not fond of the idea, reluctant to give away jurisdiction of the area to another branch of the government; Jackson Hole businessmen and dude ranchers were afraid that a national park would inhibit their commercial interests; and hunters were opposed for the obvious reason that all hunting would be banned inside national park boundaries. Although there existed great interest in setting aside the Tetons as a national park in some quarters, local opposition was prevalent.

The threat of building dams on three of Jackson Hole's lakes in 1919 became the driving force in uniting opponents of the dams and champions of a national park to agree to research a scaled-down plan that would use private funds to establish a recreation area or reserve. Such a plan would protect the area against commercialization but continue to allow hunting, grazing, and dude ranching. Ten years later, local opposition to national park status for lands above Jackson Hole had diminished enough to allow Congress to pass legislation establishing 96,000 acres of land as Grand Teton National Park, a tract encompassing only the Teton peaks and six glacial lakes at their base.

While this legislation was a good first step, many park advocates—including Yellowstone Superintendent, Horace Albright—realized the broader ecosystem of Jackson Hole deserved federal protection. However, local opposition to the expansion of the park into the Snake River valley was still strong. After visits in 1924 and 1926, John D. Rockefeller Jr. became convinced of the need to preserve this stunningly scenic area from encroaching commercial development and subsequently surreptitiously formed the Snake River Land Company. The purpose of this company was to provide a way for Rockefeller to use his vast wealth to acquire sensitive lands anonymously, thereby keeping the prices reasonable and the ultimate goal of expanding the national park a secret. Over the course of twenty years, Rockefeller spent about 1.4 million dollars to purchase 35,000 acres of Jackson Hole real estate.

Many of these acquisitions were made easier by a bad ranching economy as a result of the Great Depression.

Unfortunately, even with the necessary land in the hands of Rockefeller, the battle for expansion of Grand Teton National Park was hardly over. Local antipark sentiment flared up again in the 1930s and early 1940s. Further compounding the difficulties, the Park Service refused to accept Rockefeller's gift of his Jackson Hole properties. After holding the land for fifteen years, Rockefeller became disheartened about this lack of progress and wrote a letter to President Franklin D. Roosevelt, which in part read, "It will be my thought to make some other disposition of it or sell it in the market to any satisfactory buyers." On March 15, 1943, Roosevelt completely bypassed Congress by declaring through presidential decree 221,000 acres of Jackson Hole (Teton National Forest lands, other federal lands, and Rockefeller's 35,000 acres) as the Jackson Hole National Monument.

Roosevelt's action further antagonized the local antipark sentiment and inflamed a bitter dispute about states' rights between Wyoming and the executive branch of the federal government. Spurred on by a Wyoming legislator, both the House and Senate passed a bill abolishing the monument, only to be killed by President Roosevelt's pocket veto. As a result, the state of Wyoming unsuccessfully sued the National Park Service to have the proclamation of the monument overturned. Even the federal government was not immune to difficulties, as the transfer of land from Teton National Forest to the Park Service produced acts of vengeance by disgruntled members of the Forest Service. Hostilities between supporters of the monument and nonsupporters were even common between residents of Jackson Hole.

Postwar sentiments against the expansion of the park eased as the nation became more mobile and tourism became more profitable for the local community. On September 14, 1950, the original park was merged with the monument into the current configuration of Grand Teton National Park. The ultimate success of the park was the work of many, but was due in large part to the generosity and vision of John D. Rockefeller Jr.

Trip Description: The thrilling and spectacular ride to the top of Rendezvous Mountain via the tram is one of the more memorable experiences for some of the hordes of summer tourists who visit

Jackson Hole each year. As scenic as the ride happens to be, in hindsight backpackers will look back upon the view-packed, 9-minute journey as merely a precursor to the much more extraordinarily picturesque scenery witnessed at a slower pace from the Teton Crest Trail. After disembarking from the tram, the hiker takes a short climb to the very top of Rendezvous Mountain (see map of Teton Crest Trail [South]) and the fine vista from what has been dubbed "the top of the world." After admiring the view, drop off the high point and follow a very rocky jeep road along an open ridge, heading away from the last remnants of civilization and toward the rugged and dramatic Teton backcountry. A few tourists amble their way along the road for a spell, and a handful of day hikers and backpackers may be seen coming and going, but most of the human traffic transported by the tram is left behind after you reach a junction with a single-track trail.

At a sign for Marion Lake and Granite Canyon, follow the trail as it drops off the ridge into Grand Teton National Park, descending into the upper basin of Granite Creek. Head downhill across open flower-dotted slopes alternating with stands of scattered-to-light forest, composed mainly of Engelmann spruce with lesser amounts of whitebark pine. The trail switchbacks, crosses over a tributary of Granite Creek, and then switchbacks a couple more times before entering the signed Middle Granite Fork Camping Zone. Pass through some lovely meadows and pockets of forest on the way to South Fork Granite Creek and a signed junction with Middle Fork Cutoff Trail a short distance farther, 3.5 miles from the end of the tram.

From the junction, a moderate, 0.6-mile climb through lush flower gardens leads to a junction and the start of your journey along the fabled Teton Crest Trail. Trail signs note a number of destinations, including the nearest landmark ahead, Marion Lake at 2.1 miles.

Just beyond a boulder hop of Middle Fork Granite Creek, a short path heads over to the designated group camp. A steeper climb culminates at the top of a divide between the Middle Fork and North Fork drainages, where rolling hills carpeted with vibrant wildflowers are backdropped by rugged peaks in nearly every direction. A brief descent from the divide leads down to the floor of the lushly vegetated basin and a junction with the Granite Canyon Trail, 5.6 miles from the top of the tram.

Just beyond the junction the trail crosses the North Fork and then ascends an open hillside, crossing a log bridge over a tributary part way up the slope. At the top of the climb the trail dips into the narrow drainage of a tiny rivulet and then winds uphill through a copse of conifers on the way to Marion Lake, where signs inform passersby about the fragile nature of the lake's ecosystem, the frequency of bear visits, and the numerous camping regulations. The trail enters the basin above the level of the lake and then drops down to near the lakeshore on the far side. As there are only three designated campsites near the lake, competition is extremely fierce for the few permits available. Located near an elevation of 9,250 feet, Marion Lake reposes serenely below a band of rust-colored cliffs above a talus slope and green-tinged hillsides around the rest of the shoreline. A smattering of Engelmann spruce dots the otherwise open lakeshore.

Leaving Marion Lake, the Teton Crest Trail crosses the tiny outlet on some large rocks and heads out across open, flower-covered slopes on the way to the top of the crest, where you exit the park and enter Jedediah Smith Wilderness. With the distinctive shape of Spearhead Peak acting as a beacon, you climb mildly across sparsely vegetated slopes with constant far-ranging views of the surrounding peaks and more distant mountain ranges. A waterless campsite large enough for a couple of tents is in a small stand of trees at the crest of a rise below Spearhead Peak. Gently graded trail continues across open, tundra-like slopes toward Fox Creek Pass with fine views of the southern Tetons. Drop slightly into the head of Fox Creek Canyon and proceed to the 9,560-foot pass and a junction with the Fox Creek Trail heading west, 2.3 miles from Marion Lake.

For those who missed out on securing a permit to camp at Marion Lake, the area around Fox Creek Pass provides the next most logical camping opportunity. A short distance off the trail to the southeast, Pass Lake, which is in actuality little more than a pond, has a couple of

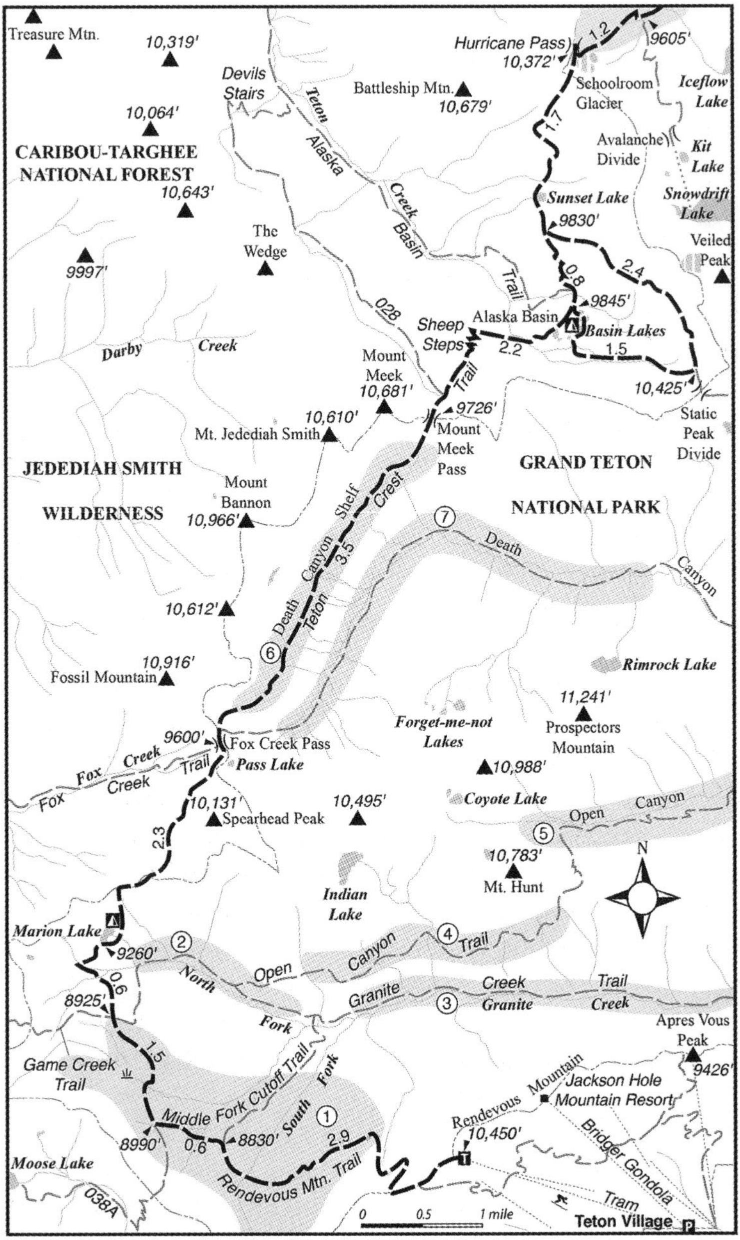

Teton Crest Trail (South)

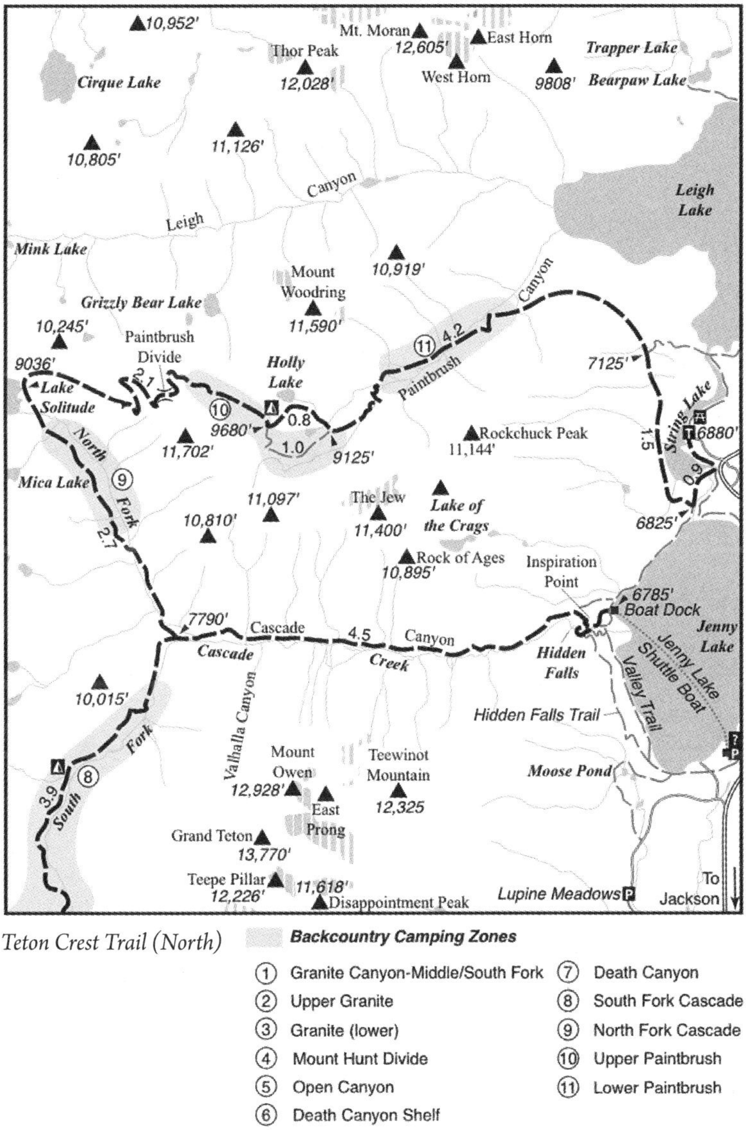

Teton Crest Trail (North)

View of the Tetons from the Teton Crest Trail

passable sites tucked into the trees above the east shore. A forested rise northwest of the pass offers a spot just big enough for a couple of tents as well. By heading downstream, you may find more campsites along Fox Creek.

Leaving Fox Creek Pass, you head back into Grant Teton National Park. A short distance from the pass is a junction with the Death Canyon Trail, which descends the canyon eastbound to Phelps Lake. Veer left here, and continue on the Teton Crest Trail into the Death Canyon Shelf Camping Zone, heading across open, flower-covered terrain and passing below a row of rugged vertical cliffs above the west side of the shelf—a prominence extending all the way north to Mount Meek. This stretch of hiking is quite pleasant, as the grade is generally mild, the flowers are quite cheery, and the views from the limestone shelf down into the deep cleft of Death Canyon are stunning. You'll probably see and hear a number of marmots along this stretch of trail, as they appear to be well suited to this alpine environment of boulder-studded meadows. Pass by an old fireplace, the only intact remnant of an old cabin, and continue to the crossing of a dwindling stream, which surely must have been the cabin's water supply in its heyday. Farther on, the trail also passes by a couple of pits that appear human made, perhaps to store water for use after snowmelt was completed. In between the two holes, a sign points the way to the designated group campsite. The journey along the shelf continues with improving views down into the immense hole of Death Canyon. The trail crosses a number of small streams before exiting the camping zone and then climbing to Mount Meek Pass, 3.3 miles from the Death Canyon Trail junction and 12.4 miles from the top of the Rendezvous Mountain tram.

Dropping away from the pass, you step into Caribou-Targhee National Forest and Jedediah Smith Wilderness across open terrain with a sweeping, westward view that extends north to the summits of the rugged Tetons. After dipping into and out of a couple of shallow drainages, you reach a junction with Teton Shelf Trail #028 heading northwest, 0.3 mile from Mount Meek Pass.

Proceed across a rocky stretch of trail composed of dolomite, and then bend around an outcrop to a marvelous view into the verdant vale of Alaska Basin. Zigzag down Sheep Steps, and head east toward the floor of the basin. Rising tread leads across some lushly lined rivulets and South Fork Teton Creek and then slabs of rock broken by small patches of meadow before reaching a junction with the Alaska Basin Trail, 2.9 miles from Mount Meek Pass.

Alaska Basin provides a wonderful overnight haven for backpackers traveling along the Teton Crest Trail. Outside of Grand Teton National Park, camping in this area is not restricted to camping zones and designated campsites, though campfires are banned and campsites must be at least 200 feet away from lakes and 100 feet from streams (grazing livestock is also banned). The handful of small lakes and tarns in the basin, known as Basin Lakes, are picturesque, bordered by flower-carpeted meadows and scattered timber and nestled beneath steep-sided cliffs and the airy summit of 11,938-foot Buck Mountain. Turning right (southeast) from the junction, Basin Lakes are just a short jaunt away, though some of the tarns sit well off the trail, requiring brief cross-country rambles to reach.

Alaska Basin Loop

The Alaska Basin Trail climbs along South Fork Teton Creek to a junction with Trail #026 near the head of the basin, before continuing up to the rocky gap of Buck Mountain Pass. The trail climbs east for another mile to Static Peak Divide, offering grand views of the Snake River coursing through Jackson Hole and backdropped by the Gros Ventre Mountains on the far side of the valley. A fine loop could be created by returning to camp via Alaska Basin Shelf Trail #026 on the north side of Alaska Basin to a junction with the Teton Crest Trail and then southeast back to Basin Lakes.

After your stay in Alaska Basin, return to the Teton Crest Trail and head northbound across a small stream and a boggy meadow, soon arriving at a junction with the westbound stretch of the Alaska Basin Trail, which follows South Fork Teton Creek through Teton Canyon to a trailhead near Teton Campground. Continuing, the trail crosses another small stream and then begins a winding climb up the north wall of Alaska Basin to the junction with the Alaska Basin Shelf Trail #026. Away from the junction, Sunset Lake pops into view, a green-tinged body of water reposing in an open bowl. A sweeping descent leads down toward the shoreline and a boulder hop across the channel. Sunset Lake is a good place for a rest stop before tackling the next section of trail, which climbs stiffly toward Hurricane Pass.

From the lake, head across wildflower-dotted slopes bisected by crystalline rivulets on the way to a series of well-graded switchbacks that zigzag up the hillside. A shorter set of switchbacks leads up through a narrow draw to an ascent across more open, rolling terrain carpeted with low-growing alpine flora. The climb eventually culminates at stunningly scenic Hurricane Pass, marked by a number of trail signs.

Perhaps the grandest view on the entire Teton Crest Trail unfolds from the vicinity of Hurricane Pass. Here the rugged and dramatic northwest face of the main Tetons springs breathtakingly into full view, totally dominating the foreground vista; from the pass, the majestic peaks appear to be so close you could seemingly hit them with a well-thrown rock. Below the rugged Tetons, South Fork Cascade

Creek plunges steeply northeast toward a union with the main branch in Cascade Canyon. A short walk from the pass toward the edge of the canyon provides an additional view of a morainal tarn filled with glacial-tinged water near the base of Schoolroom Glacier. If inclement weather or strong winds fail to propel you down the trail, at some point you'll have to force yourself to leave this picture-postcard scene.

Dropping away from the pass, the view-packed trail eventually switchbacks and descends rocky slopes toward the floor of the upper canyon. Along the way the sparse, low-growing alpine flora of the pass transitions to pockets of shrubs and taller plants. Pass below the moraine responsible for the tarn and continue onto the verdant floor of the upper canyon, which is dotted by small ponds and coursed by tiny rivulets; nestled in the shadow of the Tetons, this area is truly an alpine wonderland worthy of a layover day or two. Near the crossing of a small stream, a sign heralds the arrival into the South Fork Camping Zone, soon followed by a junction with the Avalanche Divide Trail.

Side Trip to Snowdrift Lake

The maintained section of the Avalanche Divide Trail ends at a divide at the toe of the east ridge of South Teton. From there, a straightforward cross-country route leads to the must-see alpine country around Icefloe, Kit, and Snowdrift Lakes. To see this area, turn south from the Teton Crest Trail, and make a switchbacking climb through meadows and then alpine, pond-dotted terrain for 1.6 miles to the 10,680-foot divide. Avalanche Divide offers a stupendous view of Grand, Middle, and South Teton, as well as Jackson Hole farther afield. Immediately below the divide is Kit Lake and farther downslope is scenic Snowdrift Lake, a straightforward 3/4-mile cross-country descent in the shadow of the Wall directly to the west. On the return hike, you can also visit Icefloe Lake, leaving the trail about a half-mile north of Avalanche Divide and following an easy cross-country route across meadows and rocks northeast one-half mile to the southwest shore of this usually icebound lake.

For more adventurous mountaineers, Avalanche Divide offers a frequently used, nontechnical (Class 4) route to the summit of South Teton (consult *A Climber's Guide to the Teton Range* by Ortenburger and Jackson for more information).

For the next couple of miles the trail makes a steady descent through meadowlands alongside bubbling South Cascade Creek, passing several signed laterals to campsites along the way. Where the creek plunges down the canyon at a steeper rate, a set of switchbacks leads to the bottom of a series of picturesque cascades and then into thicker forest. Cross several side streams as the trail occasionally switchbacks down South Fork canyon and passes more campsite laterals. Shortly after the trail turns east and enters the main branch of Cascade Canyon, you reach a junction with the Lake Solitude Trail heading northwest at 5.1 miles from Hurricane Pass (see map of Teton Crest Trail [South]).

Here the traveler faces a tough decision. Those pressed for time can continue down Cascade Canyon another 4.5 miles to the boat dock on the west shore of Jenny Lake. Those fortunate souls blessed with another couple of days can opt to extend their trip by climbing up Cascade Canyon to Lake Solitude, crossing over Paintbrush Divide and then descending Paintbrush Canyon to the String Lake trailhead.

Exit Via Cascade Canyon Trail: A short distance from the junction, the trail crosses Cascade Creek on a plank bridge and heads eastbound down the canyon through stands of dense timber alternating with openings in the forest. Gentle sections—where the creek slows and meanders through the deep, glacier-carved gorge between the Cathedral Group of peaks on the south and the Saint John Group of peaks on the north—provide fine rest stops on the way down the canyon. Nearing Jenny Lake, you reach a junction on the left with the horse trail, which provides the shortest route to the boat dock but is a featureless path through dense forest with the customary droppings littering the way. Continue ahead from the junction a short distance to Inspiration Point, where a fine view unfolds of Jenny Lake 400-plus-feet below, with Jackson Hole and the Gros Ventre Range beyond.

From Inspiration Point, a winding trail drops steeply south toward Cascade Creek for 0.2 mile to a junction with the lateral to Hidden Falls and the horse trail around Jenny Lake. A 5-minute walk along the right-hand path will take you to a view of the falls, but the area is usually packed with sightseers rubbing elbows to get the best view. Away from the

Hidden Falls junction, your trail traverses below Inspiration Point and then drops down past a junction with the western part of the loop to the falls and then another junction with the Valley Trail. Continue to the boat dock on the west shore of Jenny Lake. The short trip across the lake only takes a few minutes and provides some fine scenery for the conclusion of your journey. The fee is payable at the concession booth at the east dock.

Exit Via Paintbrush Canyon Trail: If your vacation allows for an extra day or two, then you are strongly encouraged to use that time by exiting this trip via the spectacular route past Lake Solitude and over Paintbrush Divide. Turn left at the junction with the Cascade Canyon Trail and hike 0.1 mile to a bridged crossing of North Fork Cascade Creek. The trail then gradually ascends through thinning forests and eventually into patchy meadows that offer nice displays of wildflowers in midsummer. After a mile, you make a second bridged crossing of the creek and immediately after enter the North Fork Camping Zone. As usual, there are several short spur paths to campsites in this zone, and you will find them to be very popular. That popularity is well deserved due to the abundant wildflowers, the fine views of towering canyon walls, and, most strikingly, the absolutely amazing scenery gazing back to the southeast of massive Grand Teton rising impressively over the mouth of North Fork Canyon. Along with that from Hurricane Pass, this is one of the most memorable vistas of the entire trip. The trail travels almost 1.5 miles through this idyllic camping zone before crossing a series of small creeks at the head of North Fork Canyon Creek. Pass beside a small, flower-banked waterfall before finally emerging at the meadow-rimmed flat holding gorgeous but incorrectly named Lake Solitude. The lake is the focal point of a classic mountain setting with abundant wildflowers, tiny rocky islands, and a ring of rugged cliffs. The lake's extreme popularity has forced the Park Service to ban all camping here, and horses are not allowed near the water.

Having enjoyed the beauties of Lake Solitude, you soon pull away from the shore on a trail curving uphill to the east. The open slopes house incredibly abundant wildflower displays including the relatively rare beauty of a type of large white columbine. The views back to Lake

Solitude and down the North Fork Canyon to Grand Teton are amazing. A couple of long, tiring switchbacks over increasingly rocky and alpine terrain finally lead you to Paintbrush Divide. At 10,720 feet, this is the highest point of the trip. This extreme elevation frequently means the pass is still covered with snow and ice until at least late July and often well into August. Check with the staff at the ranger station when you pick up your permit about the latest conditions. Before mid-July an ice axe is usually needed to safely cross the divide, and during heavy snow years that date may be extended for weeks. At any time of year, this above-timberline location is no place to be in inclement weather, or when thunderstorms are threatening. Even in good weather, expect cold and stiff winds. The view of mostly unnamed rugged summits all around is tremendous. For bird-watchers, Paintbrush Divide is an excellent place to look for relatively elusive black rosy finches, which spend their summers at these generally inaccessible heights.

From Paintbrush Divide, the wildly scenic path descends, often over snowfields and rocks, back into the land of grass and wildflowers, then spotty meadows, and finally past scattered whitebark pines. Partway down, you enter the Upper Paintbrush Camping Zone, which is a must-stay area during fair weather. The abundant wildflowers and the views of the colorful and extremely jagged ridge to the south, as well as the slopes of towering Mount Woodring to the north, contribute to an especially rewarding overnight stay. Numerous little creeks and an array of hidden locations create good spots for pitching a tent, though most sites are fairly exposed at this altitude. About 1.7 miles down from Paintbrush Divide is a junction with a side loop trail heading left on the way to Holly Lake. There are a couple of good campsites at this pretty lake, though obtaining a permit for them is often challenging.

The main trail goes right at the Holly Lake junction, continuing the uneven descent. Below the upper Holly Lake trail junction, camping is only allowed on the south (right) side of the trail, but the best sites are mostly before that junction. Although good campsites are now rare, wildlife is increasingly abundant, with lots of marmots, pikas, deer, and an improving chance of seeing black bears farther down into the forested terrain. After passing a sign noting your departure from the Upper Paintbrush Camping Zone, come to the lower junction with the loop trail to Holly Lake. The trail then descends through more terrific alpine scenery, forcing you to work hard to keep your neck from getting sore looking up at the snow-streaked canyon walls and at several long waterfalls cascading down cliffs to the south.

Descend a series of short switchbacks and then enter the Lower Paintbrush Camping Zone, where several laterals lead to pleasant campsites, though nowhere near as scenic as the ones above in the Upper Zone. In the middle of this camping zone, a bridge leads over the rampaging creek in Paintbrush Canyon. Below this point the terrain is generally more forested and the views become less impressive, not only due to the obstructing trees but because you are approaching the mouth of the canyon and the walls are no longer as tall. The path eventually pulls away from the creek and gradually curves to the southeast where you leave the mountain vegetation zone of fir trees and manzanita and enter the park's lower-elevation vegetation zone dominated by sagebrush, Douglas firs, and quaking aspen trees.

At 6.4 miles from Paintbrush Divide, you come to a junction and a choice of trails. The path to the left descends gradually for 0.8 mile to a creek crossing near the south end of large Leigh Lake and a junction. Here you turn right and follow a crowded lakeshore path rarely far from either paralleling roads on your left or the view-packed shore of String Lake to your right. After about a mile you reach the String Lake trailhead.

Alternate Route to String Lake Trailhead

The slightly longer alternative trail is less crowded than the one beside String Lake but also has fewer good views across the water back up to the rugged Tetons. To follow this route, keep straight at the junction below Paintbrush Canyon and for the next mile descend a mostly open, sagebrush-covered hillside above the waters of partly lily-pad-covered String Lake. The trail then travels over a low, forested ridge and comes to a junction. Turn left and walk through mostly open lodgepole-pine woods for about 0.3 mile to the String Lake trailhead and the end of your magnificent Teton adventure.

Possible Itinerary (exit via Cascade Canyon Trail; 27.2 miles)

	Camps and Side Trips	Miles	Elevation Gain
Day 1	Tram to top of Rendezvous Mountain		
	Hike to Marion Lake	7.1	+1,250/−2,425
Day 2	Marion Lake to Alaska Basin	8.0	+1,725/−1,550
Day 3	*Layover day*		
	Day hike to Static Peak Divide	5.0	+1,150/−1,150
Day 4	Alaska Basin to South Fork Camping Zone	4.9	+1,250/−1,800
Day 5	Cascade Canyon Trail to Jenny Lake boat dock	7.9	+0/−2,150

Possible Itinerary (exit via Paintbrush Canyon Trail; 34.9 miles)

	Camps and Side Trips	Miles	Elevation Gain
Day 1	Tram to top of Rendezvous Mountain		
	Hike to Marion Lake	7.1	+1,250/−2,425
Day 2	Marion Lake to Alaska Basin	8.0	+1,725/−1,550
Day 3	*Layover day in Alaska Basin*		
	Day hike to Static Peak Divide	5.0	+1,150/−1,150
Day 4	Alaska Basin to South Fork Camping Zone near Avalanche Divide junction	3.7	+1,275/−1,150
	Day hike to Avalanche Divide and cross-country to Snowdrift Lake	4.2	+1,650/−1,650
Day 5	South Fork Cascade Creek Camping Zone to Holly Lake	9.0	+2,875/−2,450
Day 6	Holly Lake to String Lake trailhead	6.0 7.1	+150/−2,725

Giving Back

Grand Teton National Park Foundation: WWW.GTNPF.ORG

Alternatives: Although most parties opt for riding the tram to the top of Rendezvous Mountain and meeting the Teton Crest Trail via the Middle Fork Cutoff Trail, the spine-running route technically begins farther south, directly west of Phillips Pass. To complete the entire Teton Crest Trail (and avoid paying the fee for the tram ride) drive west from Jackson on Highway 22, pass through the small community of Wilson, climb to Teton Pass, and then drop 2.5 miles to the turnoff to

Coal Creek Campground and Trailhead. Hike north along Coal Creek and Mesquite Creek to the junction with the Teton Crest Trail (008) and climb east to Phillips Pass. From the pass, the trail heads north to the west of Rendezvous Mountain, climbs to a 9,085-foot pass at the national park boundary, and then meets the route described above at the junction with the Middle Fork Cutoff Trail. This route is an extra 10 miles long, with an elevation gain/loss of +3800'/−2100'.

Perseverance

Peering out our motel room window, we saw thick, gray clouds hanging low in the morning sky above Jackson, obscuring even the lowest of the surrounding hills. Moments later, our party of four stepped outside, feeling the cold chill in the air on our walk to a nearby café for breakfast—this certainly didn't seem like mid-August (unless we had been magically transported to somewhere in the southern hemisphere). Today was supposed to be the start of our trip along the Teton Crest Trail. We had already delayed our start once because of the rainy weather, instead opting to do a six-day trip in the nearby Wind River range. After two nights in Jackson, the days were slipping away before we all had to return home and resume our normal lives—the clock was ticking.

We quietly lingered over breakfast, futilely hoping that the more time we spent in the café would somehow get the clouds to start lifting. Back at the motel, the pace of our packing was similarly lethargic, as we debated the wisdom of forging ahead versus waiting one more day for the weather to clear. Eventually, we threw caution to the wind, hopped into our two vehicles, and headed toward Teton Village, where we dropped off Tic, John, and our four packs. During the time it took for Andy and me to drive our two cars to Jenny Lake, drop off one of the vehicles, and then return to Teton Village, the clouds had at least lifted off the valley floor, though the Tetons above were still shrouded in a thick veil of gray and the temperature remained quite chilly.

The tram ride to the top of Rendezvous Mountain passed all too quickly, and, as we headed into the mountains on foot, we soon left the cozy security of any human-made shelter behind. Much of the initial route off Rendezvous Mountain was downhill, so we were all a bit chilled without the generation of body heat one usually gets from an uphill climb. A light dusting of snow had fallen the day before, some of which had melted during the day and then frozen overnight, creating slippery patches of ice on the trail, causing numerous near-slips and one bona fide fall. Soon light snow began to fall and we stopped to don our parkas, wondering silently amongst ourselves about the creature comforts we had left behind in Jackson.

Over the course of the next few miles, we would experience alternating periods of snow flurries, bone-chilling rain, and pelting hail, all accompanied by gusty winds and frigid temperatures. Longing for the much more dependable weather of my home range, the Sierra Nevada, I thought more than once about abandoning this venture, which I more than likely would have done had I not been with companions who had traveled long distances all this way at considerable expense. I broached the subject with my companions of turning back on a couple of occasions, but they encouraged me onward with an unwavering, almost Pollyanna-like optimism. We pressed on, hoping beyond hope that the weather would eventually cut us some slack.

At some point in our first day's journey, the schizophrenic precipitation abated and the cloudy skies reversed hue from an ominous dark gray to a lighter, slightly less foreboding gray. Without the tunnel vision created by the hoods of our parkas, we began noticing the vivid colors from the profusion of wet wildflowers lining the slopes next to the trail. Although the high peaks were still shrouded, the clouds had lifted enough to offer sweeping vistas of the lower mountains, causing our hearts to stir. By the time we passed Marion Lake, the weather had stabilized and we pressed on to our first night's camp at Fox Creek Pass. Setting up camp, we found that the sky was no longer threatening but the temperature was still quite cold, forcing us to bundle up in every available article of clothing we had. Without the possibility of a campfire to warm us, we piled into our tents and the warmth of our sleeping bags well before dark.

A few days later, we would crest a rise and experience the incredible view of the Tetons from the vicinity of Hurricane Pass, one of the most breathtaking vistas I've ever witnessed. From this vantage, I thought back to that first day on the trail and was thankful for the perseverance of my companions, without which I may have bailed out and completely missed the many wonders that this magnificent area offers to those willing to press onward.—**Mike**

Cloud Peak Wilderness, Bighorn National Forest

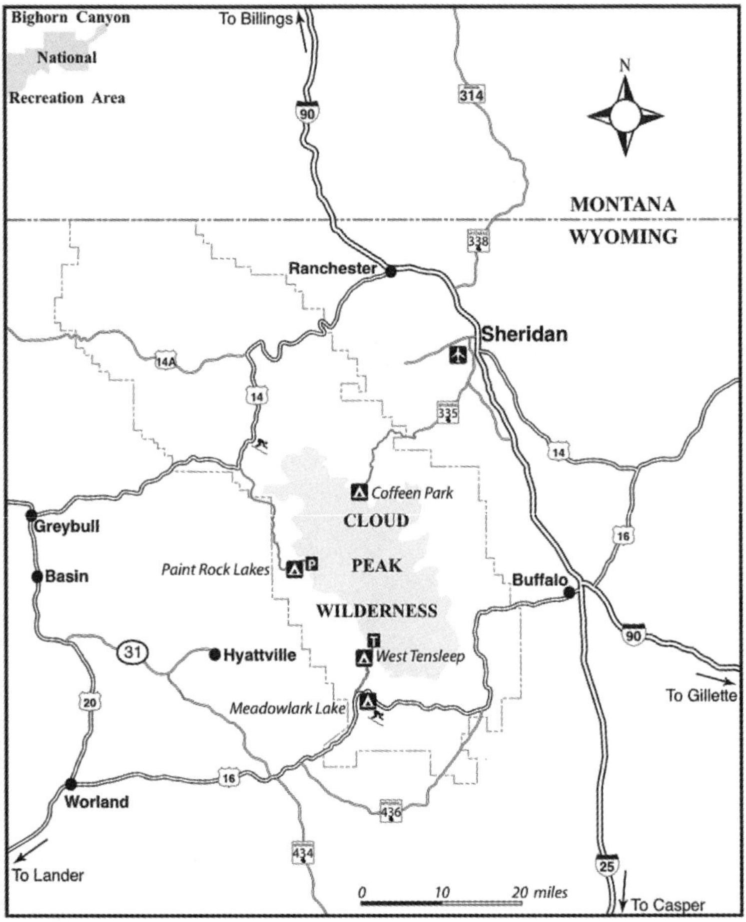

Solitude Trail Loop Location Map

TRIP 8

Solitude Trail Loop

> It is not good for man to be kept perforce at all times in the presence of his species. A world from which solitude is extirpated, is a very poor ideal. Solitude, in the sense of being often alone, is essential to any depth of meditation or of character; and solitude in the presence of natural beauty and grandeur, is the cradle of thoughts and aspirations which are not only good for the individual, but which society could ill do without.
>
> —JOHN STUART MILL, FROM *PRINCIPLES OF POLITICAL ECONOMY* (1848)

The Bighorn Mountains rise like a misplaced snowy wall above the seemingly endless rolling plains that stretch from north-central Wyoming east to the Great Lakes. This terrain amounts to almost 1,000 miles of tediously flat land, broken only by the forested bumps of the Black Hills. Since the Bighorn Mountains represent the closest "real" mountains to hikers coming from the east, it's not surprising that the trailhead parking lots here are often filled with cars sporting license plates from Indiana, Minnesota, Wisconsin, and similarly mountain-starved states. And these flatlanders have made an excellent choice, because the Bighorns provide a generous supply of mountain delights, including sheer granite cliffs, deep gorges, wildflower-filled meadows, hundreds of alpine lakes, peaks topping 13,000 feet, and even a tiny glacier or two.

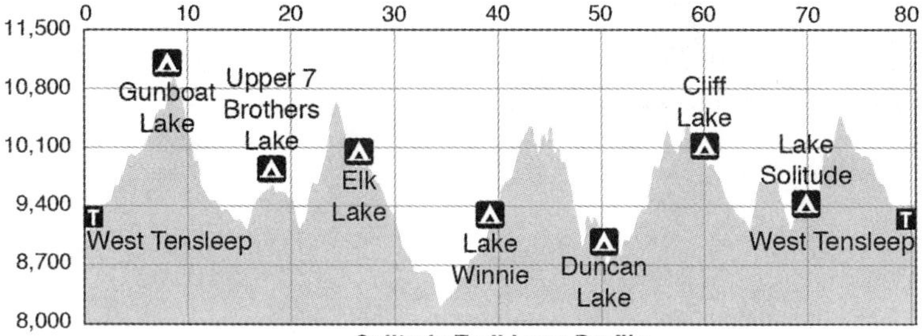

Solitude Trail Loop Profile

This popular loop trip visits all of those enticing features and more on its long course through and around the Cloud Peak Wilderness. Small portions of this trip, however, are outside of the wilderness, so you may come across motorized vehicles in one or two places. But for the most part, this is a wonderfully wild loop through outstanding mountain scenery. And if that sentence doesn't cause your feet to get itchy, then I can only ask why are you reading this book in the first place?

Days: 6–9

Distance: 80 miles (with side trips to Seven Brothers Lakes and Duncan Lake, but excluding day hike to Lost Twin Lakes)

Type: Loop

Scenery: 8

Solitude: 4

Technical Difficulty: 5

Physical Difficulty: 6

Elevation Gain/Loss: +12,700'/–12,700'

Season: July to October

Best: Mid-July through early August

Map: Trails Illustrated: *Cloud Peak Wilderness* (although frustratingly, a small section of the loop near Willow Park Reservoir is not shown)

Resources: *Hiking Wyoming's Cloud Peak Wilderness*, by Erik Molvar; *Joe Pickett* series, by C. J. Box (a better-than-average mystery series about a game warden stationed in the Bighorn Mountains)

Contact: Bighorn National Forest
Powder River Ranger District
1415 Fort Street
Buffalo, WY 82834
307-684-7806

Permits: Required—free at the trailhead.

Regulations: No fires are allowed above 9,200 feet, which accounts for most of this hike. There is a maximum group size of ten people. No camping allowed within 100 feet of water.

Nearest Campground: West Tensleep Lake Campground—0.5 mile

Nearest Airport: Sheridan County Airport (SHR)—88 miles
Caspar/Natrona County Airport (C/NCIA)—166 miles
Billings Logan International Airport (BIL)—220 miles

Nearest Outdoor Retailer:
Sports Stop—90 miles
208 North Main Street
Sheridan, WY 82801
307-672-5356

Outfitter: This is big game country, so there are several outfitters that specialize in hunting trips. There are a couple of companies that also just do horse-packing trips (try Flatiron Outfitters, for one), but no companies in the area cater to backpackers.

Transportation Logistics: There are no public transportation options to reach the trailhead, so you'll need your own vehicle. All access roads are paved or good gravel.

Backcountry Logistics: (A, BB, L, St) This is high-elevation country, with most of the trip above 10,000 feet. Anyone who lives at relatively low elevations and who has not yet become acclimated to the thinner air may suffer from shortness of breath, loss of appetite, headaches, and other symptoms of altitude sickness, especially for the first few days of the trip.

Thunderstorms are common, so bring a sturdy tent and plan your hiking days so you're off the higher ridges before mid-afternoon.

Attractions and Amenities: The cities of Buffalo and Sheridan offer the best selection of restaurants, shopping, and accommodations in the area. Of the two, Sheridan is larger and offers greater variety. You'll find the usual assortment of national chains and locally owned establishments. Granted, we're not talking about five-star destination resorts but perfectly good and comfortable motels, as well as restaurants with decent food.

The area also boasts a wide assortment of both natural and human-made attractions, some of which really should not be missed. In the small town of Bighorn, just a few miles south of Sheridan, be sure to visit the very excellent **Bradford Brinton Memorial & Museum**, which is a faithful and fascinating re-creation of upscale western ranch life. In addition to the expected displays on running a ranch and on the Plains Indians, the museum also includes a superb collection of western art, including works by such renowned painters as John James Audubon, Frederic Remington, and Charles M. Russell.

History buffs may want to visit any of the numerous battle sites from the Plains Indians Wars that are found in the area, including the most famous site of all, the **Little Bighorn Battlefield National Monument** just 60 miles north of Sheridan in southwest Montana.

In Buffalo, the **Occidental Hotel** is well worth a quick visit. This fully restored western hotel is a local landmark and includes many features familiar to fans of Old West movies, including lots of antique furnishings and a lovingly restored saloon. In its heyday, this hotel played host to such western icons as Buffalo Bill Cody, Calamity Jane, and Teddy Roosevelt.

The natural attractions in this area are perhaps even better than the human-made ones. Just off US Highway 16 on the way to the trailhead, don't miss the fine view from **Sheep Mountain Lookout** and the supremely scenic drive on a rough dirt road through the narrow defile of **Crazy Woman Canyon**. With a little more time, you can also visit some of the many attractions in the northern part of the Bighorn Mountains, including **Shell Falls**, **Bucking Mule Falls**, and the **Medicine Wheel National Historic Landmark**.

Directions to Trailhead: From Buffalo, at the intersection of Interstates 90 and 25 about 33 miles south of Sheridan, take Exit 299 off I-25 and drive 48.3 miles west on US Highway 16 to a junction not far from milepost 44. Turn right (north) onto Forest Road 27, a good gravel route that is also known as West Tensleep Road, and proceed 1.1 miles to a fork. Go right, and drive 6.1 miles to a second fork. Go right again, and continue 0.5 mile to the large trailhead parking lot.

Day Hike to Lost Twin Lakes

Before beginning the backpacking trip, take a day or two to get acclimated to the elevations here. First, spend a night or two at a campground high in the mountains near the trailhead. Another good idea is to take a day hike into the higher parts of the Bighorn Mountains. The most dramatically scenic option is the popular 11.4-mile round-trip hike to the Lost Twin Lakes, which leaves from the same trailhead as the backpacking trip described here. This hike will not only be a good test of your ability to deal with exercise in an environment with reduced oxygen, but also offers outstanding scenery at one of the most spectacular lake basins in the range.

To take this day hike, walk 25 yards along the trail that departs from the north end of the parking lot to a prominent fork where you veer right onto Trail #065. This trail takes you along the top of a wide, wooded ridge and in just 0.1 mile arrives at an unsigned but obvious junction with an unofficial path on the right toward Elk Park.

You go straight and continue along the ridgetop for another 0.4 mile before dropping to a meadow along Middle Tensleep Creek and a possible campsite. From here a steep climb takes you over another mostly forested ridge to a rock-hop crossing of the outlet creek from unseen Mirror Lake. The trail then gradually ascends in a mix of meadows and forest beside lovely Middle Tensleep Creek, as you make your way into the high country. The last 1.3 miles are a bit steeper through meadows and rocky areas to the first Lost Twin Lake. Awe-inspiring cliffs rise over 1,000 feet from the shores of this deep and scenic alpine lake, and several campsites offer options for the overnight hiker. Reaching the second Lost Twin Lake requires some scrambling, but is only about 0.5 mile away and well worth the extra effort for adventurous hikers.

Trip Description: ***Note:*** *Trails in the Cloud Peak Wilderness are usually signed only with their number. Typically, there is no indication of a trail's name or destinations. Therefore, in the following description trail numbers rather than names will be used.*

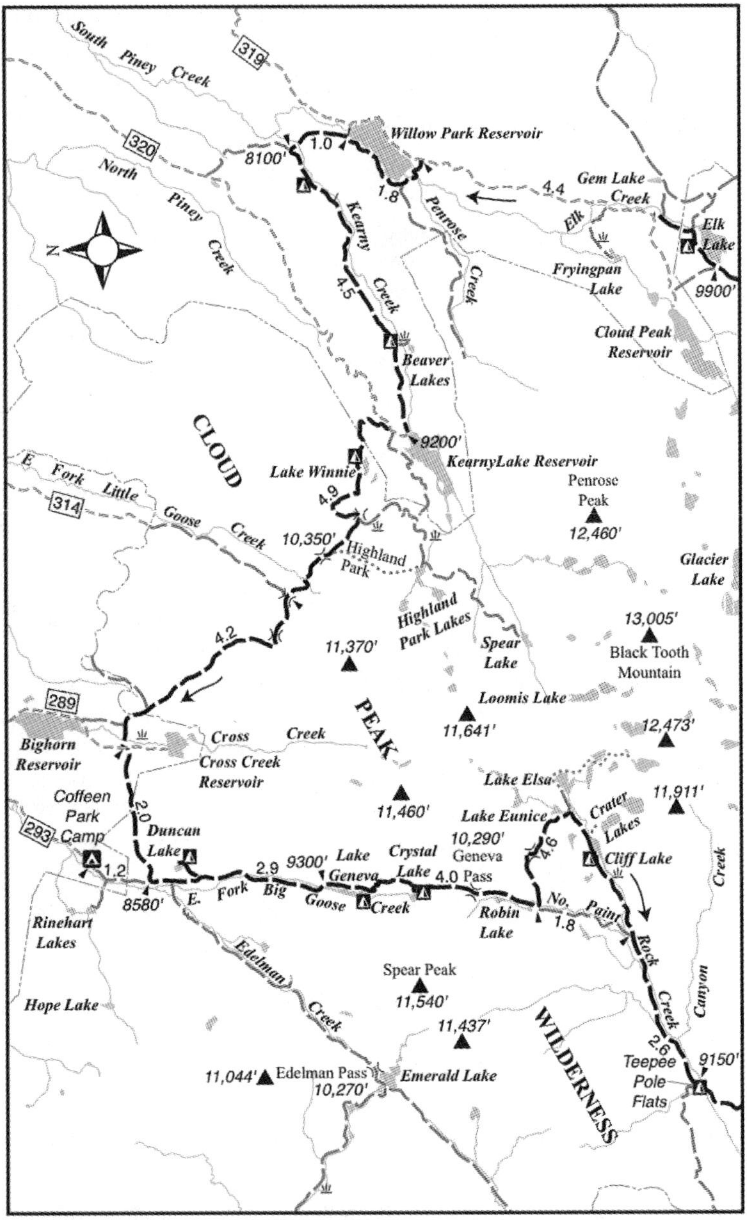

Solitude Trail Loop (North)

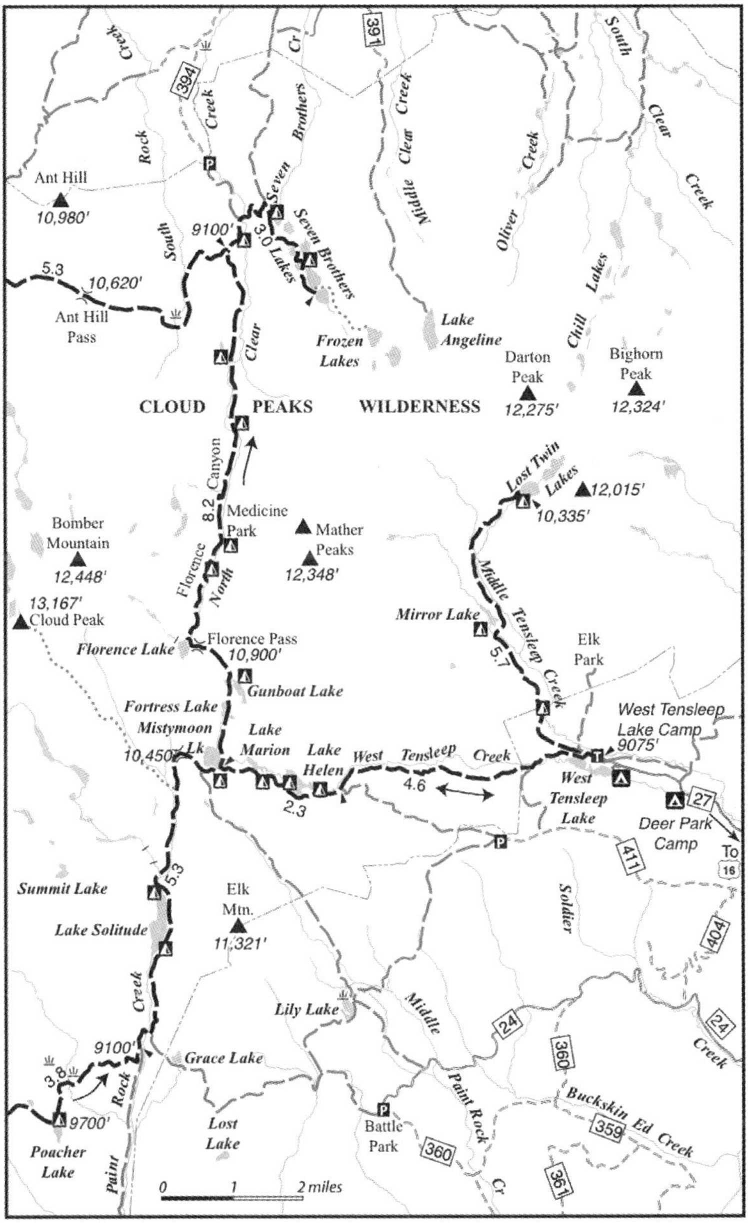

Solitude Trail Loop (South)

Similar to the day hike described above, the backpacking trip begins next to the self-issuing permit and registration box at the north end of the parking lot. After only 25 yards, the trail forks. The trail to the right is the route to Lost Twin Lakes (see the description above).

For the recommended backpacking loop, head left on Trail #063, a wide and gentle path that travels lazily through a relatively dense forest of Engelmann spruces and lodgepole pines. Pass the northern end of meadow-rimmed West Tensleep Lake, where moose are sometimes seen, then make an easy calf-deep ford of West Tensleep Creek at 0.8 mile. Immediately after this crossing is a signed junction with a very faint path heading to the left. Go straight on the main trail and gradually climb this often-rocky path through dense forest and across occasional meadows. The meadows offer tantalizing glimpses of the high peaks to the north.

At about 4.6 miles is a junction with Trail #097, which goes left (uphill). You keep right and walk another 0.2 mile to the south end of rock-lined Lake Helen. On quiet mornings, the rounded summits of several snow-covered mountains and ridges are nicely reflected in the waters of this long and irregularly shaped lake. There are good campsites near the south shore and several more along the lake's west side.

After winding around the west side of Lake Helen, the trail climbs gradually into increasingly alpine terrain with more meadows and rocks but fewer trees. In less than a mile, you walk past Lake Marion (campsites) and then climb an open slope to a junction at 6.9 miles. In the shallow basin immediately ahead is circular Mistymoon Lake. This lovely spot offers great views across its waters of Cloud Peak to the north, which at 13,167 feet is the highest point in the Bighorn Mountains. There are some good but rather exposed campsites on the ridges around the lake.

The junction beside Mistymoon Lake is the start of the recommended loop. Either direction is equally scenic, but most hikers go counterclockwise. Turn right on Solitude Trail #038, and climb away from the lake up a narrow and rocky little canyon. This trail soon takes you above timberline before leveling out beside narrow Fortress Lake,

Lake Helen

about 0.6 mile from Mistymoon Lake. This starkly scenic basin holds not only Fortress Lake but also Gunboat Lake, a larger body of water easily reached via a short walk across the rocky tundra to the south. Gunboat Lake is overshadowed by a tall cliff of very dark rock and has some possible campsites.

The trail now climbs 350 feet over rocks and tundra to 10,900-foot Florence Pass, from which you have great views especially of very scenic Florence Lake, a little below in the basin to the north. Several bulky peaks surround this alpine lake, and a small waterfall tumbles directly into the waters at the northeast end. Camping here is not recommended due to the exposed and extremely rocky terrain.

From the east end of Florence Lake the trail follows the lake's outlet stream, North Clear Creek. This stream very rapidly drops into the steep-walled defile of Florence Canyon. In less than 1.5 miles this canyon goes from flat to over 2,000 feet deep, with contorted walls rising sharply on either side. The trail crosses the creek a number of times, often where the water is buried under huge piles of boulders fallen from the canyon walls. At about 1.5 miles from Florence Lake, you come to a small meadow where there is a decent campsite sheltered by scrubby trees. For a better selection of camps in an even more scenic location, continue another 0.4 mile to Medicine Park, a larger meadow directly beneath the canyon's towering walls.

From Medicine Park the trail descends steeply for about 0.4 mile, and then levels out, where you wander through forest to a calf-deep ford of North Clear Creek. Immediately after this crossing is a particularly inviting campsite. Below this point, the canyon rapidly widens and the walls fade into rolling, forested hills. About 1 mile from the first ford, you cross the creek again just before another good campsite. This is followed by a little less than 2 miles of almost level walking in forest and small meadows on the way to a junction.

Side Trip to Seven Brothers Lakes

The continuation of your loop on the Solitude Trail turns sharply left at the junction. However, before going that way you might want to consider a side trip into the scenic basin of the Seven Brothers Lakes. To visit this popular area, veer right at the junction onto Trail #024, which takes you through a meadow and past possible campsites for 0.6 mile to a second junction. Turn right here, onto Trail #044, ford North Clear Creek, and then climb a short set of switchbacks over a forested ridge to a junction beside the first of the Seven Brothers Lakes. This rock-lined body of water offers nice views of the cliffs and peaks to the west. For even better views, go right at the junction onto Trail #045 and for the next 1.6 miles pass near or above a string of relatively large lakes progressively drawing nearer to the rugged line of peaks and cliffs to the west. Most of these popular lakes have campsites (the Forest Service prohibits camping and horse use on the west end of the sixth lake in the chain and anywhere around the seventh and last lake). After enjoying the Seven Brothers Lakes, retrace your steps to the Solitude Trail junction.

After returning to Solitude Trail #038, you go north and make a steady climb through relatively dense forest to the top of an old moraine. From the boulder-covered ridgetop are excellent views back to the west of the many high peaks at the center of this wilderness, as well as good looks to the east of the seemingly endless rolling prairies. The path now takes you across more open terrain, climbing a bit to the top of a second moraine. Openings caused by old forest fires allow additional views, including down into the basin of South Rock Creek to the north.

The trail then drops to a crossing of South Rock Creek, an easy, ankle-deep ford. Wander uphill away from the creek, mostly in meadows, toward a high pass west of Ant Hill. The long but rewarding ascent offers good vistas both near and far and lots of marmots to provide comic relief. Cairns help mark the route, which tends to disappear in places. From the above-timberline top of Ant Hill Pass you can sit and rest while enjoying stupendous views, now including a view down to shimmering Elk Lake to the north-northeast (see map of Solitude Trail Loop [North]).

To reach Elk Lake, the trail descends lazily though tundra meadows and over boulder fields, eventually making its way back into open forests shortly before arriving at the shores of this large, meadow- and forest-rimmed gem. Along the west side of this lovely lake you go right at the junction with a spur trail to Cloud Peak Reservoir, then circle around the north side of the lake to some good camping areas. These camps are ideally suited to taking in the terrific views across the lake to a series of high peaks.

Near the northeast shore of Elk Lake, and just before you cross the outlet creek, is a junction where you turn left and descend along a good horse trail (still Trail #038) in the wet meadows beside gently meandering Elk Creek. You soon leave the wilderness and, about 0.5 mile from Elk Lake, meet an old gravel road, which is still popular with the ATV crowd (expect your wilderness experience to be ruined several times over the next few miles).

You descend gradually on this old jeep road, which offers only so-so scenery and potentially far too much noise. Over the next mile, ignore junctions with faint trails that first go right to tiny Gem Lake and then left and down to larger Fryingpan Lake. The road crosses Elk Creek after about 0.8 mile (an easy crossing), and then spends the next few miles first gradually and then more steeply descending to the head of Willow Creek Reservoir. The road forks here, with the main route going straight.

You go left at the fork and follow an ATV trail, which drops to a bridge over South Piney Creek just above the lakeshore. After a brief detour upstream, the trail leaves the creek and wanders through forest to an unsigned junction with little-used Trail #118 going up Penrose Creek. Your wheel-eroded route keeps straight and soon curves to the northeast along the hillside a little above Willow Park Reservoir. Farther along the shore are some nice views back across the water to Penrose Peak and beyond. At the foot of the reservoir is an earthen dam. The trail crosses below the dam and descends gradually past the two common "p"s at this elevation: ponds and pines. About a mile from Willow Park Reservoir is a bridge over Kearny Creek and a possibly unsigned junction.

Your route, (Trail #038), goes left and heads upstream, soon leaving most of the ATVs behind. The forested route passes some pleasant but viewless campsites near the creek. Compensating nicely for the lack of views is an abundance of wildlife (look for moose and deer in the forest and meadows, and perky little dippers along the creek). After about 1.2 miles, you'll see some very attractive but short waterfalls. Above the falls, the trail passes by a couple of pretty meadows and then a large outfitter's camp. An unmaintained trail goes south here to the tiny Beaver Lakes, offering good fishing but only marginal scenery. The main trail continues straight from the outfitter's camp and steadily climbs for another 1.3 miles to the earthen dam holding back the waters of Kearny Lake Reservoir. There are good views across this reservoir to the high peaks to the west.

Right beside Kearny Lake Reservoir is a junction with another gravel jeep/ATV road, which curves uphill and to the northeast. Follow this road for 0.15 mile to a signed junction with Trail #036 to Highland Park and Spear Lakes (an excellent side trip for those with an extra day to spend). The main route stays with the road for another 150 yards to a second junction, this time with the resumption of Solitude Trail #038.

Go left here, almost immediately cross a wet meadow, and then climb past a series of good, rocky viewpoints featuring Kearny Lake

Reservoir, pyramid-shaped Penrose Peak, and jagged Black Tooth Mountain, all to the southwest. At the top of this grade is an expansive flat holding shallow Lake Winnie and an unseen slightly smaller twin. Abundant wildflowers and fine views across the lakes to the distant spires of Black Tooth Mountain argue in favor of an overnight stay, though the marshy environment and attendant mosquito population may dissuade you.

The trail climbs away from Lake Winnie, ascending through thinning tree cover to the flower-speckled meadows at the head of the basin. A final traverse across rocky slopes leads to a wide saddle and a junction at the east end of the lovely but boggy meadowlands of Highland Park.

From there, the Solitude Trail #038 goes right, following cairns and skirting the northeast side of gorgeous Highland Park. The views across this large marshy expanse to the high and rugged peaks around Black Tooth Mountain are some of the best along the entire circuit. Providing the mosquitoes aren't too bad, you should find some good campsites nearby. The trail reaches drier ground near the north end of the park and then ascends fairly gradually into alpine terrain at a wide, view-packed pass.

The trail descends fairly sharply down the north side of the pass to an easy crossing of the headwaters of trickling East Fork Little Goose Creek. You then regain virtually all of that previously lost elevation to reach a second pass and a junction with a lightly used trail heading to the right (#027). You keep left and go up and down across scenic, near-timberline terrain before beginning a long descent. The steady decline leads across the slopes above a partly forested basin with numerous strip meadows supporting a wealth of wildflowers. After descending about 450 feet, top a rocky knoll from which you have excellent views to the south of the rugged but unnamed peaks at the head of Cross Creek. More downhill ensues through a forest recovering from an old fire. After a mile-plus-long descent from the knoll, you veer left at a junction and then leave the wilderness to make a short but fairly steep downhill to a second junction. The route to Bighorn Reservoir goes to the right, but your trail stays to the left, dropping a bit to a marshy area and a bridged crossing of Cross Creek. About 0.1 mile after this crossing is a junction with an ATV road.

Go briefly left on this road before Solitude Trail #038 resumes on the other side. You leave the heavily wooded valley of Cross Creek on a short but steep ascent to the top of a minor ridge, then go up and down for the next 0.6 mile and reenter the Cloud Peak Wilderness. Shortly after crossing this boundary, the trail makes an extended viewless descent into the valley of East Fork Big Goose Creek. At the bottom of the descent is a junction with Trail #592, which goes right on its way to Coffeen Park Campground.

You turn left (south) and follow this wide and well-used trail for 0.2 mile to a junction with Trail #025, which goes right. Keep straight on Solitude Trail #038 and gradually climb for 0.5 mile in forest until you come to a junction shortly past a collapsed miner's cabin. The trail to the left (#125) goes 0.4 mile to lily-pad-covered Duncan Lake, which offers a nice campsite and good views of a cluster of snowy peaks to the southwest.

The main trail goes straight at the Duncan Lake junction and ascends very gradually to an easy ford of East Fork Big Goose Creek. From here, another 1.5 miles of gentle uphill takes you to the north end of long and narrow Lake Geneva. This scenic and relatively deep lake provides fine views of several craggy peaks to the southwest. The lake is heavily used, so be especially careful to follow all no-trace principles if you decide to camp here. The trail stays close to the eastern shore of the lake until reaching a meadow and some excellent campsites at the lake's south end.

A steep 450-foot climb now leads up a series of switchbacks to an unsigned but obvious junction with a short side trail that goes right to some good campsites beside dramatic Crystal Lake. This very scenic and nearly circular pool nestles directly beneath the hulking ramparts of an unnamed peak.

More climbing takes you up to and through a lovely alpine meadow, and then back above timberline to the narrow gap of Geneva Pass. Away from the pass, a relatively gentle downhill leads across the open slopes just above teardrop-shaped Robin Lake, and then past a series of smaller ponds to a junction with Trail #060.

The Solitude Trail goes straight, descending along pretty North Fork Paint Rock Creek for 1.8 miles through forest and meadows to a reunion with Trail #060. For a longer but more scenic alternate route to this same lower junction, turn left at the first junction with Trail #060, soon cross the splashing headwaters of North Paint Rock Creek, and wind uphill to a minor saddle. From here some up-and-down hiking across alpine meadows and rocky areas takes you to scenic Lake Eunice. The trail then descends along a rushing creek to extremely scenic and appropriately named Cliff Lake, which offers excellent (but popular) campsites at its west end and sits immediately beneath a huge mass of dark rock.

If your schedule allows for an extra day, spend it exploring from a base camp at Cliff Lake. There are no official trails, but reasonably easy cross-country routes take you up to the two dramatic Crater Lakes to the south and a series of several stunning alpine lakes in the basin above Lake Elsa to the east.

Once you've had your fill of the off-trail possibilities beyond Cliff Lake, get back on Trail #060 and walk southwest (downstream) past a marshy lake and through open forest and pretty meadows to a calf-deep ford of the outlet from Cliff Lake. From there, an easy 0.3 mile of gentle downhill leads to a junction and the reunion with Solitude Trail #038.

From the junction the trail goes downhill and generally west-southwest for 0.6 mile to an easy ford of North Fork Paint Rock Creek. Continue another 2 miles to a junction at the edge of the large meadow called Teepee Pole Flats. Although there are good-looking campsites here, they are often dusty and smelly due to repeated use by horse parties.

Go straight at this junction, still on Solitude Trail #038, and quickly come to a calf-deep ford of North Paint Rock Creek. From here, the trail leaves the meadow and rapidly regains altitude, traveling most of the way beneath the shade of a primarily Engelmann spruce forest. Granite outcroppings offer occasional breaks in the tree cover on this winding ascent, offering fine views to the north. The route eventually levels out and then passes a couple of small rock-lined ponds and a large meadow before reaching shallow Poacher Lake (see map of Solitude Trail Loop [South]). This somewhat marshy lake offers pleasant scenery, lots of wildlife, and some adequate campsites near the east shore.

The trail turns east away from Poacher Lake, remaining mostly level until reaching a large marshy area with a fair-sized creek, plenty of mosquitoes, and nice views across the damp foreground to multitudinous peaks to the east. Beyond, the trail reenters forest, climbs a bit to the top of a rounded ridge, and then begins a lengthy descent. The zigzagging course generally takes you through relatively open forests with plenty of nice views on the way down to a junction with Trail #062 a little above the main branch of Paint Rock Creek.

Keep left at this junction and head upstream for 0.2 mile, passing some huge granite boulders and outcroppings along the way to a chilly, knee-deep ford of the creek. On the other side of this crossing is another junction, this time with Trail #120.

Veer left, now on a trail badly chewed up by a cavalry of horses, and parallel the cascading stream for 0.8 mile to Lake Solitude, the largest natural lake in the Bighorn Mountains. This understandably popular spot offers wonderful scenery, including a glimpse of the rounded top of Cloud Peak to the east, decent fishing, and several inviting campsites. On the north side of the lake are towering granite domes and cliffs, often with a reddish tint. The trail stays on the gentler terrain on the south side of the almost mile-long lake, eventually reaching some large meadows and a ford of the inlet. Additional good campsites may be found under the trees near this knee-deep crossing.

A short walk now leads to a bridged crossing of a side creek, which tumbles down a series of lovely waterfalls just a little above the bridge. A bit more climbing around a narrow gorge in the creek leads you to the top of a granite outcropping from which you can look back to Lake Solitude, now far below. You parallel the creek past grassy knolls for about another mile before coming to another crossing of Paint Rock Creek, this time usually accomplished via a rock hop. About 0.2 mile later, the creek forks, with the main branch angling off to the northeast.

> **Side Trip to Cloud Peak**
>
> Hikers interested in bagging Cloud Peak, the highest summit in its namesake wilderness, should leave the trail here. The route is nearly 4 miles one way (although seemingly longer) and gains 2,100 feet. Initially the off-trail route goes up the creek valley but then angles left and follows a ridgeline to the top. The higher parts of this fun but challenging route are rugged and steep, including lots of above-timberline boulder travel. The view from the top is truly breathtaking and worth the difficulties, but the scrambling is Class III in spots and the peak is very exposed, making this no place for a novice or for anyone in a thunderstorm. Watch the weather carefully and beat a hasty retreat if there is any build-up in the clouds.

Meanwhile, the main trail continues east soon ascending above the last of the scraggly fir trees and leading back above timberline. The views to the east and northeast of Cloud Peak and Bomber Mountain are outstanding. The surroundings are quite scenic as you wander over meadow knolls and through tundra-covered valleys. Eventually you reach a broad saddle, from where you'll enjoy excellent views across the waters of numerous tarns and small ponds to the nearby mountains. A short, scenic descent leads down to Mistymoon Lake. As you round the eastern shore, keep left at a junction with Middle Paint Rock Creek Trail #066 and soon close the loop at the junction above the south shore of Mistymoon Lake. Turn right, and retrace your steps 6.9 miles back to your car at the West Tensleep trailhead.

Possible Itinerary

	Camps and Side Trips	Miles	Elevation Gain
Day 1	West Tensleep TH to Gunboat Lake	7.8	+1,650/−200
Day 2	upper Seven Brothers Lakes	10.3	+1,100/−1,950
Day 3	Elk Lake	8.7	+1,600/−1,400
Day 4	Lake Winnie	12.3	+1,850/−2,050
Day 5	Duncan Lake	11.2	+2,100/−2,900
Day 6	Cliff Lake	9.8	+2,100/−1,100
Day 7	Lake Solitude	9.8	+950/−1,550
Day 8	Out to West Tensleep TH	10.2	+1,350/−1,550

Giving Back

Wyoming Wilderness Association: WWW.WILDWYO.ORG

Don't Forget to Update Your First-Aid Kit

I could have sworn the damn pills were in here somewhere. And I certainly was swearing when I couldn't find them.

I was almost three days into a backpacking trip in the Teton Wilderness southeast of Yellowstone National Park, and the pills that I so desperately wanted to find were my emergency iodine tablets. I carry a small vial, or so I thought, in my first aid kit just in case the water filter breaks, which, unfortunately, had just occurred. When all else fails, the pills serve to effectively purify water, thus avoiding any nasty little organisms upsetting my digestive system. They do *not* work, however, when they cannot be found. Apparently, this was the inopportune moment to realize I had not been sufficiently careful to fully restock the first aid kit last winter.

I'm usually careful about the water I drink on a backpacking trip, especially since I often hike alone and can be gone for weeks at a time. As a consequence, coming down with a debilitating digestive illness is never a good plan. That evening I boiled water, which is an effective method of purification, but without enough extra fuel for this unexpected chore this would be a short-term solution. Building fires to boil water is dirty and inconvenient, so I foolishly took what I thought at the time was a reasonably calculated risk.

Although all water in the backcountry should be treated as suspect, most of the time it isn't contaminated at all. In addition, there are certain steps you can take to further reduce your chances of ingesting any unwanted little nasties. Water collected closer to the spring or snowfield from which it originates is less likely to be contaminated by offending animal feces than water in larger streams further down the drainage. Also, high-elevation lakes, which are necessarily subject to extended exposure to bacteria-killing sunlight, are less prone to contamination than lower-elevation streams. Following these rules of thumb for the last couple of days of my trip, I carefully collected water only from the smallest creeks at the highest elevations and hoped for the best. These precautions apparently fell short, however, as somewhere along the way at least a few unwanted giardia parasites found their way past these defenses.

Now the "good" thing about giardia (if that adjective can ever be used for this miserable protozoan) is that typically symptoms don't begin until several days after exposure—enough time for the unknowing victim to return to civilization and obtain any necessary medical assistance. Unfortunately, I was in the middle of an extended trip of guidebook research and had already returned to my vehicle and moved on to the next backpacking adventure in Wyoming's Bighorn Mountains. Two days into this trip I began to notice something was definitely wrong.

With extended bouts of nausea, gas, vomiting, and diarrhea, I rapidly ran out toilet paper. Fortunately I had brought along reading material, and the novel wasn't nearly as bad as the use to which I was forced to put its pages. My apologies to the author—he deserved much better. I also experienced an incredible amount of weakness, as the miserable microorganisms sapped all the energy out of my system. I remember sitting down on a log to rest and the next time I looked at my watch, fully two hours had somehow elapsed about which I had absolutely no memory.

The photographs I somehow still managed to take and looked at weeks later indicate that the Bighorns were truly spectacular—I had to return for a later trip to confirm this. My recollections, however, center almost exclusively on unmitigated discomfort and misery.

Once I finally managed to stagger back to my car, drive to a nearby small town, and half-crawl into a hospital, the doctor did a cursory examination and declared the obvious diagnosis of giardia. He then told me that he could prescribe a drug that would "knock 'em back, but not kill them entirely." After a couple of days the drug did a nice job of eliminating the symptoms, but apparently the dastardly little bugs stay in your system and rapidly return upon future exposure. I now have to carry the drug around on all my trips, just in case.

The moral of this story: similar to dealing with mosquitoes, even though humans enjoy an enormous size advantage, when the enemy has you out-numbered several million to one, you're still going to lose. Don't play the odds, just play it safe and only drink purified water. Oh, and don't forget to do the first thing I did once I got home: make sure your emergency supply of iodine tablets is refilled and doesn't get lost!—**Doug**

Bridger Wilderness, Bridger-Teton National Forest

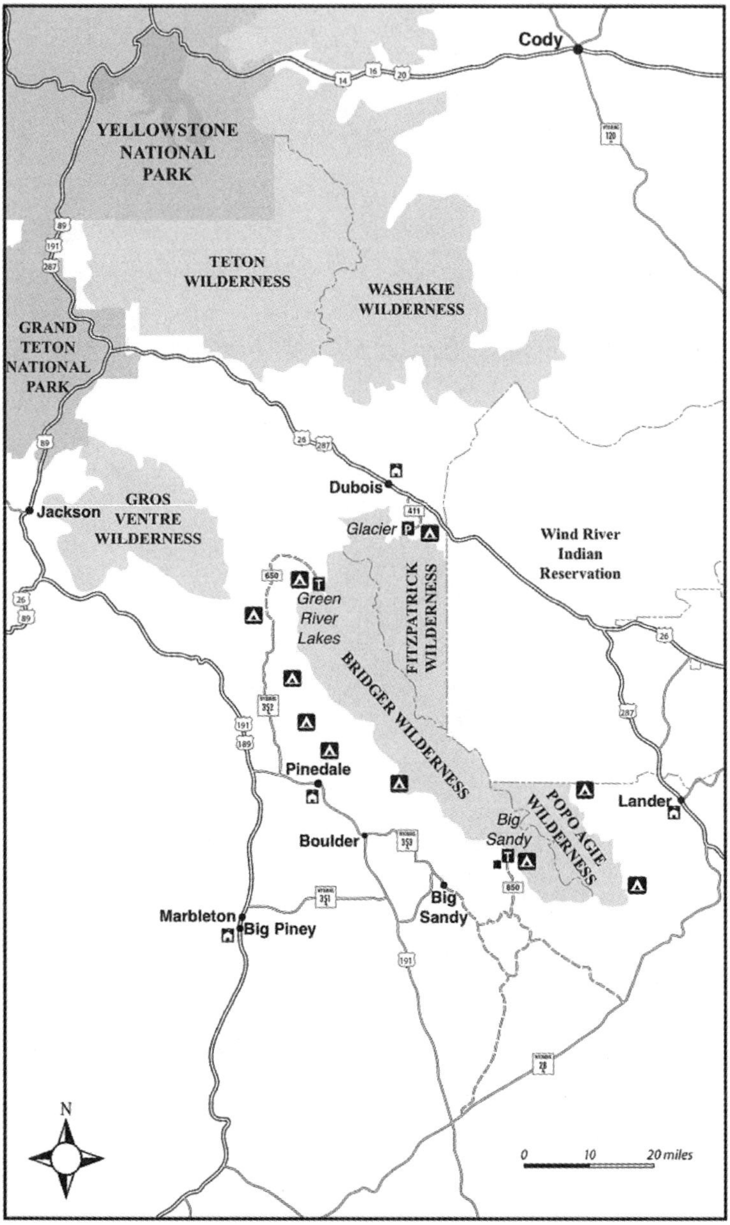

Wind River Highline Traverse Location Map

TRIP 9

Wind River Highline Traverse

> A mountain is the best medicine for a troubled mind. Seldom does man ponder his own insignificance. He thinks he is master of all things. He thinks the world is his without bonds. Nothing could be farther from the truth. Only when he tramps the mountains alone, communing with nature, observing other insignificant creatures about him, to come and go as he will, does he awaken to his own short-lived presence on earth.
>
> —FINIS MITCHELL, PIONEERING MOUNTAINEER, FORESTER, AND NATURALIST IN THE WIND RIVER RANGE

Any short list of the greatest hikes in North America (even *really* short lists of just three or four) *must* include this magnificent adventure through Wyoming's Wind River Range. The English language lacks the number of superlatives to adequately convey the beauty of these mountains. Towering granite cliffs, breathtaking alpine lakes, sky-scraping peaks, idyllic mountain meadows, voluminous wildflowers . . . the list of spectacular features goes on and on. The Wind River Range is a backpacker's paradise, and the Highline Trail (or the older and even more scenic Fremont Trail paralleling the Highline Trail) is arguably the best of the best. At the first taste of such magnificent mountain scenery, you'll want to add into your itinerary some of the many outstanding side trips this route offers (you'll kick yourself if you don't). Be sure to bring along plenty of extra food, as you'll probably end up taking

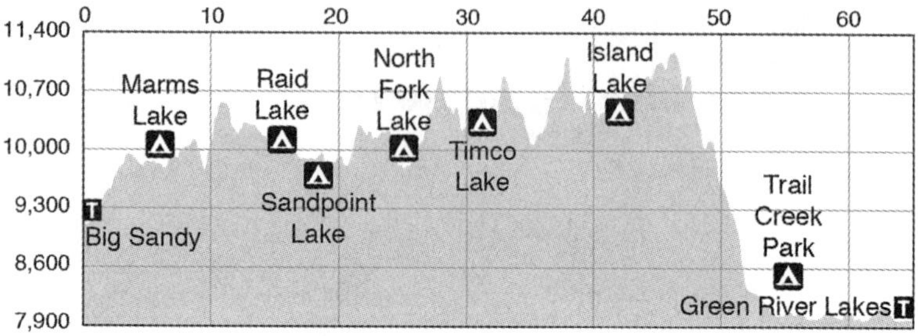

Wind River Highline Traverse Profile

a bunch of unscheduled vacation days. Use that extra time to marvel at the beautiful scenery while thinking up some sort of imaginative excuse for your boss back home—trust me, it'll be worth it.

Days: 8–15

Distance: 64 miles (minimum point-to-point trip), 124 miles (with just the bare-bones recommended side trips). You could easily stretch this to 200 miles or more with the countless other excellent explorations available.

Type: Shuttle

Scenery: 10

Solitude: 6

Technical Difficulty: 4 (much higher on some of the off-trail side trips)

Physical Difficulty: 6

Elevation Gain/Loss: +8,500'/–9,650'; +15,550'/–16,700' (with minimum recommended side trips)

Season: July to October

Best: Mid-July through August

Map: Earthwalk Press: Southern Wind River Range and Northern Wind River Range

Resources: *Wind River Trails*, by Finis Mitchell; *Climbing and Hiking in the Wind River Range*, by Joe Kelsey; *Wind River*, by Tom Morrisey; *Sky's Witness: A Year in the Wind River Range*, by C. L. Rawlins.

Contact:
Bridger-Teton National Forest
Pinedale Ranger District
29 East Fremont Lake Road
PO Box 220
Pinedale, WY 82941
307-367-4326

Permits: No permits are required.

Regulations: No fires are allowed above timberline. Maximum group size of 15 people and 25 stock. No camping within 100 feet of streams and 200 feet of lakes or trails.

Nearest Campground: Big Sandy Campground—0 miles from starting trailhead.

Green River Lakes Campground—0.5 mile from ending trailhead.

Nearest Airports: Rock Springs / Sweetwater County Airport (RKS)—100 miles (from southern trailhead)

Jackson Hole Airport (JAC)—122 miles (from northern trailhead)

Salt Lake City International Airport (SLC)—285 miles (from southern trailhead)

Nearest Outdoor Retailer: Neither Pinedale nor Rock Springs have any stores that cater to the needs of backpackers. In Jackson there are several possible locations for last-minute supplies, but it's a long drive if coming from the south. The better plan is not to forget anything.

Outfitter:
Wildland Trekking Company
Montana Office
2304 North Seventh Avenue, Unit K
Bozeman, MT 59715
800-715-4453
www.wildlandtrekking.com

Transportation Logistics: A rather long (about 107 miles) and complicated car shuttle is required to make this trip. The access roads are usually drivable in a passenger car, but they can be very rough and slippery. After heavy rains, a basic rental car may not be able to safely negotiate the roads.

Although finding and hiring a local dude ranch or trail-riding outfit to help you with the car shuttle may be possible, generally there are no easily available public transportation options to reach these trailheads. Realistically, you must bring two cars.

Backcountry Logistics: (GB, BB, St, Sn, A, L) Black bears are common throughout these mountains, and a few grizzly bears have recently migrated into the northern Wind River Range, so camp and act accordingly.

Long stretches of this trail are above 10,000 feet. Expect thin air, and take the usual steps to become acclimated.

A few parts of the trail get a bit sketchy at times, though nothing that any reasonably experienced hiker can't easily handle. Some of the side trips and off-trail wanderings require competent navigation and scrambling skills to safely negotiate.

You'll have to ford a few streams along the route, though with the possible exception of East Fork River and, if the bridge is washed out, the Green River, none of the crossings are dangerous or more than about calf-deep.

Thunderstorms can be epic in these mountains (see "The Windy 'Winds' below), especially when camping at or above timberline, which is often required along this route. Bring a sturdy tent, stay off the higher ridges in the late afternoon, and come prepared for all possible weather conditions.

Attractions and Amenities: The tiny hamlet of Pinedale is the closest form of civilization to the trailhead, where choices for gas, food, and lodging are available. The **Wind River Brewing Co.**, located on the main drag at 402 W. Pine Street, offers award-winning, handcrafted beers for sipping and decent pub fare for eating. Even in the middle of cowboy country you can satisfy a hankering for a burrito at **Rock Rabbit** at 23 W. Pine. The **Sugar Shack** (310 E. Pine) is the place in town to grab an old fashioned burger, fries, and shake on the way to or from the trailhead. An interesting attraction worth thirty minutes of your time is the **Museum of the Mountain Man** in Pinedale (700 East Hennick Road), a small facility offering historical displays and artifacts from early fur trappers, guides, and other explorers who opened the American West to later pioneers.

One-half mile from the Big Sandy trailhead, rustic **Big Sandy Lodge**, founded in the 1920s by Finis Mitchell, has been hosting overnight guests for several decades in ten rustic but cozy cabins, furnished with oil lamps, old-fashioned wood burning stoves, and down quilts. Meals are served family style in the main lodge, which is warmed by two large stone fireplaces. Advanced reservations are highly recommended. For more information consult their website at www.big-sandy-lodge.com.

Hikers interested in history should consider a visit to **South Pass**, which is 45 miles northeast of Farson along Highway 28. This was an important (and relatively low) crossing of the Continental Divide that has been used for centuries by Native Americans, trappers, and westward-bound settlers. There are interpretive signs here, a few places where you can still make out the original ruts from wagons on the Oregon Trail, and a historic old ghost town to explore.

Groups flying into or traveling through Jackson Hole should spend at least one night in the town of **Jackson** (see Amenities and Attractions in Trip 7). Rock Springs offers a full range of amenities for travelers as well.

Directions to Trailheads: Begin by making your way to Pinedale. This small town is located along US 191, either 76 miles southeast of Jackson or 102 miles north of Rock Springs.

To reach the ending trailhead, drive 5.3 miles west on US 191, then turn right (north) on State Highway 352, following signs to Green River Lakes. This road is paved for the first 25.7 miles but then enters national forest land and quickly deteriorates into a gravel road with lots of washboards, ruts, and potholes. Driving this road with care is usually reasonable for passenger cars, but can become difficult after a rainstorm. Stay on the main road at all intersections until you come to a fork about 45 miles from the turnoff from US 191. To reach the trailhead, bear left at the fork and drive 0.4 mile to the signed hiker's parking area. The road straight ahead at the fork goes a short distance to Green River Lakes Campground.

To reach the starting trailhead, backtrack to Pinedale, drive 12 miles south on US 191, and then turn left (east) onto State Highway 353. This route is paved for its first 18 miles, but then turns to decent (sometimes washboarded) gravel for 0.7 mile to a junction. You bear left, drive 2.8 miles to a fork, and then go right for another 4.7 miles, still on rough but decent gravel roads, reaching a junction about 0.5 mile after a bridge over Big Sandy River. Turn left and proceed 7.1 miles to another junction, where you go left again, following signs to Big Sandy Campground. Stick with this very rough dirt-and-gravel road, which eventually becomes Forest Road 850, for 9.3 miles, and then go straight at a junction with a side road to a summer home area. About 0.9 mile later is a fork in the road, where you go right and drive a final 0.8 mile to the large and usually crowded trailhead parking area and campground. Please do not park in the campground slots, as these are for the use of those paying a fee to camp here.

Finis Mitchell "Lord of the Winds" (1901–1995)

No one is more closely associated with Wyoming's magnificent Wind River Range than Finis Mitchell, a pioneer, naturalist, mountaineer, backcountry guide, writer, and general jack-of-all-trades who made this range his home for fully eighty-five years. Eventually known as "The Lord of the Winds," Finis (sounds like "highness") Mitchell came to Wyoming from Missouri in 1906 with his parents, "a span of mules, a wagon and a cow." They settled on the west side of the mighty Wind River Mountains and tried to eke out an existence in the harsh Wyoming environment. His father repeatedly took him into the mountains on hunting trips, where Finis fell in love with the Wind Rivers and caught the climbing bug along the way. As a young adult, Finis migrated to the town of Rock Springs and worked for the Union Pacific Railroad for seven years until he was let go during the Great Depression.

With no job to be had, Finis and his young wife, Emma, returned to the southern Wind River Mountains in 1930, bought a tent, borrowed ten horses and saddles from nearby ranchers, and started Mitchell's Fishing Camp near Mud Lake in Big Sandy Opening, the present-day site of Big Sandy Lodge. Charging $1.50 a day for the horses, 50 cents for meals, and usually nothing for their time, the Mitchells were able to provide for themselves. When they began their camp, only a few lakes had any fish in them and they would take their clients fishing in Dads, Black Joe, and Big Sandy Lakes. Occasionally, they would transport some of their catch in oilcans or 5-gallon milk cans and then plant them in some of the surrounding lakes—Finis's first efforts of stocking fish in the mostly barren lakes of the range. By the time he was done, Finis would stock over 300 lakes in the Wind Rivers with over 2.5 million trout (they would migrate on their own to another 700-plus lakes). The big catch that today's anglers typically pull out of these lakes is due almost entirely to the efforts of Finis Mitchell.

Along with stocking trout, Finis eventually hiked every trail in the Wind Rivers, logging over 15,000 miles. He also climbed all but 20 of the range's peaks, making nearly 300 different ascents, and soloing the vast majority. He climbed until the age of eighty-four, reaggravating a previous knee injury during a fall into a crevasse at seventy-three, when he was forced to construct makeshift crutches and painfully hobble 18 miles out of the wilderness to reach a doctor.

As an avid photographer, Finis shot hundreds of thousands of photos of the Wind River range, and used them in numerous presentations to a wide variety of groups and organizations—he was willing to talk to just about anyone about his beloved Winds. He wrote a pocket guidebook to the range, *Wind River Trails,* which was first published in 1976 and, thankfully, is still available today. With his wealth of experience, he was certainly the preeminent authority on the Wind River Mountains.

Later in life, Finis went on to serve two terms in the Wyoming legislature. He also received an honorary doctorate from the University of Wyoming. Perhaps his finest honor was the naming of Mitchell Peak by the U.S. Congress, making him one of the few people to have a landform named after him while still living. Finis Mitchell passed away at the age of ninety-four.

By all accounts, Finis was a very affable soul when people would meet him on the trail or on top of a peak. Thanks in part to his love for these mountains and the enthusiasm for them that he expressed to others, the Wind River Mountains have become a highly desirable destination for backpackers, equestrians, mountaineers, photographers, and anglers from all over the world. Any visitor to these mountains is certainly blessed by the activities of this compelling figure.

Today, atop Mitchell Peak, a distinctive 12,482-foot mountain a little east of Jackass Pass above the famous Cirque of the Towers, climbers will find a bronze commemorative plaque, the only such memorial in the entire Wind River Range, to honor the man for whom this mountain was named—a man who is rightfully thought of by the title that he, and only he, could have possibly earned: "The Lord of the Winds."

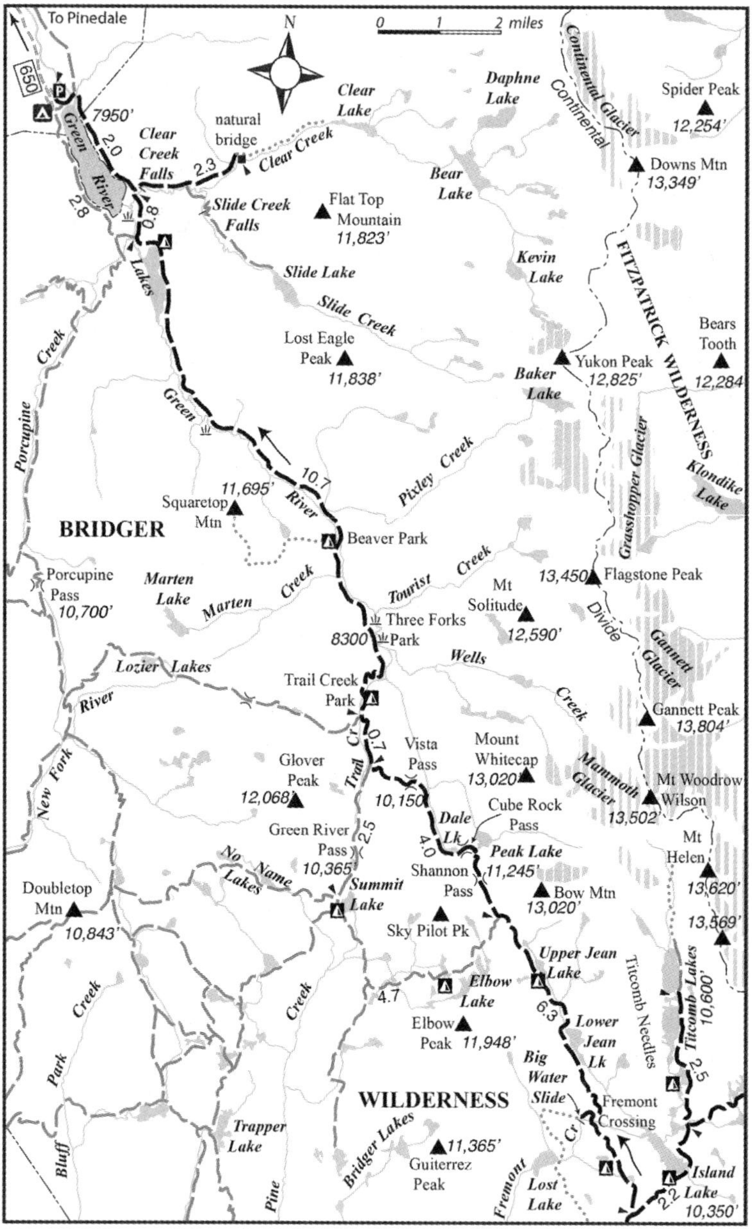

Wind River Highline Traverse (South)

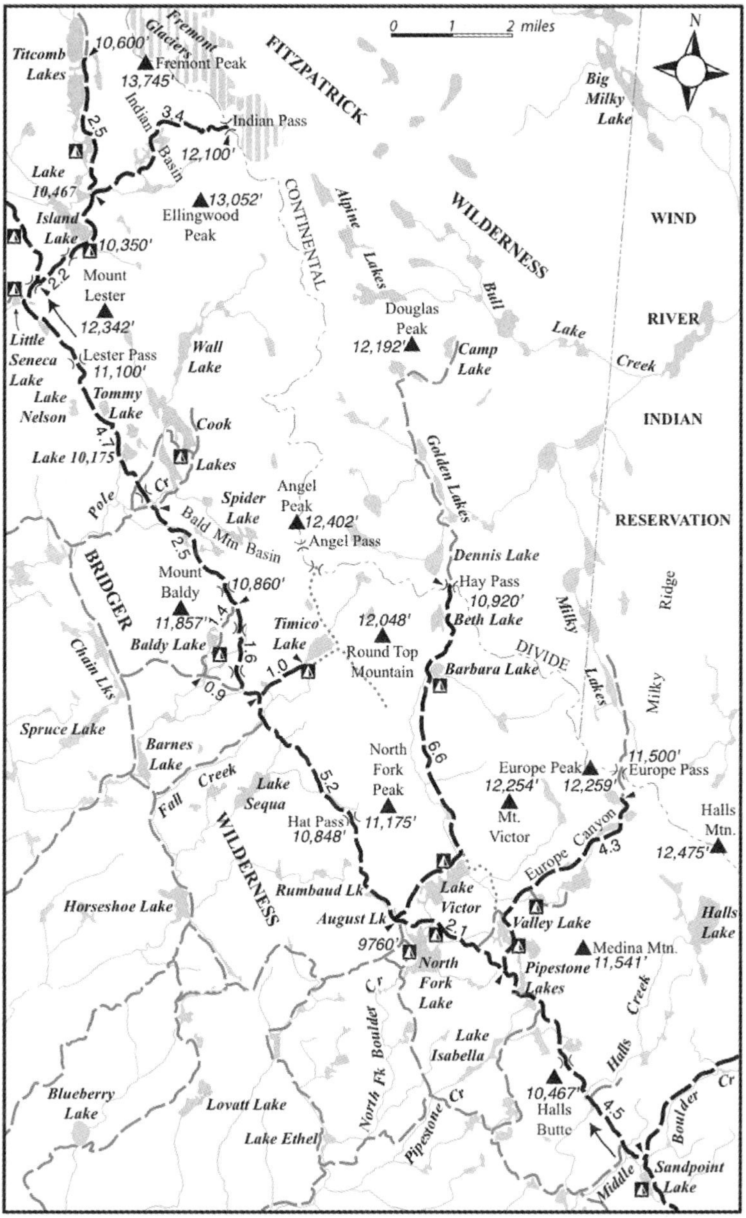

Wind River Highline Traverse (Middle)

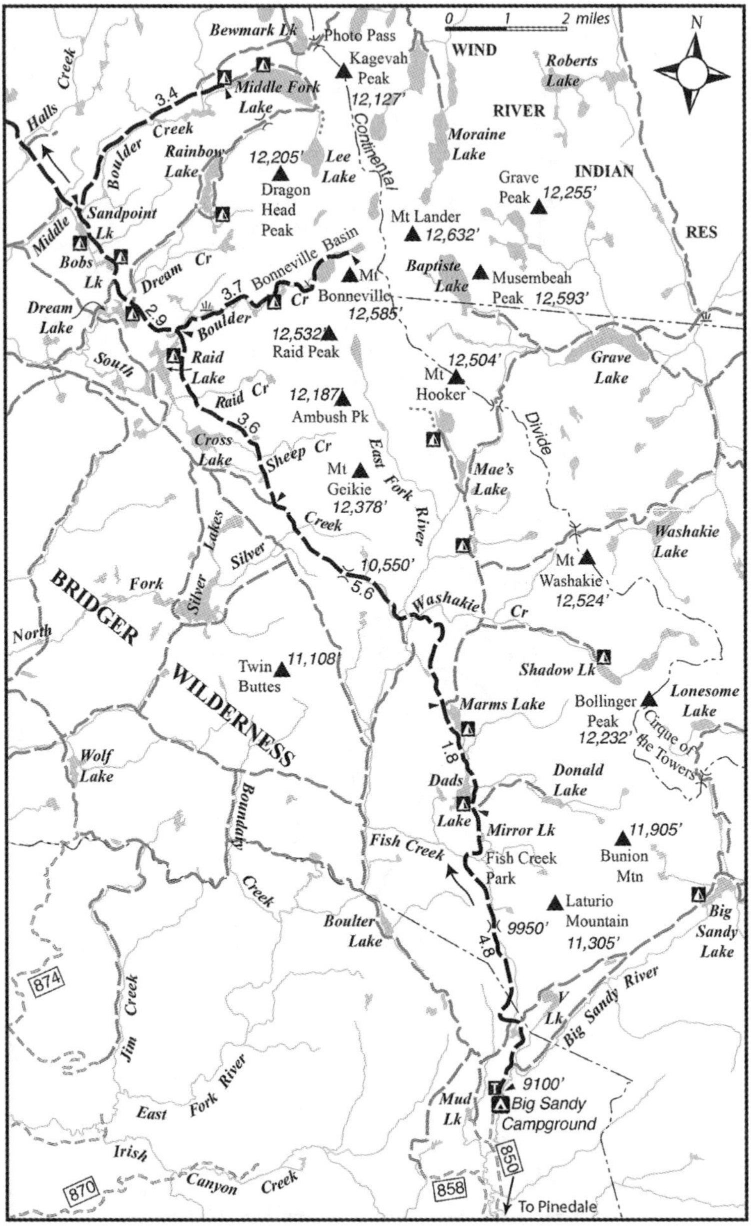

Wind River Highline Traverse (North)

Trip Description: ***Note:*** *This description includes only a handful of the many outstanding side trips that branch off from the main trail. My recommendation is to take all of them. Even better, study the map and simply wander off on your own at any of several dozen enticing locations to discover some of the many private off-trail lakes, meadows, peaks, and other beautiful spots found in abundance throughout this range.*

The trail starts near a large signboard at the north end of the parking lot (see map of Wind River Highline Traverse [South]) and wanders gradually uphill through a relatively open lodgepole-pine forest. The route parallels the clear waters of Big Sandy River, soon passes a junction with an alternate trail from an equestrian corral at Mud Lake, and then reaches a junction at 0.6 mile. Turn left (uphill), walk 0.8 mile to the next junction, and then veer left across a meadow to yet another junction, this time with the Fremont Trail coming up from Mud Lake.

Go right and steadily climb through open forest for 1.5 miles to a large meadow near the top of a minor ridge. This meadow offers good views to the east of the jagged pinnacles on top of Laturio Mountain and north to several distant but impressive peaks. The trail now descends a bit, goes around the west side of Fish Creek Park, and comes to tiny Mirror Lake. Just beyond this lake, you go left at the junction with the trail to Donald Lake and descend to island-studded Dads Lake. There are good views of Mount Geikie across this meadow-rimmed lake, as well as some nice campsites.

After passing around the east side of Dads Lake, you ascend to very attractive Marms Lake, which features more good campsites and has lots of hungry trout to tempt the backpacking angler. Just 0.1 mile north of Marms Lake is a junction.

The trail to the right heads for Mae's Lake, Hailey Pass, Grave Lake and the backcountry beyond (see Trip 10 for a description). Your trail veers left and makes a gentle ascent through meadows and past small ponds to an open area with excellent views to the north of a number of tall and very scenic peaks. The sometimes-rocky path then descends in meadows and forest to the grassy bottom of the valley of

East Fork River. Here you must make two fords. The first takes you over sluggish Washakie Creek, a simple crossing, while the second is the much more challenging ford of East Fork River. The water here is relatively swift and at least knee deep, so be careful and choose your crossing point wisely.

Shortly after the ford of East Fork River, you stay straight on the main trail, where a poorly marked route comes in from the left. The trail then makes a fairly strenuous climb for the next 1.3 miles, most of that distance beside a tiny creek, before you finally top out at a pass and the start of a huge area of rolling grasslands. The view about 2 miles north to the pyramid of Mount Geikie is stunning, as well as to the east of the crags around the distant Cirque of the Towers.

From here you descend gently past a shallow lake to an easy rock-hop crossing of North Fork Silver Creek. ***Tip:*** *For some worthwhile exploring, consider checking out the several small ponds and tarns that dot the gentle landscape to the southwest.*

A short climb through meadows and near-timberline forest takes you to a fork in the trail. The Highline Trail veers left on the way to the meadows around large Cross Lake and the start of a long course past subalpine lakes and through forests. However, that route includes large areas recently scarred by forest fires and is generally both lower in elevation and less scenic than the Fremont Trail (sometimes called the "Old Highline Trail"). A better choice is to bear right on the Fremont Trail and wander happily across rolling, boulder-strewn meadows. After about a mile, you splash across or rock-hop small Sheep Creek, making sure to look up the valley to the looming summits of Mount Geikie and Ambush Peak.

Staying near the northeast side of the vast meadows that characterize this area, you pass well above Cross Lake, rock-hop small Raid Creek, and then travel in and out of strips of forest. About a mile from the crossing of Raid Creek, you splash across South Fork Boulder Creek near the northern tip of an arm of irregularly shaped Raid Lake and reach an unsigned but obvious junction.

Side Trip to Bonneville Basin

The unofficial but easy-to-follow trail to the right makes a particularly outstanding side trip to the incredibly beautiful lakes in Bonneville Basin. To reach them, head up the valley of South Fork Boulder Creek, gently at first, then steeply across a forested slope to a small, unnamed lake. From there, a short uphill ramble leads to spectacular Little Bonneville Lake. This lake has a stunningly scenic campsite with amazing views across the lake's waters to extremely rugged Mount Bonneville. Adventurers can continue from here up an extremely steep scramble route past a waterfall to Bonneville Lake, which sits right at the base of the towering pinnacles and cliffs of Mount Bonneville. From there you can explore further up to starkly scenic Sheila Lake. When the time comes, retrace your steps to the junction.

Back on the sometimes-faint Fremont Trail, you wander north past a small, shallow lake, and then pass through more scenic, rolling meadows above large Dream Lake, which offers excellent fishing and camping possibilities. Keep left at a junction with the obscure Middle Fork Trail up to Rainbow Lake, and then rock-hop shallow Dream Creek. A short additional climb takes you to a narrow little lake and a junction at the north end. Keep straight (slightly right), shortly loop around the east side of pretty Bobs Lake (good campsites), and then wander up and down in forest for about 0.5 mile to very attractive Sandpoint Lake. This lake has good campsites at both the southeast and north ends. Just past the north end of Sandpoint Lake, you make a calf-deep ford of Middle Fork Boulder Creek and immediately reach a junction.

Side Trip to Middle Fork Lake

The trail to the right at the junction is another superb side trip, which climbs relatively gently for 3.4 miles to enormous and stunning Middle Fork Lake. From this 1.6-mile-long, brook trout-filled gem you can look up to hulking Kagevah Peak to the east, towering Dragon Head Peak to the southeast, and various other unnamed summits spread all around. A sketchy trail goes around the north side of the lake to a terrific (and very easy) off-trail wander over rocks and tundra to Lee Lake, which sits right beneath the soaring cliffs of Dragon Head and Pronghorn Peaks.

Other faint paths lead up to outstandingly beautiful Bewmark Lake, the stunning views from aptly named Photo Pass, and other worthwhile destinations. When your visit is over, return to the junction.

From the junction to Middle Fork Lake, head north on the Fremont Trail past a pretty meadow to an unsigned and easy-to-miss junction with a trail on the left toward Junction Lake. Keep straight and pass more meadows and small, unnamed lakes for the next mile to a junction with an unofficial route marked only with a cairn. Keep left on the main trail, and soon cross ankle-deep Halls Creek. You then climb to a saddle on the east flank of flat-topped Halls Butte and go downhill past an unnamed and irregularly shaped lake sitting in a shallow basin to the east (right). The trail now travels in and out of a burned area on the way to the first of the scenic Pipestone Lakes and a junction with the Lake Isabella Trail (see map of Wind River Highline Traverse [Middle]). Keep right on the Fremont Trail and soon come to the second Pipestone Lake, which has excellent views across its waters of bulky Mount Victor to the north. The trail then climbs away from the lake and in 0.2 mile comes to another junction.

Side Trip up Europe Canyon

The initially obscure trail angling to the right is another excellent extended side trip option. In less than a mile you come to some nice campsites near large Valley Lake. At the north end of this meadow-rimmed lake is a junction marked only with a small sign on a tree several yards to your right reading Trail Abandoned—Not Maintained. To explore the wonders of the upper parts of magnificent Europe Canyon, turn right onto this unmaintained trail and climb steeply up good tread for 0.6 mile to an obscure junction very shortly before reaching a pretty, unnamed lake. Go left on an initially faint route that heads north up Europe Canyon. Over the next 3 miles this increasingly grand route takes you up to several above-timberline lakes, over lovely alpine meadows, and finally to a high pass right on the Continental Divide. The trail is not always distinct, but actually becoming lost is fairly difficult in the mostly open terrain. The views of craggy summits and sparkling alpine lakes are terrific. Retrace your steps to the Fremont Trail junction.

From the Valley Lake junction, you head west-northwest on the Fremont Trail, going up and down for 0.7 mile to another junction, this time with a very faint path marked with cairns heading north-northeast toward the west side of Valley Lake. Keep straight here, and wind downhill in open forest for less than a mile to the flat basin holding large and popular North Fork Lake, where you will find a number of good campsites. After circling the meadows on the north side of this lake, you make a calf-deep ford of North Fork Boulder Creek, and then wander through more meadows before reaching a junction with a trail on the left toward the west side of North Fork Lake. Go straight here, and come to a four-way junction 0.1 mile later, where another possible side trip heads to Hay Pass.

Side Trip to Hay Pass

The outstanding viewpoint atop Hay Pass is 6.6 miles from this junction, well worth the distance and almost 1,200-foot elevation gain to get there. The maintained trail takes you up past the northwest side of long and island-studded Lake Victor, fords North Fork Boulder Creek, and then ascends the canyon of this large creek all the way up to Barbara and Beth Lakes, a pair of above-timberline gems with great scenery and good fishing. The path finally tops out at wide and rocky Hay Pass, from where you can look out on a seeming infinity of tall peaks, deep lakes, and rugged canyons. Perhaps most impressive is large and very deep Dennis Lake, several hundred feet below you to the north-northwest. If you are really feeling spry, a sketchy path continues down to Dennis Lake and beyond to yet more mountain wonders. After marveling at the scenery around Hay Pass, return to the Fremont Trail junction.

Following signs to Hat Pass, the Fremont Trail goes north from the junction near North Fork Lake and soon comes to scenic little August Lake, which features fine views across its waters to dramatic North Fork Peak. From this lake you make a long climb, which first takes you past Rumbaud Lake, and then up through increasingly alpine terrain to 10,848-foot Hat Pass, offering marvelous views of countless scenic peaks both near and far.

From Hat Pass the trail goes downhill through open tundra and meadows before finally returning to forested terrain. About 1.9 miles from the pass, you will notice large but trailless Lake Sequa in a wooded basin to the west. Walk another half mile to a junction marked only with a post just before an easy ford of Fall Creek. Go straight and climb 300 feet in the next 0.4-mile to a signed junction.

Side Trip to Timico Lake

This is the start of one of the shortest and most outstanding side trips off the Fremont Trail. Veer right at the junction onto a sometimes-faint path leading a mile over rolling tundra meadows to Timico Lake, one of the most spectacular bodies of water in the Wind River Range. Surrounded by rocky peaks, almost all of which top 12,000 feet, the scenery around this large and deep lake is absolutely breathtaking. Camping here is rather exposed, but is highly recommended in decent weather for the beautiful surroundings. There is also good fishing at Timico Lake, if you needed any additional reasons to make the side trip. Adventurers can explore scramble routes leading to high passes both southeast and north of Timico Lake. Both destinations feature fine views and are well worth visiting, but the route to the north is more scenic because you pass a marvelously scenic alpine lake a little below the pass. Retrace your steps to the junction.

After returning to the Fremont Trail, you continue your northerly trek across meadows for 0.1 mile to a four-way junction with the Bell Lakes Trail. Here you have a choice of routes.

Fremont Trail Alternate

For a higher and more rugged trip, go straight on the Fremont Trail, which rapidly ascends 350 feet to a saddle beside a rocky knoll. The trail then loses almost all of that elevation to a basin above the Baldy Lakes, regains every foot once again on the way to a second high saddle, and finally goes back down 300 feet to a junction with the Baldy Lakes Trail. This up-and-down route offers good views along the way and is 0.7 mile shorter than the alternative, but offers no decent camping options and misses the Baldy Lakes.

Baldy Lakes Alternate

The other option from the four-way junction west of Timico Lake is to take the trail past Baldy Lakes. This route involves less up and down and takes you to possible campsites beside the scenic Baldy Lakes, but is 0.7 mile longer, so take your pick. This route goes 0.8 mile west on the Bell Lakes Trail, which travels gently downhill through mostly forested terrain to a junction. Turn right (north) on the sometimes-rocky Baldy Lakes Trail and gradually climb beside small Baldy Creek for 0.5 mile to very attractive Baldy Lake, with its good campsites, large cutthroat trout, and fine views of rugged Mount Baldy to the northwest. The trail goes around the east side of Baldy Lake, and then climbs steadily past a couple of smaller ponds, a marshy area, and a very pretty waterfall to a reunion with the Fremont Trail.

From where the two alternates converge, head north on the Fremont Trail and continue trudging uphill on a rocky and eroded track to a 10,860-foot pass. The view, especially to the north, from this alpine grandstand is spectacular, with Spider Lake and several other smaller bodies of water in the Bald Mountain Basin almost directly below. Further to the north are the large Cook Lakes and a cluster of unnamed domes at the head of Pole Creek. In the distance are multitudinous 12,000- and 13,000-foot peaks scratching the Wyoming sky, including Ellingwood Peak, Fremont Peak, Jackson Peak, Elephant Head, and too many others to name.

The often badly eroded route now descends across rocky tundra into Bald Mountain Basin, where off-trail routes go east to several attractive lakes and a tough (but reasonable) scramble to the viewpoint at Angel Pass (an excellent side trip for experienced cross-country hikers).

The Fremont Trail descends to a series of ponds near the bottom of Bald Mountain Basin, and then follows the basin's outlet creek back down into forested terrain. About 0.4 mile below the last pond is an easy ford or rock-hop crossing of this small stream. You soon cross a wet meadow, then go over a little rise, before a short but steep descent takes you into the valley of Pole Creek. At a junction here, a trail goes right (northeast) to the large Cook Lakes, the first of which is only 0.5

mile away and well worth visiting. Your trail goes left at this junction and just 0.1 mile later comes to another junction and a reunion with the Highline Trail, whose route you departed from all the way back near East Fork River.

You turn right and in less than 100 yards reach a potentially difficult crossing of Pole Creek. Rock-hopping the flow of this boisterous stream a little above or below the horse ford is usually possible, but during high water you can expect a tricky, thigh-deep ford. After the ford, you walk north through a little saddle between two rocky buttes, and then descend to a junction with the upper trail to the Cook Lakes. You go straight (northwest) and hike up and down through open forest for 0.4 mile to the crossing of the outlet creek of meadow-rimmed Lake 10,175. This scenic lake offers good fishing for both brook and lake trout but offers only mediocre campsites.

From Lake 10,175, the sometimes-rocky trail ascends back above timberline and crosses the wide swatch of rocky terrain between Tommy Lake on the right (east) and Lake Nelson on the left (west), both of which have been stocked with golden trout. More climbing over rocky alpine terrain finally leads to the wide, grassy saddle of Lester Pass, which, at a little over 11,100 feet, is the highest elevation reached along the official Highline Trail. Given this lofty elevation, you might expect the view to be outstanding, and you would be right. Looking southeast, back the way you came, the mostly unnamed peaks and crags that rim Bald Mountain Basin dominate the view. Taking in the new terrain to the north, you get your first good look at the dramatic spires and granite summits that enclose Titcomb Basin.

With such a grand and enticing view, you will probably be anxious to get closer to these lofty peaks. So, head northwest and downhill from Lester Pass, steadily losing elevation over less rocky and increasingly vegetated terrain to an unnamed lake. Walk around the northeast side of this pretty lake, and then descend back below timberline to an easy crossing of a small creek and a junction, located just below a small, unnamed lake and just above somewhat larger Little Seneca Lake. The latter lake has possible campsites.

Most of the long route you've hiked from Marms Lake to here has been devoid of crowds and generally a solitude lover's delight. However, things are about to change, as you've now intersected the most popular hiking route into Titcomb Basin, one of the most famous and beautiful spots in the Wind River Range. The trail is wide and well beaten by legions of admirers, so you can no longer expect to be alone. But all those crowds are coming here for a good reason, and you'll definitely want to share in the fun. So turn right (northeast), still on the Highline Trail, and make a moderate, switchbacking ascent of a rock-strewn gully for 0.4 mile to a narrow, above-timberline pass. This pass has excellent views to the north and northeast of dozens of craggy peaks along the Continental Divide. Only a few yards on the other side of this pass is a junction.

Side Trip to Titcomb Basin

The Highline Trail goes left, but unless you are almost out of either time or food, or the weather is absolutely atrocious, then you'll want to spend at least an extra day or two on an exploration of magnificent Titcomb Basin and the nearby surroundings.

Turn right at the junction just below the pass northeast of Little Seneca Lake, drop briefly into a little basin, and then ascend to a tarn between a pair of low passes. From the second pass, there is a wonderful view of huge Island Lake, which fills much of the basin below. The trail now descends to the south shore of this gorgeous lake, which is surrounded by boulders and stunted alpine trees. There are numerous (but very popular) campsites scattered all around this lake. The trail loops around the southeast shore of the lake and then heads away from the water to a junction near Lake 10,467. The trail on your right climbs steeply to the stark, rugged grandeur of Indian Basin, which should be a mandatory side trip, at least as far as the dramatic lakes below the towers of Ellingwood Peak. If you have the additional time and energy, continue to the amazing views from Indian Pass.

The main Titcomb Basin Trail goes straight at the Indian Basin junction, fords the stream coming down from the basin, and then travels through alpine rock gardens to the lower end of otherworldly Titcomb Basin. The bottom of this alpine paradise is filled with several unusually large lakes surrounded on three sides by towering 13,000-

foot peaks and pinnacles of unusual beauty and grandeur. Despite the exposed nature of this area, campers often fill every nook and cranny in this basin, using the place as a convenient jumping-off point for climbs of the various peaks. Nonclimbers, who just want to marvel at the scenery, can happily do so for hours as they wander north along a trail generally following the east shore of this increasingly spectacular string of lakes. Be sure to go at least as far as Upper Titcomb Lake, which may be the most impressive of the bunch. With a little more time and energy, you can continue on past this gem into the rocky alpine meadows of upper Titcomb Basin, which sits directly beneath so many peaks, spires, glaciers, and pinnacles, naming them all would take several pages. Eventually you'll have to tear yourself away from this spectacularly beautiful area and return to the Highline Trail junction.

Having reluctantly left Titcomb Basin, turn north and wander up and down over rocky terrain (see map of Wind River Highline Traverse [North]). Proceed to an easy creek ford and past numerous small tarns, all offering water for the many good campsites in this vicinity. ***Tip**: By camping in this area you'll have much less crowded overnight conditions than at Island Lake or Titcomb Basin and still be close enough to those destinations for a reasonable day hike.* About 2.3 miles from the junction with the Titcomb Basin Trail is Fremont Crossing, where a sturdy metal bridge spans Fremont Creek, a raging torrent that would present a very difficult ford otherwise.

Just 0.1 mile past Fremont Crossing is an unsigned junction with a trail on the left. This is the upper terminus of the Lost Lake "Trail," actually a well-worn cross-country boot path winding down to Lost Lake. ***Tip**: If you turn left (west) and follow this unofficial route for about 0.5 mile you'll come to Big Water Slide, which, like Fremont Crossing, carries a rather mundane name, but the feature itself is far from boring, as the waters of Fremont Creek cascade down a sloping granite ledge in a thunderous display of hydropower.*

North of Fremont Crossing, the Highline Trail gradually ascends back above the land of scraggly trees and into an alpine landscape of rocks, tarns, and wildflower gardens. After about a mile you come to Lower Jean Lake, a long and irregularly shaped lake with nice views across the surface to the Titcomb Needles and Bow Mountain. Unfortunately, the ground here is too rocky for comfortable camping.

The trail goes around the west side of Lower Jean Lake and then follows the inlet creek, fording its ankle-deep flow twice before taking you to Upper Jean Lake. Although smaller than its lower neighbor, this lake is more scenic, with stupendous views to the north of Bow Mountain and Mount Arrowhead. There are good campsites at this lake, though exposed to the elements and rather uncomfortable during a big thunderstorm. Above Upper Jean Lake, the trail goes gradually uphill past a fairly small and unnamed lake to the top of a minor rise. From here, another 0.3 mile of gentle downhill through tundra and rocks leads to a junction and yet another choice of routes.

Highline Trail Alternate

The official Highline Trail goes left at the junction, a quite attractive route down to a point a little above long and lovely Elbow Lake (just going as far as this lake makes an excellent side trip). Beyond Elbow Lake the trail passes fine views of Sky Pilot Peak, and then curves to the north to reach beautiful Summit Lake. This large lake is ringed by meadows and quite scenic, but is often crowded with horse parties, creating rather muddy and aromatic conditions. The trail then goes north over wide Green River Pass and heads downhill along the headwaters of Trail Creek. Although very scenic and well worth hiking, this 7.2-mile route is not the recommended one.

Shannon Pass / Glacier Trails Alternate

For most hikers, the better choice from the junction north of Upper Jean Lake is to follow a wildly scenic course on the Shannon Pass and Glacier Trails. This route is more rugged than the official Highline Trail, but is 3.2 miles shorter and more dramatically scenic. To take this trail, go right at the junction and hike north-northwest over gentle alpine meadows to 11,245-foot Shannon Pass. On the north side of this pass the trail rapidly descends a rocky slope to very impressive Peak Lake, a deep gem that is nearly surrounded by rocky peaks, all of which top out at over 12,000 feet. ***Warning:*** *The way down to Peak Lake from*

Shannon Pass is subject to rockslides and is often icy. Ask about current conditions before starting your adventure.

From Peak Lake the trail turns west, goes through Cube Rock Pass, and then descends a rocky defile to tiny Dale Lake. Shortly beyond this lake the trail goes back below timberline and descends beside a small creek forming the headwaters of Green River, one of the most significant streams of the American West. After about 0.6 mile, you head away from the stream and make a brief climb to Vista Pass. With a foreground of meadows and small ponds and a background of impressive peaks and ridges, this is yet another wonderfully scenic spot in the Wind River Range. A section of fairly steep downhill switchbacks through open forest leads west-northwest from Vista Pass to a junction and a reunion with the Highline Trail.

Where both alternates converge, you turn right and steadily descend on the Highline Trail through forest for 0.7 mile to a junction, where you go straight and soon find yourself at Trail Creek Park, a popular meadow featuring fine scenery and good campsites, offering an excellent locale for a final night on the trail. At the north end of Trail Creek Park you cross Trail Creek and then descend a fairly steep grade for almost 2 miles to the large and rather swampy expanse of Three Forks Park. Extremely photogenic cliffs and pinnacles rim this nearly mile-long meadow but camping here is not recommended, as the few sites are only mediocre and the wet environment produces mosquitoes in abundance. The trail heads downstream through forest, paralleling the course of the increasingly large Green River. About 1.5 miles below Three Forks Park, you break out of the trees at Beaver Park (campsites).

Side Trip to Squaretop Mountain

Beaver Park makes a good base camp for those who want to climb Squaretop Mountain, one of the most famous landmarks in the Wind River Range. The unsigned and unmaintained scramble route to the top goes west from Beaver Park, starting from the north end a little before the crossing of Green River. The often-sketchy route then steeply ascends a partially forested hillside to lovely Granite Lake, and

Three Forks Park

then charges up a rocky gully a bit south of the lake to the ridgetop. From here, simply walk north over relatively gentle terrain to the top of Squaretop Mountain. The view from atop this 11,695-foot hulk of a mountain is superb, especially to the north over the Green River Lakes.

The Highline Trail crosses Green River at Beaver Park, where most of the time a large and sturdy bridge offers easy access to the other side. Unfortunately, this bridge has been washed out more than once over the years. Without the bridge, the ford can be cold, at least thigh deep, and potentially dangerous. Inquire at the Pinedale Ranger Station before departure to make sure this bridge is in place, or that the water level is low enough for a safe crossing.

The trail now heads downstream, following the northeast bank of the river. For the most part, the next few miles are in dense forest, with only occasional glimpses of Granite Peak and Squaretop Mountain across the river. The forest does provide welcome shade, and water is abundant with several tributary creeks crossing the trail. At just over 3 miles from Beaver Park, the forest opens up and a very gentle trail travels through or beside a delightful meadow, bisected by the milky waters of Green River and beneath the massive cliffs on the north side of Squaretop Mountain. Moose are frequently seen feeding on the marsh vegetation in this wet habitat.

Eventually you come to the south end of Upper Green River Lake and follow the eastern shore for almost 1.5 miles. The view from the northeast side of the lake looking south to the sheer cliffs of well-named Squaretop Mountain is one of the most famous views in Wyoming, justifiably appearing on numerous calendars and postcards. Campsites are nearby if you want an extended time to enjoy the scene, but they are usually very crowded.

From Upper Green River Lake, the Highline Trail travels over a forested knoll and then comes to a junction at the edge of another meadow. Either trail will take you back to the Green River Lakes trailhead in 2.8 miles, though superior views recommend staying on the Highline Trail. Therefore, continue straight at the junction and walk beside a willow-choked meadow (watch for moose) for 0.7 mile to a crossing of Clear Creek. Most of the time a bridge spans this large, rollicking creek, but it also often gets washed out, which will require a tricky ford. A little less than 0.1 mile later is a junction with the Clear Creek Trail.

Side Trip to Clear Creek Natural Bridge

Investing a couple of extra hours in a side trip up the Clear Creek Trail is well worth the effort. This path climbs past some good views of Clear Creek Falls and Flattop Mountain on the way to Clear Creek Natural Bridge, 2.3 miles from the Highline Trail. Here Clear Creek has cut a hole through the bottom of an imposing wall of dark limestone. The feature is too massive to fit into your camera frame, but is worth the time to admire the powerful forces of nature and the thousands of years necessary to carve the bridge. After fully admiring the scene, retrace your steps to the junction.

From the junction, follow the Highline Trail south along the hillside a bit above Lower Green River Lake. Most of the up-and-down route is across open slopes covered with wildflowers, sagebrush, scattered trees, and meadows. The open terrain offers decent views across the large lake to the forested slopes of Big Sheep Mountain to the southwest. After 1.7 miles, you come to a junction just past the north end of the lake. Turn left, almost immediately cross a large, metal bridge over the Green River, and hike gradually uphill for 0.3 mile to a fork in the trail. Keep right and walk a short distance up a draw to the trailhead parking lot (see map of Wind River Highline Traverse [North]).

Possible Itinerary

	Camps and Side Trips	Miles	Elevation Gain
DAY 1	Big Sandy TH to Marms Lake	6.6	+1,100/−300
DAY 2	Raid Lake	9.2	+1,300/−1,250
	Side trip to Bonneville Basin	7.4	+1,100/−1,100
DAY 3	Sandpoint Lake	2.9	+250/−400
	Side trip to West Fork Lake	6.8	+650/−650

continued on next page

Possible Itinerary—*continued*

	Camps and Side Trips	Miles	Elevation Gain
Day 4	North Fork Lake	6.6	+800/−850
	Side trip up Europe Canyon	8.6	+1,000/−1,000
Day 5	Day hike to Hay Pass	13.2	+1,450/−1,450
Day 6	Timico Lake	6.2	+1,650/−900
Day 7	Island Lake	11.0	+1,450/−1,600
Day 8	Day hike to Titcomb Basin and Indian Pass	13.8	+2,200/−2,200
Day 9	Trail Creek Park	12.3	+1,750/−2,800
	Side Trip to Big Water Slide	1	+100/−100
Day 10	Out to Green River Lakes TH	13.4	+550/−1,900
	Side Trip to Clear Creek Bridge	4.6	+300/−300

Alternatives: For a slightly shorter version of this traverse with paved road access to the northern trailhead, you could exit via Elkhart Park. Simply hike west on the heavily used trail from the junction just above Little Seneca Lake (but only after you do the recommended side trip into Titcomb Basin.)

Giving Back

Wyoming Wilderness Association: www.wildwyo.org

The Windy "Winds"

In August, Dave and I were off on one of our annual backpacking vacations. Over the years we have trekked through dozens of the American West's most spectacular hiking spots, including Idaho's Sawtooth Mountains, Wyoming's Teton Range, Oregon's Wallowa Mountains, Washington's rugged Olympic Coast, southern Utah's Escalante Canyons, Colorado's San Juan Mountains, and numerous others. For this trip we had particularly high expectations, as this was a return engagement to one of our favorite areas. After months of planning, we were making the long drive out from our homes, which were then in western Oregon, to Wyoming's Wind River Range. We'd been on a weeklong hike in the Winds a couple of years before and had such a grand time amid the soaring granite peaks and sparkling alpine lakes that we just had to return to see more of what this magnificent range had to offer.

The long and tiring drive was absolutely worth the effort. After just a few days on the trail, we both agreed that the trip was exceeding even our lofty expectations. On day 1 we sat and quietly watched a huge bull moose feeding amid the marshy shallows near Upper Green River Lake. On day 2 we had walked over a pass that was, we noted with amazement, higher than the top of Mount Hood, the highest point in our entire home state of Oregon (no wonder the air seemed thinner and we had less stamina than back at home). And on day 3 we stood in upper Titcomb Basin for hours, absolutely awestruck while we marveled at the amazing array of 13,000-foot peaks ringing this otherworldly basin. We were having a great trip and our usual wonderful time in the backcountry.

On day 4 we stopped early in the afternoon at an above-timberline gem known as Upper No Name Lake, which sported the usual absolutely amazing scenery so abundant in the Winds. After a while such outstanding scenery becomes so commonplace that if it doesn't rate at least a 9.7 on a scale of 1 to 10, then taking out your camera is not even worth considering. On this day the early stop was necessitated by a concern about the rapid build-up of thunderclouds filling the mountain sky. I would have strongly preferred camping someplace below timberline, but the nearest trees along our planned route were two or three hours away, and the speed at which the weather was deteriorating didn't make such a journey feasible. The clouds had been thickening and getting darker for more than an hour and were now roiling around and looking pretty ominous. The first clap of thunder sealed the decision as we quickly dropped our packs and started pulling out our gear.

Dealing with thunderstorms in the Wind Rivers is a fairly common occurrence. The mountain ranges of western Wyoming are famous for afternoon cloudbursts and, since large expanses of this range are above timberline, backpackers frequently must forgo their afternoon hiking plans and sit out the storms in the relative safety and comfort of their tents. We weren't particularly concerned because we knew from previous experience that thunderstorms are common in this range and don't typically pose a significant problem. Usually, after an hour or so of rain and loud thunderclaps, the storm dissipates, which would allow Dave to spend the evening fishing while I explored the area and took pictures. This particular evening Mother Nature had more robust plans.

Dave and I quickly pitched the tent, but we weren't exactly thrilled with the arrangements. Without any trees or even bushes more than a foot or so tall, cover was nonexistent. We'd chosen a spot tucked between a couple of large boulders to use as a partial but generally ineffective windbreak. In addition, the area was so rocky that getting tent stakes into the ground ranged from very difficult to impossible, requiring us to rely on weighing things down with piles of rocks. As the first gusts of wind came up and drops of rain began to fall, we crawled into our nylon home-away-from-home, reasonably confident we could easily wait out the expected short-term storm. Almost five hours later, we were still waiting and considerably less confident.

This time the storm hit with a violence that was well beyond anything we had experienced on our previous trip. The rain pelted down in sheets as mini-waterfalls cascaded off the tent's rainfly. As the winds howled, buffeting us from different directions seemingly all at once, the tent struggled to remain in place, compelling the occupants to utter silent prayers for the care and competence of the manufacturers. Lightning and thunder were seemingly everywhere—huge blinding flashes followed almost immediately by deafening booms that reverberated all across the basin. Though very exciting for the first hour or two, the storms refused to let up for more than a few minutes, and we soon grew worried. Finally, approaching early evening, Dave and I cautiously peeked out the tent flap during a moment of relative calm to see some very welcome breaks in the clouds, allowing us to tentatively explore outside.

The next ten minutes were spent shoring up our shelter, hastily piling up more rocks to strengthen the guy lines, building up a mini wind break of large boulders, and shunting away the rivers of rain water. Dave then announced his intention to try some angling, while I was tasked with cleaning out and rearranging the inside of the tent. Just five minutes later the lightning was back, forcing Dave into a rapid retreat. Through the tent walls I could hear him hustling up the hillside and, rather surprisingly, calling me to come out of the tent.

"What's up? I asked, sticking my head out around the rainfly. "The sunset," he exclaimed. "Grab your camera, it's amazing." With Nikon in hand, I crawled out of the tent to an evening sunset that was beyond stunning. The orange, yellow, and purple colors took our breath away, and the billowing thunderclouds were perfectly backlit by the last rays of the sun. Most striking of all, those sunrays streamed through holes in the clouds creating columns of

Perfect Mountain Sunset

contrasting light and dark that shot out for miles across the evening sky. I've since learned that meteorologists refer to this phenomenon as crepuscular rays, but I prefer the term "God Fingers," a better description of the feeling I had at the time. Sadly, this scene didn't last long, as the storms were back upon us in just a couple of minutes. However, I'll never forget that perfect mountain sunset.

The rest of the night was extremely hair raising, as the thunderstorms returned with a violence that seemed to make those we experienced earlier in the day look like the unknown warm-up act before a Rolling Stones concert. And boy were the stones (and everything else, it seemed) rolling!

For hours, a series of incredibly violent storms continued to pass over our location. The atmosphere felt and sounded like a war zone. Cooking dinner was out of the question, so we sullenly snacked on granola bars and gorp. We nearly lost our voices, having to yell to be heard over the din. Sleep was impossible, as the howling winds and loudly pounding hail passed over in wave after wave. Dave and I were forced to take turns holding up the tent poles so our little nylon shelter didn't completely collapse on us during the night.

The morning finally dawned, with deceptively clear, cool, and stunningly beautiful skies. The entire basin of Upper No Name Lake was buried under drifts of hailstones piled inches deep, from a distance appearing like a nice gentle snowfall. Although exhausted and bleary-eyed from lack of sleep, we were grateful to be otherwise unscathed. As often happens after such experiences, we were actually quite upbeat as we used our hands to shovel the hail away from our shelter and worked to repair the tent's damaged rainfly.

And why wouldn't we be happy? After all, we'd survived the night. And, more important, we would forever savor the exciting memory of witnessing the finest sunset either of us could remember. We definitely no longer had any question about why this range is referred to as "The Winds."—**Doug**

Bridger and Popo Agie Wildernesses,
Bridger-Teton and Shoshone National Forests

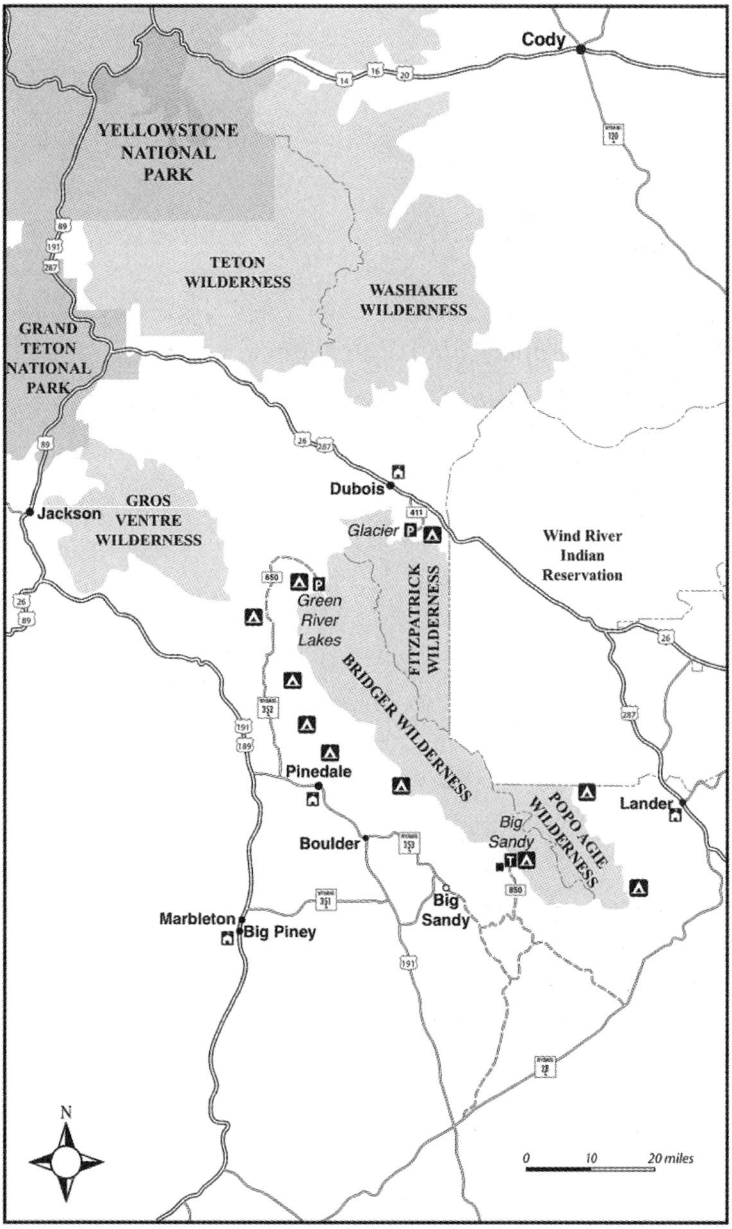

Cirque of the Towers Loop Location Map

TRIP 10

Cirque of the Towers Loop

> We don't stop hiking because we grow old—we grow old because we stop hiking.
>
> —FINIS MITCHELL

Over the years I have had the privilege of completing several weeklong backpacking trips into different areas of the Wind River Range, which encompasses a spectacular, 100-mile-long stretch of high mountains along the spine of the Continental Divide in west-central Wyoming. Each one of those trips has been both memorable and spectacular—the Winds never disappoint. The range boasts nearly fifty summits over 12,000 feet and is home to the highest mountain in Wyoming, 13,804-foot Gannett Peak (34 feet higher than the much more renowned Grand Teton, 70 miles to the northwest). Not surprisingly, climbers flock to the area due to an abundance of good rock and challenging routes. Backpackers, equestrians, and photographers come for the incomparable scenery, in part from an abundance of towering peaks, cirque-bound lakes, rushing streams, and wildflower-carpeted meadows. Plentiful, good-size fish draw anglers to the area as well. Although not as well known among the masses as the nearby Tetons, the majestic Wind River Mountains have full awareness on the part of knowledgeable mountain lovers.

Selecting just one trip from the numerous possibilities presented by the Wind River Mountains is a difficult task. Undoubtedly, those who

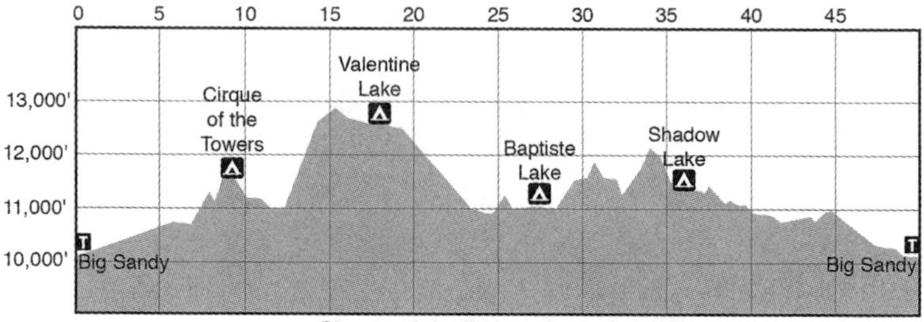

Cirque of the Towers Loop Profile

visit this area and sample some of the range's delights will surely want to return again and again. The trip described here is a 40-mile loop in the southern Winds around some of the range's most dramatic and awe-inspiring collection of peaks, known as the Cirque of the Towers, where several classic-looking granite spires rise up into the sky from a horseshoe-shaped cirque to elevations of over 12,000 feet. These peaks were relatively unknown until the writings of Orrin Bonney publicized the area after he and Frank and Notsie Garrick made a climbing trip in 1940. Since then, the area has increasingly grown in both stature and attention, so much so that the Forest Service has instituted a camping ban within 0.25 mile of poorly named Lonesome Lake near the head of the cirque—as far as I know, the only such ban in the wilderness.

Dramatic-looking peaks are not the only attraction to this route, as the loop travels to several fine examples of Wind River lakes and streams, where overnighters should have plenty of choices for view-packed campsites and anglers should find the fishing to be characteristically good. Early- to mid-season visitors will be treated to a vibrantly colorful display of wildflowers, but should be prepared for hordes of mosquitoes at that time as well. With short side trips off the main loop, you can also visit some equally beautiful, but somewhat less popular, highlights at Baptiste and Shadow Lakes. Overall this may be one of the most scenic mountain hikes in the United States, so come prepared to be awed.

Days: 5–7

Distance: 47.5 miles (plus side trip to Pyramid Lake)

Type: Loop

Scenery: 9

Solitude: 8 (away from Cirque of the Towers)

Technical Difficulty: 5

Physical Difficulty: 7

Elevation Gain/Loss: +7,540'/–7,540'

Season: Mid-July to mid-September

Best: Mid-July through August

Maps: USGS: *Big Sandy Opening, Temple Peak, Lizard Head Peak, Mount Bonneville*
USFS: Bridger Wilderness
Earthwalk Press: Southern Wind River Range

Recommended Resources: *Wind River Trails*, by Finis Mitchell
Climbing and Hiking in the Wind River Mountains, by Joe Kelsey

Contacts:

Bridger-Teton National Forest
Pinedale Ranger District
29 East Fremont Lake Road
PO Box 220
Pinedale, WY 82941
307-367-4326
www.fs.fed.us/r4/btnf

Shoshone National Forest
Wind River Ranger District
1403 W. Ramshorn
Dubois, WY 82513-0186
307-426-2466
www.fs.fed.us/shoshone

Nearest Campgrounds: Big Sandy—at trailhead

Nearest Airports: Rock Springs / Sweetwater County Airport (RKS)—100 miles
Jackson Hole Airport (JAC)—143 miles
Salt Lake City International Airport (SLC)—285 miles

Nearest Outdoor Retailers:

Great Outdoor Shop—57 miles
322 W. Pine St. (Hwy. 191)
Pinedale, WY 82941
307-367-2440

Wild Iris Mountain Sports—77 mi
166 Main Street
Lander, WY 82520
307-332-4541

Outfitters: Contact the Pinedale Ranger District for a current list of permitted commercial outfitters.

Wildland Trekking Company
Montana Office
2304 North Seventh Avenue, Unit K
Bozeman, MT 59715
800-715-4453
www.wildlandtrekking.com

Lander Llama Company
2024 Mortimore Lane
Lander, WY 82520
307-332-5624
www.landerllama.com

Permits: Permits are not required at this time, except for organizational groups and parties traveling with stock.

Regulations: Maximum group size: 15. No camping within 0.25 mile of Lonesome Lake. Campfires are banned above timberline.

Transportation Logistics: Private automobile or rental car (Jackson Hole Airport) is about the only way to reach the Wind Rivers, although there is an unconfirmed rumor of shuttle service from Jackson.

Backcountry Logistics: (A, BB, L, Sn, Su, W) The weather can be fickle at times at this high of an altitude this far north in the Rocky Mountains. Backpackers should be prepared to handle inclement weather, including severe thunderstorms, bringing with them the possibility of high winds and hail, as well as the occasional snowstorm. This is also bear country, where black bears are active throughout the range and a small population of grizzly bears has been reestablished in the northern part of the Wind River Mountains. Although not required, backpackers should use bear canisters.

Amenities and Attractions: The tiny hamlet of Pinedale is the closest form of civilization to the trailhead, where choices for gas, food, and lodging are available. The **Wind River Brewing Co.**, located on the main drag at 402 W. Pine Street, offers award-winning, handcrafted beers for sipping and decent pub fare for eating. Even in the middle of cowboy country, you can satisfy a hankering for a burrito at **Rock Rabbit** at 23 W. Pine. The **Sugar Shack** (310 E. Pine) is the place in town to grab an old-fashioned burger, fries, and shake on the way to or from the trailhead. An interesting attraction worth thirty minutes of your time is the **Museum of the Mountain Man** in Pinedale (700 East Hennick Road), a small facility offering historical displays and artifacts from early fur trappers, guides, and other explorers who opened the American West to later pioneers.

One-half mile from the Big Sandy trailhead, rustic **Big Sandy Lodge**, founded in the 1920s by Finis Mitchell, has been hosting overnight guests for several decades in ten rustic but cozy cabins, furnished with oil lamps, old-fashioned wood-burning stoves, and down quilts. Meals are served family style in the main lodge, which is warmed by two large stone fireplaces. Advanced reservations are highly recommended. For more information, consult their website at www.big-sandy-lodge.com.

Hikers interested in history should consider a visit to **South Pass**, which is 45 miles northeast of Farson along Highway 28. This was an important (and relatively low) crossing of the Continental Divide that has been used for centuries by Native Americans, trappers, and westward-bound settlers. There are interpretive signs here, a few places where you can still make out the original ruts from wagons on the Oregon Trail, and a historic old ghost town to explore.

Groups flying into or traveling through Jackson Hole should spend at least one night in the town of **Jackson** (see Amenities and Attractions in Trip 7). Rock Springs offers a full range of amenities for travelers as well.

Orrin Bonney (1903–1976)

Orrin Hanning Bonney was born in the tiny mining town of Idaho Springs, Colorado, located in Clear Creek Canyon in the mountains west of Golden. As a young lad he did some climbing in the Indian Peaks area, but his climbing career would not really take off until later. After graduating from the University of Colorado in 1926, he moved to Houston, Texas, to practice law, where he would maintain a primary residence. However, in 1930 he established a practice that would continue all his years, spending most of his summers in the Rockies. Becoming an avid mountaineer, Bonney would leave Texas each summer to climb mountains, initially in the Longs Peak area and then in the Tetons, climbing the Grand for the first time in 1933. As his skills and interests grew, he climbed extensively in the Wind Rivers, the Canadian Rockies, Mexico, and the Alps. On one of his forays to Canada, he met and then later married his wife, Lorraine Gagnon.

Tremendously fascinated by the Tetons and the Winds, he spent most of his summers in his beloved second home of Wyoming. He extensively explored unmapped areas in the Wind Rivers, making numerous first ascents and naming some of the peaks. Aside from Finis Mitchell, no one knew more about the Winds than Orrin Bonney. With the assistance of his wife, he updated a couple of existing guidebooks and then wrote a guide to the mountains of Wyoming. He and his wife penned several books, including a climbing and backcountry guide to the Wind River mountains, *Field Book, Wind River Range,* as well as *Bonney's Guide to Grand Teton National Park and Jackson's Hole, Absaroka Range and Yellowstone Park Field Book, Teton Range Field Book,* and *Battle Drums and Geysers* (a journal of Lieutenant G. C. Doane, an early explorer of the greater Yellowstone region). His extensive research was also useful in authenticating a number of early Teton climbs. Many of his guides are still available and a welcome addition to the library of anyone who loves the mountains of Wyoming.

In the 1960s, Bonney joined the Sierra Club and was instrumental in establishing the Lone Star chapter, the first in Texas, serving as vice Chairman and then chairman. He also was an active member in the American Alpine Club, serving as central vice president in the mid-1950s. Following passage of the original wilderness bill in 1964, he was very influential as an advocate for wilderness areas in Wyoming, his research and activism playing an important role in the eventual designation of the Cloud Peak Wilderness in the Bighorn Mountains. Some of his other accomplishments included conceiving the Lone Star Hiking Trail through the Sam Houston National Forest in southeast Texas, and preservation efforts in the Big Thicket (also in southeast Texas), the Guadalupe Mountains, and Big Bend Wilderness. However, his first love seemed to be the mountains of Wyoming and many a Teton climber will recall being entertained by Bonney at his big teepee near Jenny Lake and later at his home in Kelly. After Orrin's death in 1976, Lorraine continued their work from their Wyoming home.

Driving Directions to Trailhead: From Pinedale, follow U.S. Highway 191 about 12 miles to the tiny town of Boulder (last gas), and turn east onto State Highway 353. Follow 353 for 18 miles to the historical site of Big Sandy and the end of paved road. Watching for road signs, turn left and proceed east then southeast for 9 miles to a junction with the Emigrant Trail (Lander Cutoff) just after crossing Big Sandy River. Turn left (east), and roughly follow the course of the river for 7 miles to another junction. Turn left and head north, entering Forest Service land after 4 miles, where the road becomes FS Road 850. Pass the turnoff to Dutch

Joe Guard Station and continue another 5 miles, eventually passing through Big Sandy Opening on the way to a junction with a road on the left to Big Sandy Lodge. From the junction, proceed ahead for 0.75 mile to the parking area loop just shy of Big Sandy Campground. Due to the distance and rough nature of some of the roads, allow about 1.5 hours for the drive from Boulder to the trailhead. There is a vault toilet just up the hill above the parking area.

Trip Description: Head northeast away from the parking area on the wide track of the Big Sandy Trail through light forest, immediately passing by a lateral on the right from the campground and a couple of posts bearing information about camping limits. The grade from the trailhead all the way to Big Sandy Lake is quite gentle, which allows backpackers the opportunity to knock off the first 6 miles of trail fairly quickly. The trail follows the course of meadow-lined Big Sandy River for 0.4 mile to a junction with a trail on the left, a stock trail angling in from the corrals at Big Sandy Lodge. Continue upstream another 0.3 mile to a junction with the Highline Trail headed north past Meeks Lake. (Between the Big Sandy and Green River Lakes trailheads, the Highline Trail travels across the west side of the Continental Divide for about 80 miles, offering a fine Wind Rivers backpacking experience—see Trip 9.) Approximately 40 miles later, this trail will be your return route to the trailhead. As a further distinction, the Highline Trail is also the designated route of the Continental Divide Trail through the southern Winds.

Bear right at the junction, hop over a small stream, and follow a bend in the river before the trail resumes a northeast bearing. Pass over a low hill into some meadowlands, where the river cuts a lazy and sinuous course through the lush vegetation, which includes wildflowers such as yarrow, daisy, lupine, and cinquefoil. Through this opening, the high peaks west of the Continental Divide make their first appearance, including Big Sandy Mountain, Mitchell Peak, War Bonnet Peak, Temple Peak, and Schiestler Peak. In the midst of this clearing, the trail passes into Bridger Wilderness and then continues

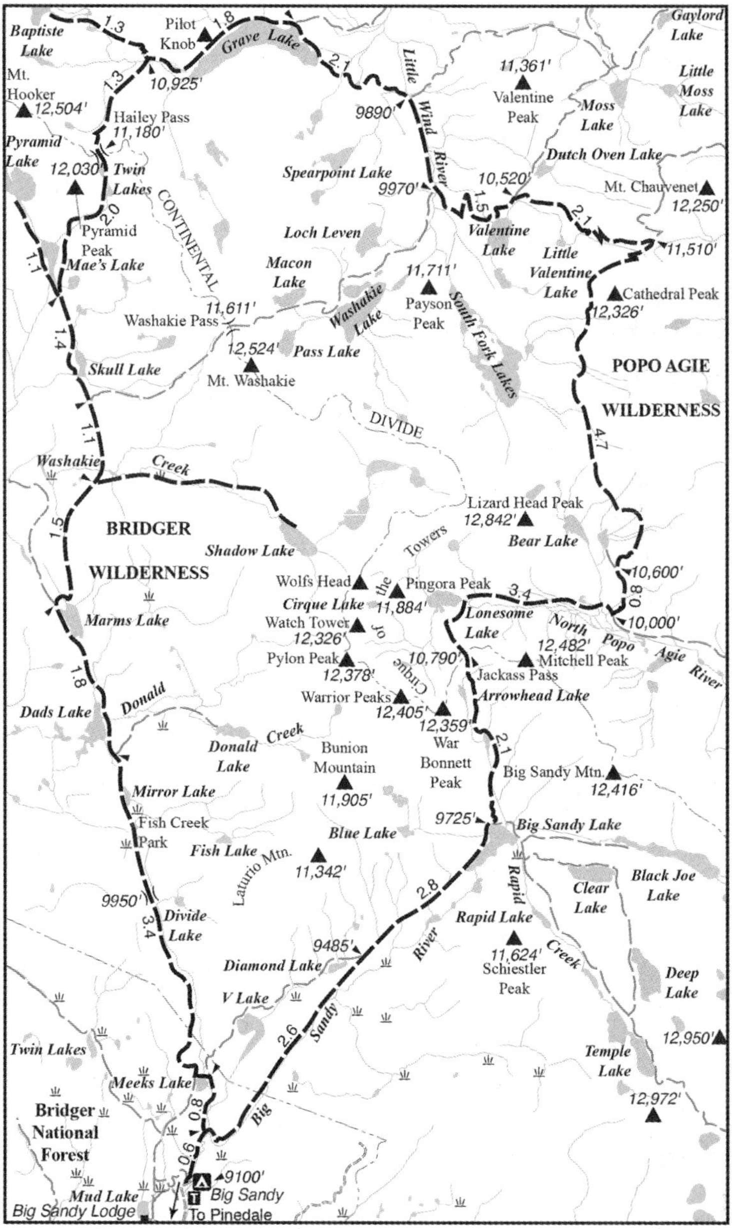

Cirque of the Towers Loop

upstream through stands of light lodgepole pine forest alternating with small pockets of meadow. The trail moves away from the river a bit on the way to another junction at 3.75 miles with a trail to Diamond and Vee Lakes. Continue ahead from the junction, passing through another picturesque, flower-carpeted meadow and a long stretch of forest, with Engelmann spruce and whitebark pines joining the lodgepoles. Hop over a side stream and then break out into the open near the west side of lovely Big Sandy Lake.

Fed by four named streams and surrounded by high peaks, most prominently pyramidal-shaped, 12,476-foot Big Sandy Mountain, scenic Big Sandy Lake is popular with day hikers, overnight backpackers, and anglers alike. Late starters can find campsites around the 57-acre lake, complete with bear-proof food lockers, down a path leading around the east shore. Dropping a line may yield a catch of cutthroat or brook trout, although both the fishing and the camping might be better at some of the lakes nearby to the east and southeast (Black Joe, Clear, and Deep), where there should be slightly less competition.

Continue around the lakeshore to the north end of Big Sandy Lake and a junction, 5.2 miles from the trailhead, where the route turns left (north) and begins a steep, zigzagging climb up the Jackass Pass Trail across the slope directly west of North Creek. After the easy stroll to Big Sandy Lake, the trail to Jackass Pass may seem quite laborious, steeply gaining, losing, and then regaining precious elevation along the way. On the way to the top of a set of switchbacks, the trail wanders among scattered whitebark pines and through flower fields of larkspur, lupine, daisy, goldenrod, bistort, bluebells, arnica, and yarrow. Above the switchbacks, the trail crosses a shallow bowl, dips down to cross boulder-lined North Creek, and then climbs steeply again, as you wend your way around granite boulders and over slabs before dropping down towards Shaft Lake (unnamed on maps and also referred to as North Lake). Pass the north side of the lake and then bend around to follow the creek north toward Arrowhead Lake. The main trail avoids the upper lake, but a use trail provides access to Arrowhead Lake for those who are inclined to visit. (From this lake there is an established route over the divide to the upper basin below Cirque of the Towers, which would eliminate the need to return to the main trail.) Ascend the rocky lower slopes of Mitchell Peak to a fine viewpoint of the Towers, drop down into the drainage of Arrowhead Lake's inlet, and then climb again to finally reach Jackass Pass (also known as Big Sandy Pass). On the way to the pass, midsummer hikers should see a sprinkling of vibrant alpine flowers, including sky pilot, phlox, alpine cinquefoil, bistort, and pussytoes.

Although the view from the actual pass at the Continental Divide is hemmed in a bit by the topography, a short uphill climb away from the trail allows a stunning view of Cirque of the Towers. Here a supreme vista unfolds and one quickly sees why rock climbers and mountain lovers from all over the globe flock to this area, where smooth granite faces rise up to culminate in a semicircular ridge of sharp pinnacles along the crest. Below, Lonesome Lake sparkles beneath an azure sky near the base of the Towers, the crowning touch to a near-perfect alpine scene. From the pass the Cirque of the Towers sweeps around the headwaters of North Popo Agie River with named summits including War Bonnet Peak, Warrior I and II, Laturio Mountain, Bunion Mountain, Pylon Peak, South Watchtower, Watchtower, Easy Day Peak, Elizabeth Peak, Block Tower, Shark's Nose, Overhanging Tower, Pingora Peak, Wolf's Head, Bollinger Peak, Skunk's Knob, Camel's Hump, and Lizard Head Peak. Finer alpine scenery is hard to imagine.

Entering Popo Agie Wilderness, the trail drops steeply from Jackass Pass across open, grass-covered slopes onto the floor of the cirque and soon reaches the outskirts of lovely Lonesome Lake, 9 miles from the Big Sandy trailhead. Due to overuse (this lake was the first in the Wind Rivers to experience contamination from human fecal matter), camping within 0.25 mile of the shore has been banned. Fortunately, plenty of fine campsites exist throughout the basin, most of which are hidden away into nooks and crannies of the upper part of the cirque. Despite the heavy visitation this area receives, with a modicum of exploration campers should be able to find secluded spots where they can pitch their tents. Although encircling the lake is possible, a defined trail is absent along the east shore, as boggy sections of shoreline force the route up into the rocks. Anglers may find fishing for cutthroat trout in Lonesome Lake to be better than at Big Sandy Lake. Plenty of fine routes on the Cirque of the Towers will tempt rock climbers, as well as on the massive north face of nearby Mitchell Peak. Peak baggers can ramble up an easy route (Class 2) to an awesome view from the top of 12,482-foot Mitchell Peak by leaving the Jackass Pass Trail near Shaft (North) Lake.

Tearing yourself away from the sheer beauty of the Cirque of the Towers may be the most difficult aspect of this trip. However, after a night or two in this majestic area the trail beckons you onward. After hopping rocks over the outlet, the North Fork Trail heads down the canyon and passes along the fringe of lush meadows lining the banks of nascent North Popo Agie River. Farther down the canyon the forest cover increases, as the trail crosses a couple of tributaries and passes by a pair of ponds before breaking out into the broad expanse of meadowlands known as Lizard Head Meadows. Campsites are tucked into the trees along the fringe of the meadows, with fine views of the surrounding terrain. Cross a few more side streams and climb mildly over a low rise on the way to a junction with the Lizard Head Trail, 2 miles from Lonesome Lake.

Turning left (northeast) up the Lizard Head Trail, you begin a strenuous 3-mile climb to the loop trip's high point on a plateau northeast of the namesake peak. Ascend through lodgepole-pine forest, crossing a refreshing-looking brook on the way, which might be a good place to fill up your water container for the grueling climb ahead. The stiff grade momentarily eases on the approach to a junction with an unmaintained side trail on the left leading to Bear Lakes, which are tucked into a cirque on the east side of Lizard Head Peak. Beyond the junction, a steep ascent leads out of the diminishing trees to increasingly impressive views of Cirque of the Towers and the surrounding terrain. A long, ascending traverse across a hillside watered by a pair of rivulets provides a temporary respite from the steep climbing, which resumes all too soon. Eventually the steep grade eases, and you can catch your breath on the top of a broad, windswept plateau. Soon the view-packed high point is reached, 2.25 miles from the North Fork Junction.

Follow a gently descending route across the expansive, open plateau through sparse patches of alpine tundra and acres and acres of broken rock. The tread disappears for stretches, but cairns aid in keeping you on route. After bottoming out at the crossing of a seasonal stream, the trail climbs moderately but shortly to a notch directly west of Cathedral Peak. From the notch, the trail makes an angling descent across the rocky, northwest side of Cathedral Peak toward the crossing of a nascent stream that eventually drains into the Valentine Lakes. Just beyond the crossing is a junction with the Bears Ears Trail, 2.75 miles from the high point.

Now headed west on the Bears Ears Trail, you make a steady descent down an open, rocky canyon with fine views of the peaks along the Continental Divide across the deep cleft of South Fork Little Wind River below. Eventually, the occasionally switchbacking trail leads down to more hospitable climes and an increasing cover of conifers. Pass above slightly distant 23-acre Little Valentine Lake and continue the descent to a junction just below a notch, through which passes the Moss Lake Trail headed north toward Dutch Oven Lake. Only 0.25 mile off the main route, Dutch Oven Lake is a fine place to spend a night. A little over a half-mile farther down the canyon, the Bears Ears Trail bends sharply south to come above 45-acre Valentine Lake, 2.5 miles from the Lizard Head Trail junction. Use trails branch away from the main trail to campsites along the north shore and near the outlet. Anglers can fish for small cutthroats and goldens. Cross-country enthusiasts can push on another mile or so beyond Valentine Lake on an off-trail route to the more remote South Fork Lakes, nestled into a glaciated cirque below Payson Peak (also known as Buffalo Head) and Lizard Head Peak.

From Valentine Lake, the Bears Ears Trail continues down toward South Fork Little Wind River through mostly forested terrain. Switchbacks lead down to the lush clearing of Ranger Park, backdropped by the north face of 11,717-foot Buffalo Head (shown as Payson Peak on the USGS map), so named for the striking resemblance to the shaggy symbol of the Great Plains. From Ranger Park, head back into the trees for a spell before emerging onto the floor of the canyon and a

Ford of the Little Wind River

ford of the river. Just beyond the ford is a junction with the Washakie Trail, 1.4 miles from Valentine Lake. Those in need of a campsite can head southwest along this trail to any of the five lakes situated below Washakie Pass.

Your route turns north on the continuation of the Bears Ears Trail, headed downstream alongside willow-lined South Fork Little Wind River. Gently descending trail leads into more forested terrain on the way to a junction, 1 mile from the previous junction, where the Moss Lake Trail heads northeast to arc around Valentine Mountain on the way to Moss Lake.

Remaining on the Bears Ears Trail, proceed ahead through forest cover, boulder-hop a creek, and then follow a short climb over a rise before dropping down to the east shore of lengthy 200-acre Grave Lake, 1.5 miles from the Moss Lake Trail junction. At an elevation of 9,964 feet, Grave Lake seems to go on forever, bending around below the southeast face of Pilot Knob near the far end. A meadow at the near end offers the first of numerous campsites scattered around the shoreline. Anglers should find the fishing for cutthroat and lake trout to be quite good this far into the backcountry.

From the east end of the lake, follow the lakeshore briefly before the trail dips into the canyon of the east fork of Grave Creek to cross the outlet on a stout wood bridge. Arc back around to the shoreline, and continue past a junction of a trail to Onion Meadow to the crossing of the west fork of Grave Creek. The long journey around the lake continues to where the trail climbs steeply below the face of Pilot Knob in order to circumvent an expansive talus slope. From the high point, a fine view of the surrounding terrain unfolds. Drop down steeply on rocky tread before a short ascent above the far end of the lake leads into the canyon of Baptiste Creek and a view of a scenic waterfall. Climb above the fall, and then follow a rising traverse over to a junction with the 1.5-mile-long trail to Baptiste Lake.

Side Trip to Baptiste Lake

The trip to 178-acre Baptiste Lake is well worth the slight diversion, not only for the picturesque setting nearly surrounded by tall peaks, but also for an unobstructed view of the massive wall of granodiorite forming the northeast face of Mount Hooker along the way; at 1,600 feet this is the highest vertical wall in Wyoming, and, not surprisingly, it offers accomplished rock climbers several challenging routes. Turn left at the junction and climb through open forest, view-packed meadowlands, and rocky areas for 1.5 miles to the south shore. Although most of the lake is in the Wind River Indian Reservation and thus off limits without a special permit, this far southern part is on public land and more than amply rewards your efforts. The views are particularly stunning across the cold waters to Musembeah Peak, Mount Lander, and dozens of other (mostly nameless) mountains. Camping is rather austere at this high-elevation location, but in good weather the scenery is marvelous. After your stay at Baptiste Lake, retrace your steps 1.5 miles to the Bears Ears Trail junction.

Away from the junction, the trail leaves the trees behind, briefly dips down to cross Baptiste Creek, and then begins a stiff climb through rock-studded terrain and across slopes of scree and sand on the canyon's headwall (early season hikers may encounter snowfields here). The ascent eventually culminates at 11,200'± Hailey Pass on the

Continental Divide, from where the view ahead is somewhat hemmed in by the topography, but the view behind you is quite striking.

Initially, the tread of the Hailey Pass Trail down from the pass and into the Twin Lakes cirque is a bit indistinct, but a more defined route appears after a short distance. Soon rocky trail passes above the upper lake and then continues down across the creek toward the lower lake. Beyond the lower lake, the trail follows the outlet around a bend that heads west around the slopes of Pyramid Peak. Farther down, the canyon opens up allowing views of East Fork River's canyon, which is bordered by a rugged wall on the west side. Rocky tread leads across the creek three more times on the way down into more hospitable terrain, where first shrubs and then scattered Engelmann spruces and whitebark pines soften the slope. Eventually, the trail turns south, passes around the shore of a large, unnamed lake (known locally as Mae's Lake). Anglers can fish for rainbow, brown, and lake trout, where plenty of campsites are scattered around the shore of the 26-acre lake. Continuing, you hop across a stream draining a smaller unnamed lake above and to the east. A short way farther, you reach the floor of the canyon and a junction with the Pyramid Lake Trail, 2 miles from Hailey Pass.

Side Trip to Pyramid Lake

A fun side trip to 55-acre Pyramid Lake is well worth the investment of a couple of hours. Continue north from the Hailey Pass junction, walk around the left (west) side of long Mae's Lake, and then climb steeply for about 0.6 mile to rock-lined Pyramid Lake. This large jewel is very impressive looking, sitting right at the base of the towering cliffs of Mount Hooker and Tower Peak. Pyramid will tempt anglers with the possibility of catching two-pound goldens. Do not plan to camp here, however, since the shore is rather exposed and windy. Adventurous hikers can continue their side trip with a relatively easy ramble on game trails and over grassy slopes west of the lake for 0.4 mile to a rocky saddle, from where you can look across the deep canyon of East Fork River to the enormous granite cliffs of Mount Bonneville, Raid Peak, Ambush Peak, and Mount Geikie. These sheer cliffs tower fully 2,000 feet above a series of trailless lakes, so the awesome sight is well worth the relatively limited extra sweat required to see this vista.

Headed south-southeast from the junction, the trail passes by a small pond, crests a low hill, and then descends through the vale of East Fork River on the way to Skull Lake. Nearing the lake, the trail climbs above the north shore and then traverses around the west shore across some sloping rock slabs, with a fine view across the surface of Mt. Washakie and the area around Washakie Pass. The lake is bordered by rolling slopes carpeted with lush vegetation amid slabs and boulders and dotted with scattered, small conifers. The open terrain is well suited to anglers plying the waters for brook trout. Plenty of potential campsites can be found in nooks and crannies above the lakeshore.

A short, mild to moderate climb away from Skull Lake leads out of the basin and up to the top of a rise and a junction with the Washakie Pass Trail, 1.4 miles from the Bears Ears Trail junction.

With the west side of the summits of the Cirque of the Towers in full view, you descend through mostly open terrain toward the Washakie Creek drainage, followed by a half-mile stretch of forest before breaking out into the open again in the broad meadowlands bordering the creek. Depending on the season and stream flows, the crossing of Washakie Creek will require either a ford or a boulder hop. Just beyond the crossing is a junction with the Shadow Lake Trail, 1 mile from the Washakie Pass Trail junction.

Turn left, and head east on the relatively gentle grade of the Shadow Lake Trail. Near the halfway point you make a fairly easy creek crossing, and continue upstream through improving scenery to the shore. Shadow Lake is a large and spectacularly beautiful lake sitting right at the base of the lesser-known west side of the dramatic peaks of Cirque of the Towers. An evening spent at a camp here is rewarded with outstanding views across the lake to these soaring peaks and spires. After a night at Shadow Lake, retrace your steps 2.1 miles back to the junction with the Hailey Pass Trail.

Away from the junction, gradually rising tread leads through beautiful open territory with fine vistas of the surrounding terrain. A long, gradual descent leads to the crossing of a shallow stream, followed by a short, moderate climb over a rise leading to a view of Marms Lake ahead. Descend through a narrow swale, and then swing around the nose of a low ridge to the north shore of the 33-acre lake and a junction with the Fremont Trail, 1.6 miles from the Shadow Lake Trail junction.

Proceed ahead around the west shore of Marms Lake, which is bordered by pockets of light timber and open hillsides. The area around the lake is peppered with passable campsites, perhaps signaling the realization that the Big Sandy trailhead is now less than a day's journey away. Fishing may also be less productive than at some of the more remote lakes visited previously, as seemingly only small brook trout inhabit these waters.

For almost the next mile, the trail follows the course of the creek draining Marms Lake through a low gully before emerging into a large meadow. In the meadow the trail crosses the creek and travels around to the east side of island-dotted Dads Lake, skirting a smaller meadow on the way to a boulder hop of Donald Creek. Farther on, the main trail bends away from the lake, where a use trail leads to numerous campsites spread around the south shore. Anglers will have to be satisfied with a catch of 6- to 8-inch brookies.

A short climb from Dads Lake brings you to a junction with the trail to Donald Lake, a 1.5-mile path providing a possibly more secluded alternative to camping at Marms, Dads, and Mirror lakes, all situated along the main trail.

A brief walk from the junction leads to the north shore of the much smaller Mirror Lake, bordered by alternating stands of forest and flower-covered meadow, where anglers can fish for both rainbow and brook trout.

Beyond Mirror Lake, the trail drops into the large meadowland of Fish Creek Park and an easy boulder hop of Fish Creek via good-size stones. From the crossing, the trail follows gently rising tread across open slopes to a junction on the right with the seldom-used Francis Lake Trail. Continue the mild ascent over a low divide southwest of Divide Lake before descending into moderate forest cover. Supposedly, 134-acre Divide Lake is far enough off the trail to offer decent fishing for several species of fish, despite its close proximity to the Big Sandy trailhead.

The mostly forested descent continues for the next couple of miles, broken only by an occasional patch of small meadow. Seemingly in the middle of nowhere, the trail starts to switchback on the way to a junction just north of Meeks Lake, 3 miles from the crossing of Fish Creek in the middle of Fish Creek Park.

Veer left at the junction and pass well above the north side of Meeks Lake, crossing the inlet on the way to a second junction. Veer right here, and pass to the east of the lake before bending west to cross the outlet, and then follow this stream through the forest down to a junction with the Big Sandy Trail. From there, retrace your steps 0.7-mile to the Big Sandy trailhead.

Possible Itinerary (40 miles)

	Camps and Side Trips	Miles	Elevation Gain
Day 1	Big Sandy trailhead to Cirque of the Towers	9.0	+2100/−1000
Day 2	*Layover day*		
	Explore Cirque of the Towers		
Day 3	Cirque of the Towers to Valentine Lake	9.2	+2250/−2050
Day 4	Valentine Lake to Baptiste Lake	9.5	+1,325/−875
Day 5	Baptiste Lake to Shadow Lake	8.7	+1,325/−1,875
	Side trip to Pyramid Lake	2.4	+300/−300
Day 6	Shadow Lake to Big Sandy trailhead	11.1	+ 450/−1,650

Giving Back

Wyoming Wilderness Association: www.wildwyo.org

The Tale of Cowboy Bill

While headed to the start of our Wind River trip, our group of four had one of those serendipitous moments that are not easily forgotten. Originally, we had planned to do a trek along the Teton Crest Trail, but the western Wyoming sky looked foreboding and far from ideal—dodging lightning bolts along the open crest of a mountain range was not our idea of a good time. Instead, we headed toward the Winds hoping for initially safer travel under the cover of forest. By the time we arrived at the Big Sandy trailhead, the gray skies turned black, a steady downpour set in, and the temperature plummeted. The longer we watched the constant rain come down, the idea of a wet and cold start to our trip became less and less appealing. Even the prospect of setting up our tents in the Forest Service campground near the trailhead seemed totally unappealing in such a deluge. On the off chance that the Big Sandy Lodge nearby had any vacancies, we left the trailhead and drove the short distance seeking shelter from the storm, acquiring the last two available cabins. After settling into our very rustic but cozy cabins and having successfully lit the old woodstoves to ward off the chill, any feelings that we had wimped out by postponing our trip for a day quickly disappeared as we saw several similarly distressed but less fortunate backpacking and climbing parties inquire about vacancies and then drive away with dour countenances.

Appreciative of our warm and dry surroundings, but feeling a tad hemmed in by the small dimensions of our temporary shelters, we walked over to the main lodge, which, when compared to our tiny cabins, seemed cavernous. Warmed by two large stone fireplaces, we marveled at our good fortune while lounging in the old overstuffed furniture. Soon, a tall, white-haired man with a handlebar moustache sauntered into the lodge, clad in the typical cowboy garb of a long-sleeved flannel shirt, neckerchief, jeans held up by a belt with a large silver buckle, slightly muddy cowboy boots, and a 10-gallon hat. With firm handshakes all around, he introduced himself to our party as Cowboy Bill. Although Bill was a quiet man by nature, the lines on his face suggested a lifetime of interesting adventures worth the telling.

My best friend, Tic, is one of those people who immediately befriends everyone in a room—a trait that I, as a complete introvert, have always admired. Within a few minutes, Tic had drawn the normally reserved Cowboy Bill into a lively question-and-answer period, where, with slow and deliberate speech, he regaled us with stimulating vignettes of his life as a cowboy in the West. With a slight smile on his face and a bit of a far away look in his wistful eyes, he recounted stories about his favorite horse, the hard but satisfying work on the range, and his love of the cowboy life. As his story unfolded, Bill informed us that he and his wife have come to Big Sandy for the last several years to oversee the workings of the lodge; he works as handyman and wrangler, and his wife does all the cooking and cleaning. During the off-season, they left Big Sandy to live in the slightly more hospitable climate of Elko, Nevada. Sadly, Bill mentioned that, due to their advancing years, they didn't know how much longer they would be able to manage the rigors involved in taking care of Finis Mitchell's old lodge each summer. After a time, the conversation came to an inevitable lull, and Bill ambled off to take care of some chores. Remaining in our chairs for a spell, we four city slickers drifted into a period of our own silence, contemplating the gift we had just been given—an hour of entertaining stories about the American West from a real-life cowboy.—**Mike**

Fitzpatrick Wilderness, Shoshone National Forest

The wild places are where we began, and when they end, so do we.

—DAVID BROWER

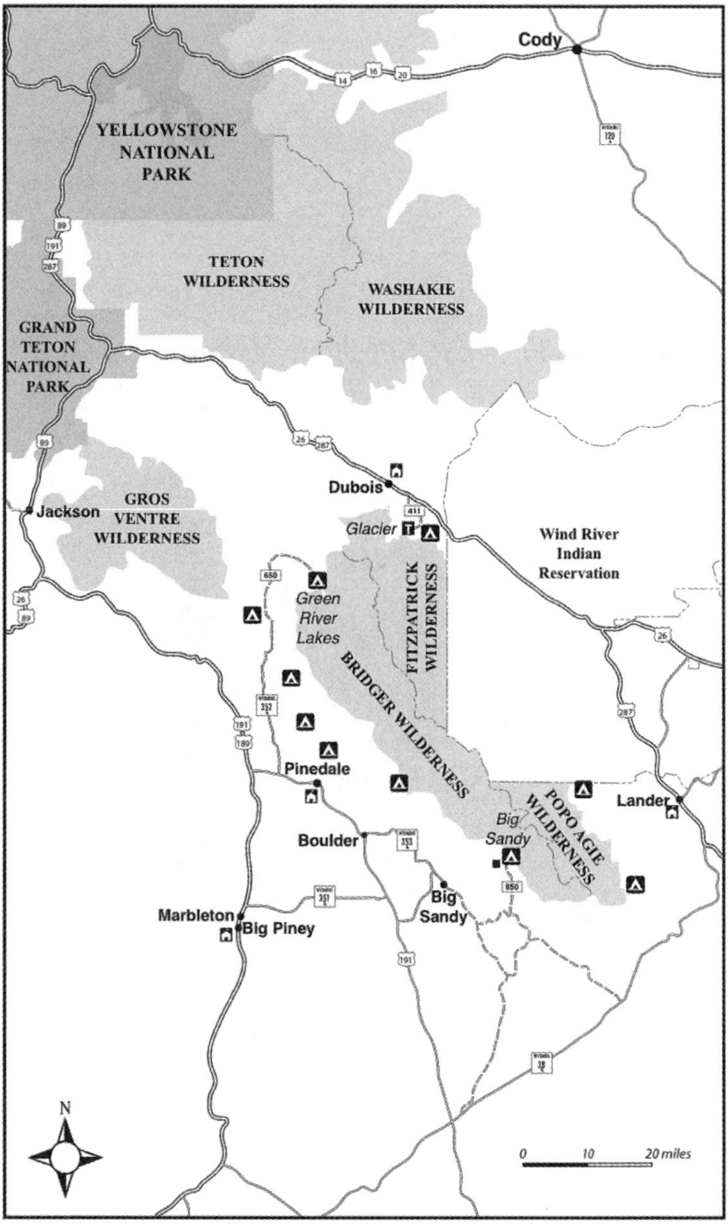

Glacier Trail to Gannett Peak Location Map

TRIP 11

Glacier Trail to Gannett Peak

As the principal access into the northeastern part of the Wind River Range, the Glacier Trail provides the preferred trail approach (although 25 miles long) for climbers heading to Gannett Peak. At 13,804 feet, this challenging glacier-clad summit is the highest point in Wyoming, making it a favorite destination for mountaineers. Unlike the Tetons, Gannet remains mostly unseen from a distance, hidden from view by the surrounding mountains. Besides the lofty height, the rugged peak is quite striking once the mountain is in sight. Orin Bonney in his classic guide to the Wind River Range said this about Gannett, "There is no more truly alpine peak in the Rocky Mountain states than this granite summit rising from ice fields hundreds of feet thick." Any lover of mountains will revel in the alpine scenery of Gannett Peak and its neighboring summits.

Backpackers not interested in bagging a state high point would be foolish to overlook this popular trail, as the route also offers excellent scenery. On the long journey to the peak, the trail passes through an amazing array of landscapes and life zones. Starting in semidesert flats covered with sagebrush and cacti, the trail ascends through a diverse forest to alpine meadows and an above-timberline pass (10,895 feet). Dropping into Dinwoody Lakes Basin, the trail visits a handful of sparkling lakes before descending to a mountain valley bisected by

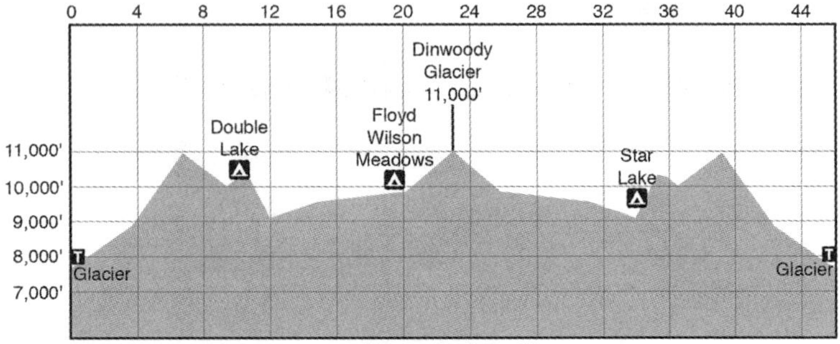

Glacier Trail Profile

Dinwoody Creek, a large, glacial melt stream. The trail follows this creek through stunning meadows all the way to the headwaters right under Gannett Peak and a host of glacier-clad, 13,000-foot summits. The route ends at the base of Dinwoody Glacier, one of the largest ice sheets in the American Rockies. For the really adventurous and experienced, this route offers access to rugged and wildly scenic off-trail routes leading to enough stunningly scenic alpine lakes, glaciers, and ridges to fill an extra week or more of rambling.

Days: 4–7

Distance: 45 miles

Type: Out-and-back

Scenery: 8

Solitude: 3

Technical Difficulty: 5

Physical Difficulty: 7

Elevation Gain/Loss: +8,450'/–8,450'

Season: July through October

Best: Mid-July to early September

Map: Earthwalk Press—*Northern Wind River Range*

Resources: *Hiking Wyoming's Wind River Range*, by Ron Adkison

Contact: Shoshone National Forest
Wind River Ranger District
1403 West Ramshorn
Dubois, WY 82513
307-455-2466

Permits: No permit is required. Just sign in at the trailhead.

Regulations: No fires are allowed above timberline. Maximum group size of 15 people and 25 stock. No camping is allowed within 100 feet of streams and 200 feet of lakes or trails. All food and other odorous items must be stored away from bears.

Nearest Campground: Trail Lake Campground—2 miles

Nearest Airports: Casper/Natrona County Airport (C/NCIA)—206 miles
Rock Springs / Sweetwater County Airport (RKS)—205 miles
Jackson Hole Airport—100 miles

Nearest Outdoor Retailer:
Wind River Gear—14 miles
19 North First Street
Dubois, WY 82513
307-455-3468

Outfitter:
Suda Outfitters (horse trips)
PO Box 1182
Dubois, WY 82513
307-455-2866

Transportation Logistics: There are no public transportation options, so the easiest way to reach the trailhead is to drive your own vehicle.

Backcountry Logistics: (GB, BB, A, L, St, W) As with all trips in the Wind River Range, hikers need to be prepared for high-altitude travel and the likelihood of afternoon thunderstorms.

Black bears sometimes visit the more popular campsites near Double Lake and at both Big and Floyd Wilson Meadows. In recent years, grizzly bears have expanded their range into the Wind River Range, so hikers must camp and act accordingly.

The trail is popular, especially with climbers, so you should expect plenty of company.

In early summer the crossing of Gannett Creek near the end of this hike can be treacherous, though typically a rope is in place to assist hikers.

Mosquitoes are abundant around Double Lake in July.

Amenities and Attractions: The nearest community is Dubois, a charming small town where every business has an address on the same street because there is only one main drag. Despite having fewer than 1,000 residents, Dubois is tourist oriented and offers a nice selection of surprisingly good accommodations and restaurants. For your typical hungry backpacker, a good option is the **Cowboy Café** (115 E Ramshorn Street), which sounds like a greasy spoon but actually offers excellent service and both filling and tasty food. The pies are especially recommended. **Mom's** (106 E Ramshorn) is a log cabin with great ambience, patio dining right on the river, and especially tasty breakfasts. For finer dining, **Nostalgia Bistro** (202 E Ramshorn) offers unexpectedly high-end options for such a small town with innovative and delicious food.

Dubois has a couple of national chain motels, but for local charm and comfort try **Rocky Mountain Lodge** (1349 E Ramshorn). There are also two or three bed-and-breakfast establishments worth investigating.

For wildlife lovers, an interesting museum in Dubois is the **National Bighorn Sheep Interpretive Center** (907 E Ramshorn), where you can learn all about this iconic species of the American West.

Directions to Trailhead: From Dubois, drive a little over 3 miles east on U.S. Highway 26/287 to a poorly marked and easy-to-miss junction with a gravel road to the right (south). The sign here points to the Dubois Fish Hatchery but makes no mention of the trailhead. Turn onto this road, and almost immediately bear left at a fork onto Forest Road 411. Follow this washboarded and pothole-filled route for 8.7 miles, passing the campgrounds at Trail Lake along the way, to a fork where you turn right. Drive another 0.6 mile to the large Torrey Creek trailhead turnaround and parking area.

Henry Gannett (1846–1914)

For whom was Wyoming's tallest peak named and what did he accomplish in his life to deserve such notoriety? Any competent backpacker is familiar with topographic maps, especially the 15- and 7.5-minute quadrangles produced by the United States Geological Survey. The pioneering work of geographer Henry Gannett laid the foundation for these maps and much more, which garnered him the title of the "Father of American Map Making."

Henry Gannett was born in Bath, Maine, and later obtained a BS from Harvard University (1869) and Hooper Mining School (1870). In the wake of the Civil War, Gannett left the east coast to experience the wonders of the western frontier. On his first expedition in 1871, he accompanied Ferdinand V. Hayden to the Yellowstone area of the Wyoming Territory as part of the ongoing "Geological and Geographical Survey of the Territories." Each summer he would return to continue the difficult work of the survey. In 1872, he was climbing an unnamed summit in the Gallatin Range of southwestern Montana when a thunderstorm started to develop. Shortly below the top he experienced tingling sensations and his hair standing on end. Surviving this brush with lightning, Gannett gave the name Electric Peak to the mountain. The next year Gannett and his companions made a daring, middle-of-the-night escape from a band of Indians near the Utah-Colorado border. Although he penned a prolific number of reports, not much is known about Gannett's personal life, other than he married Mary E. Chase in 1874, as his reports were factual, to the point, and totally lacking in personal touch or detail.

After Congress created the USGS in 1879 with John Wesley Powell as the first director, Gannett went to work for the agency and quickly ascended through the ranks, becoming chief cartographer in 1882. In 1884, he published his first work, A Dictionary of Altitudes in the United States, which included a listing of all the elevations of known summits in the country. He also wrote extensively on boundaries and place-names. During his tenure, he was involved in numerous censuses, both in the United States and abroad. Perhaps his most significant work was Manual of Topographic Methods, which set the standards for mapping for many decades. In addition to influencing American mapmaking, Gannett was a cofounder of the National Geographic Society and served as president from 1910 to 1914. Whenever you pull a topo map out of your pocket or backpack, you can thank Henry Gannett for his pioneering groundwork in cartography.

Trip Description: The wide trail departs from the west end of the parking area and soon begins to switchback up a dry hillside covered with hardy grasses, sagebrush, junipers, and a few prickly pear cacti. The gravelly, well-graded route gains elevation for the first 0.6 mile on the way to a junction with the Whiskey Mountain Trail on the right. The path then enters the Fitzpatrick Wilderness and 0.2 mile later reaches a signed junction with the Lake Louise Trail. Turn left here, and almost immediately cross a wooden bridge over boisterous Torrey Creek, which roars through a narrow chasm right under the bridge.

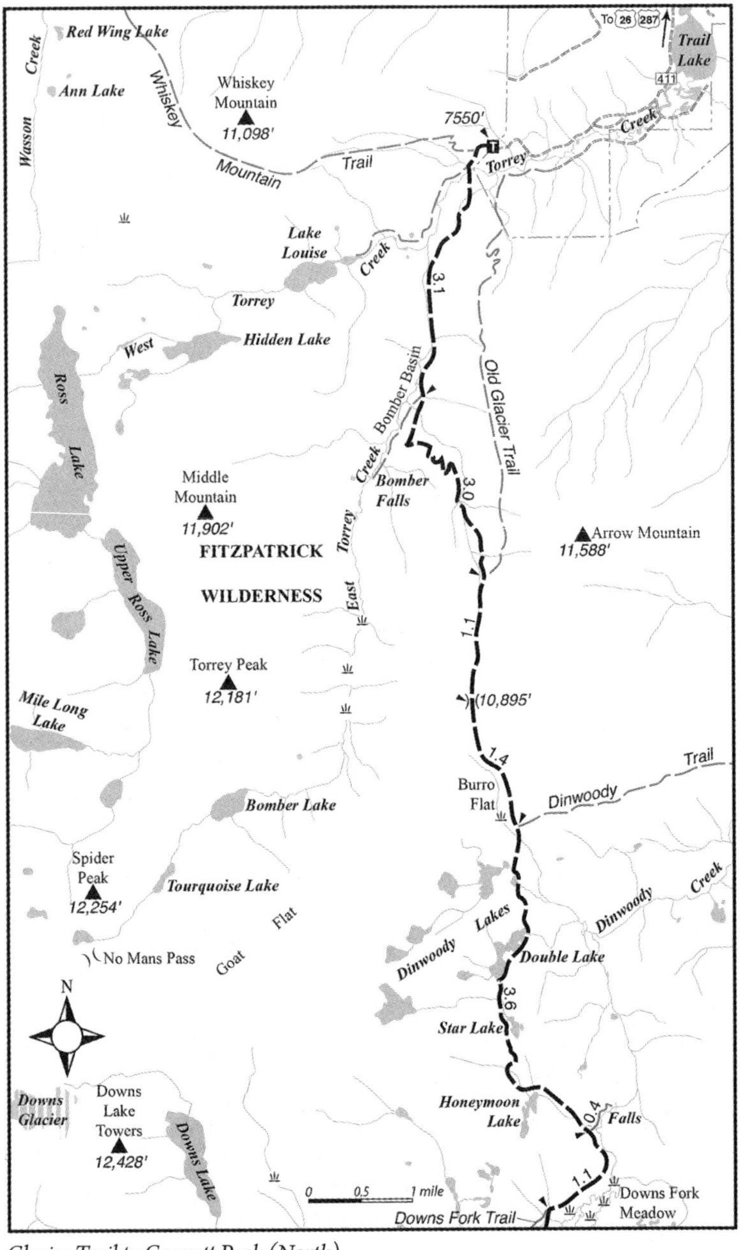

Glacier Trail to Gannett Peak (North)

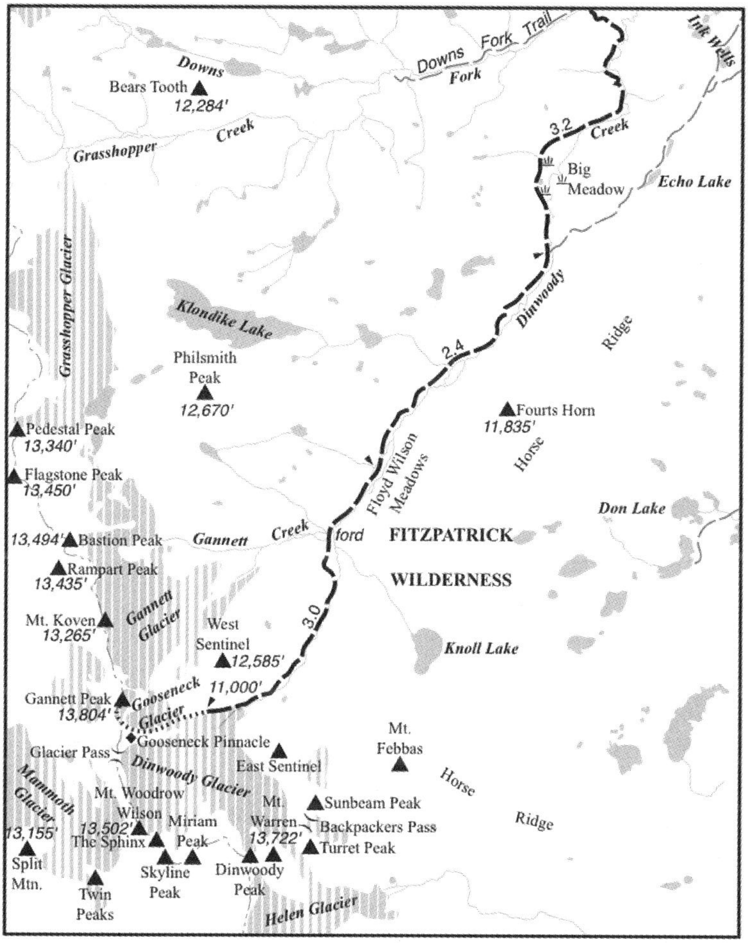

Glacier Trail to Gannett Peak (South)

The trail now takes you on a tour of an array of rounded rock buttresses and outcroppings on an ascent into increasingly forested terrain. At the top of this intermittent climb, enter Bomber Basin, a relatively flat subalpine meadow along East Torrey Creek with at least one good campsite for those who got a late start to their hike. At the southern end of this meadow is a junction, where an abandoned trail forks to the right and heads to Bomber Falls.

Bear left at this fork and settle in for a long climb, which is accomplished with a set of thirty gently graded switchbacks gradually offering improving views of brown-tinged Middle Mountain to the west. At the top of the ascent, you reach an open ridgetop with rolling terrain and lots of midsummer wildflowers. The route leads to a hop-over crossing of a small creek, near which you could camp, before making a long, gradual climb through beautiful open terrain to a junction with the old Glacier Trail angling in from the left. Go straight, and complete the gentle climb to a windy 10,895-foot saddle. From here a wonderful and relatively easy off-trail side trip travels about 3 miles southwest over a wide tundra-covered ridge to the excellent viewpoint at Goat Flat. Since you have already climbed almost 3,500 feet to reach this pass, however, most hikers are more interested in finding a place to spend the night than exploring.

Descend from the pass along the Glacier Trail over open terrain to the large expanse of Burro Flat, where you'll find a tiny creek and a junction with the start of the faint Dinwoody Trail next to a cairn, which heads east over the tundra. Keep straight on the main trail, and descend through a partially burned forest of scraggly whitebark pines to a shallow oversized pond called Phillips Lake. Much larger and more scenic Upper Phillips and Golden Lakes are in the higher basins to the west and offer both secluded campsites and good fishing.

The main trail descends from Phillips Lake on the way to very scenic Double Lake. This large and irregularly shaped gem offers views across the water of a number of cliff-edged peaks and rock outcroppings and has excellent campsites—the best ones near the southern end. However, the area is very popular with both tired backpackers and hordes of mosquitoes in July. Despite the insects' determination to suck what little energy is left from the exhausted hikers, most put on the bug dope and call this lake home for their first night on the trail.

The trail climbs away from Double Lake, gaining a little over 300 feet in several switchbacks on the way to slender and very attractive

Star Lake. Although the lake is less dramatically scenic, the usually less crowded campsites are nearly as good as those at Double Lake.

A little beyond Star Lake the trail tops a little rise and begins a lengthy downhill, most of which is accomplished via a series of short, rocky switchbacks. During this descent, you pass rock-lined Honeymoon Lake, which many hikers may not notice since the trail never approaches the water. Dinwoody Creek greets you at the bottom of the downhill, where you can rest on a log and admire the rushing stream full of silty meltwater from the large glaciers below the divide. An unsigned and easy-to-miss trail goes downstream along the north bank of this creek for about 0.4 mile to a thundering but unnamed waterfall (see map of Glacier Trail to Gannett Peak [South]).

The trail now travels very gently upstream, detouring around the north side of marshy Downs Fork Meadows to a signed junction. The Downs Fork Trail goes right, offering 2.5 miles of maintained tread before petering out in an attractive upper meadow. From there, adventurous hikers can go off-trail toward the excellent scenery around Downs Lake, No Man Pass, and the Ross Lakes.

The much more heavily traveled Glacier Trail goes left at the Downs Fork junction and almost immediately crosses a bridge over Downs Fork. The color of this sizable stream indicates the water carries considerable meltwater from the glaciers above. Beyond the bridge, climb through a mostly burned forest, reconnect with Dinwoody Creek above Downs Fork Meadow, and then travel around a rugged butte to reach aptly named Big Meadows. This large, mostly flat expanse of grasses, wildflowers, and rocks offers excellent scenery with fine views of the rounded peaks on either side.

The sandy trail goes around the right (northwest) side of Big Meadows, taking hikers to a campsite just before the path reenters the forest at the south end. Another 0.5 mile of gentle walking leads to a junction with the Ink Wells Trail, which heads sharply left and crosses a bridge over Dinwoody Creek. On the other side of this bridge is a fine campsite.

Staying on the Glacier Trail, you soon round a corner and enjoy the first good views up the canyon toward Gannett Peak. This tower-

Dinwoody Creek above Big Meadows

ing behemoth is an impressive looking peak, towering above the other 12,000- and 13,000-foot summits in the area. Large glaciers blanketing the peak add to the remarkable appearance of the mountain. Even more striking views of Gannett Peak and the surrounding summits increase farther up the drainage of Dinwoody Creek. The next few miles also offer numerous fine campsites for you to sit back and enjoy the show in relative comfort.

The trail crosses rushing Klondike Creek near the north end of the flats known as Floyd Wilson Meadows, which is replete with scenic and very popular campsites often used by climbers establishing a base camp for an ascent of Gannett Peak. Just after the stream crossing, a rough cross-country route goes up Klondike Creek toward large and exceptionally beautiful Klondike Lake. For backpackers with a couple of extra days to spend in Floyd Wilson Meadows, Klondike Lake makes a fine day-hike destination, but be prepared for a difficult and very steep climb over rough terrain.

As you work your way toward the high peaks ringing the southwest end of Floyd Wilson Meadows, the trees thin and the terrain becomes more dramatically scenic. Shortly after the climb begins more noticeably from the end of the meadows, reach a crossing of Gannett Creek. As expected, the waters of this glacial stream are bone-chillingly cold and may be rather intimidating looking early in the summer. Usually, previous hikers/climbers have put a rope in place across the flow to aid in making the ford across such tricky footing—more than likely you'll be quite happy for its presence.

Above this crossing, the trail passes through increasingly alpine terrain, forcing you to negotiate a sometimes steep tread beside rushing Dinwoody Creek, passing through areas of grasses, rocks, and old moraines. The trail ends at the base of the rapidly retreating Dinwoody Glacier, where the cold waters of the namesake stream pour out of the melting ice. Impressive Gannett Peak towers above you along with such other notable summits as East Sentinel, West Sentinel, and Mount Woodrow Wilson adding to the spectacular scene. All of these summits require technical climbing gear and expertise; backpackers without the requisite equipment and skill should turn around here and head back the way they came.

Possible Itinerary

	Camps and Side Trips	Miles	Elevation Gain
Day 1	Torrey Creek TH to Double Lake	10.3	+3,500/−1,100
Day 2	Floyd Wilson Meadows	8.8	+1,150/−1,300
	Side Trip to falls on Dinwoody Creek	0.8	+100/−100
Day 3	Day hike to Dinwoody Glacier	6.6	+1,300/−1,300
Day 4	Star Lake	8.2	+1,300/−750
Day 5	Out to Torrey Creek TH	10.9	+1100/−3,900

Alternatives: Short but worthwhile side trips by trail reach destinations such as Lake Louise and the upper valley of Downs Fork. For longer options you need to be an experienced off-trail hiker willing to expend considerable time and energy. If up for the challenge, consider turning this into a long and glorious cross-country loop by returning via the route past Downs Lake, No Mans Pass, and the two huge Ross Lakes.

Giving Back

Wyoming Wilderness Association: WWW.WILDWYO.ORG

The Legend of the Girl in the Flip-Flops

Many years ago, back before lightweight hiking boots became vogue, I made my first trip to the Wind Rivers with my wife, Robin; best friend, Tic; and his neighbor, Wayne. We rendezvoused in Salt Lake City and then proceeded east toward what would become one of my all-time favorite ranges. My wife had just completed a very challenging first year of medical school and had a week off before the exhausting grind would resume all over again. Having purchased a new pair of full-leather boots a couple of months prior, I had reminded her several times about the importance of breaking them in before our trip. Unfortunately, school consumed almost all of her waking moments, with little time on the schedule for fully breaking in hiking boots.

We headed out on the trail under the sunny skies of early July soon after snowmelt, passing through moist meadows carpeted with an amazing display of colorful wildflowers. Water was seemingly everywhere and so were clouds of mosquitoes. Despite the winged pests, we had a great first day and the scenery was outstanding. After a 7-mile hike, we found a fine camping spot near a lake and began to set up camp. Gingerly pulling off her boots and socks, Robin revealed two ruptured, silver-dollar-shaped, nasty-looking blisters on each heel. While she doctored up her feet, I tried to conceal my utter disappointment, figuring we would have no choice but to abandon the trip after driving hundreds of miles to get here. However, as I would learn repeatedly over the years, never underestimate the tenacity and determination of my wife.

After breakfast the next morning, we anxiously turned to Robin and awaited her proclamation on the fate of our trip. Much to our amazement, she proposed continuing, wrapping her ankles with ace bandages and hiking in the flip-flops she had brought along for water crossings and camp shoes. We skeptically distributed some of the weight in her pack among the three of us and tentatively set off, fully believing her plan had no chance of succeeding. Much to our surprise, she performed admirably in her makeshift but far-from-ideal footwear, not even substantially slowing her pace. Our hopes soared with the dawning realization that our trip may not be doomed after all.

As is usually the case on the trail, we would meet fellow hikers periodically and stop for a chat, exchanging the customary information about where we had come from and where we were going. Everyone we encountered over the next several days marveled at the girl in the flip-flops.

Near the end of our last day, we gathered near a bridge to filter some water before the final climb up to the Elkhart Park trailhead, where we met some Canadian hikers who were just beginning their weeklong trip into the Winds. After exchanging the customary pleasantries, they wanted to tell us the most unbelievable story they had heard about a girl who backpacked all the way over Green River Pass in flip-flops. In a week's time, Robin had become momentarily famous in the backpacking community of the Wind Rivers. "You don't say," one of us replied. "Well, we can confirm that wild story, because she's right over there." With the good fortune of pleasant weather, our trip turned out to be a success. Fortunately, we never again had to deal with boots that weren't properly broken in.–**Mike**

PART 3

Colorado

Flat Tops Wilderness, White River and Medicine Bow–Routt National Forests

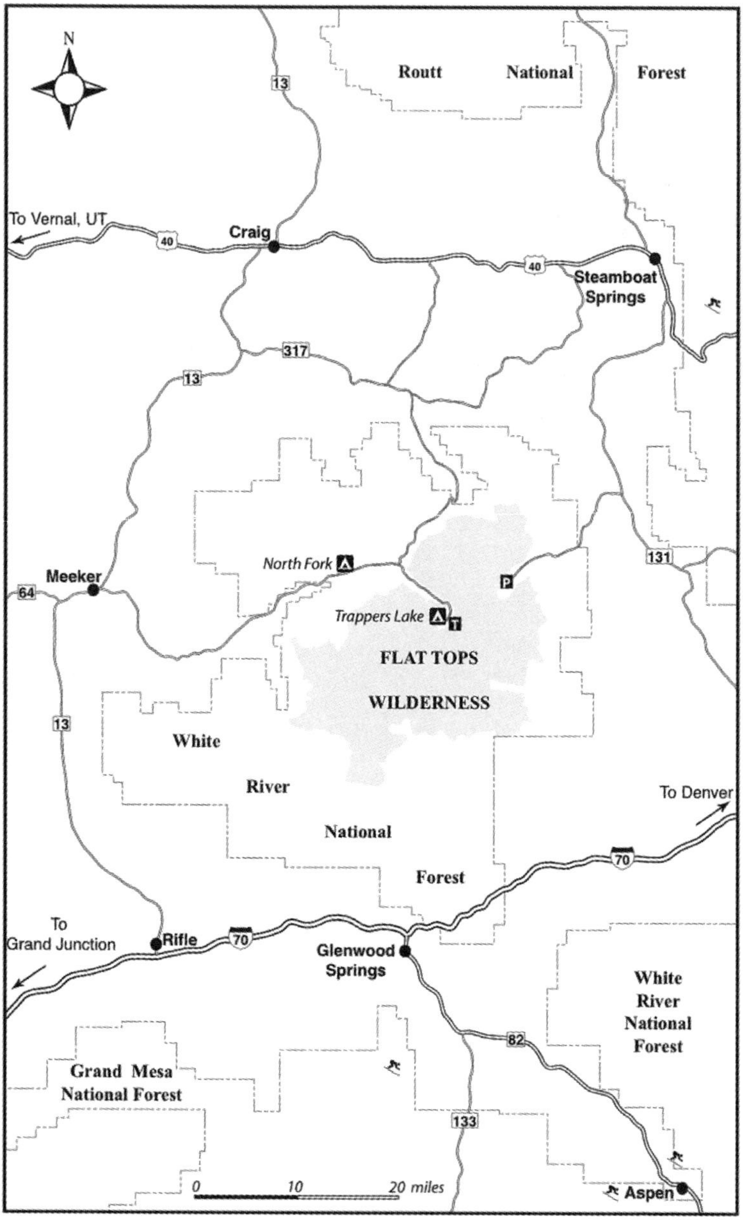

Trappers Lake–Devils Causeway Loop Location Map

TRIP 12

Trappers Lake–Devils Causeway Loop

> There are a number of places with scenic values of such great worth that they are rightfully the property of all people. They should be preserved for all time for the people of the Nation and the world. Trappers Lake is unquestionably a candidate for that classification.
>
> —ARTHUR CARHART, IN A REPORT THAT HELPED TO MAKE TRAPPERS LAKE THE NATION'S FIRST OFFICIAL WILDERNESS

Colorado is full of great trails exploring some of North America's most dramatic high peaks, but the Flat Tops Wilderness is unique. The mountains here look nothing like the jagged pinnacles found elsewhere in the state. In fact these "mountains" are really more like high mesas surrounded by tall volcanic cliffs. On top of these mesas you'll revel in beautiful, rolling alpine plateaus with just a few somewhat taller points sticking up above the general flatness. Extremely scenic lakes dot these plateaus and fill the even more scenic glacial basins that sit beneath the surrounding cliffs. All of this adds up to a fun hiking experience, even though you may not feel as though you are in Colorado. But despite their unfamiliar appearance, the Flat Tops make a terrific hiking destination, with all the mountain scenery a backpacker could ever reasonably desire.

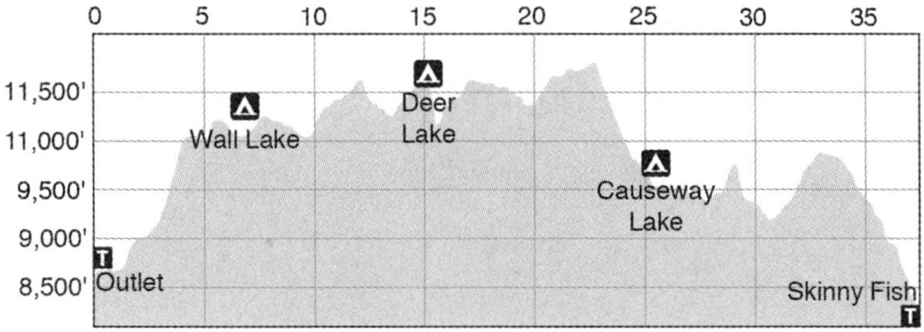

Trappers Lake – Devils Causeway Loop Profile

Days: 3–5

Distance: 37 miles (excluding 1.4-mile road walk between trailheads)

Type: Loop

Scenery: 8

Solitude: 6

Technical Difficulty: 7 (higher if you are afraid of heights and still want to cross the Devils Causeway)

Physical Difficulty: 6

Elevation Gain/Loss: +5,650'/–6,050' (excluding road walk, with its almost 400 feet of elevation gain)

Season: July to October

Best: July through September

Map: Trails Illustrated: Flat Tops NE, Trappers Lake #122

Resources: *A Hiking and Camping Guide to the Flat Tops Wilderness*, by Al Marlowe; *Arthur Carhart: Wilderness Prophet*, by Tom Wolf

Contacts:
White River National Forest
Blanco Ranger District
220 East Market Street
Meeker, CO 81641
970-878-4039

Medicine Bow–Routt National Forest
Yampa Ranger District
300 Roselawn Avenue
PO Box 7
Yampa, CO 80483
970-638-4516

Permits: Permits are not required.

Regulations: The usual no-trace principles apply. Maximum group size is 15 people. Campfires are prohibited within 100 feet of any lake, stream, or trail.

Nearest Campground: Trappers Lake Campground—1 mile

Nearest Airport: Grand Junction Regional Airport (GJT)—149 miles

Nearest Outdoor Retailer:
REI—150 miles
644 North Avenue
Grand Junction, CO 81501
970-254-8970

Outfitter: Commercial outfitters in this area tend to cater to big-game hunters. A few also provide overnight horse-packing trips in the summer. Try Sable Mountain Outfitters 970-878-4765, www.sablemountainoutfitters.com. There are no outfitters offering guided backpacking trips.

Transportation Logistics: There are no public transportation options to reach this trailhead, so you must have your own vehicle. The access roads are good paved or gravel routes and easy to drive.

Backcountry Logistics: (BB, A, L) Thunderstorms are common, especially in the afternoon, so plan to be off the high ridges and plateaus by no later than 2 PM. Also, bring a sturdy tent that can survive the hail, rain, and strong winds that often accompany these extreme thunderstorms.

The hike across Devils Causeway isn't dangerous for an experienced hiker, but is a significant mental challenge involving crossing a 25-yard section of rocky and uneven terrain only about 2 or 3 feet wide, with a drop-off of hundreds of feet down sheer cliffs on either side. Anyone who is afraid of heights should avoid this section and take a shorter loop instead.

Typical for the Colorado Rockies, almost the entirety of this hike is above 10,000 feet (much of it *well* above). As a result, the air is quite thin, especially for anyone arriving directly from a near-sea-level home. If you are not yet acclimated, expect a few days of discomfort (headaches, lack of appetite, inability to sleep, and so on) before you start to feel "normal." In a few cases, the symptoms may be so severe that you will be forced to retreat to lower elevations and abandon your trip.

Attractions and Amenities: Meeker has a limited number of motels, restaurants, and shops, none of which will bowl you over with their quality. For greater selection, try Craig, about 50 miles north-northeast of Meeker. This city has a much larger population, though the businesses there tend to cater to the energy extraction industry rather than to tourists. In addition to Grand Junction, the nearest town with a good selection of outdoor-oriented retailers is Steamboat Springs, where, although quite pricey, you should be able to find just about anything you would reasonably need.

Directions to Trailhead: From Grand Junction, drive 58 miles east on Interstate 70 to exit 90 for the town of Rifle. Go north here on Highway 13 and follow that route for 42 miles to the small city of Meeker. Continue on Highway 13 to a junction a little over 1 mile east of town where you go right on County Road 8, following signs to Buford and Flat Tops Trail Scenic Byway. Follow this good paved road up the scenic valley of White River, staying on the main road at several minor intersections. At 31.2 miles from Highway 13, you reach the end of pavement at the Lost Creek Guard Station. Now on excellent, smooth gravel, you proceed another 8.6 miles to an important junction. Turn right on Road 8A (also known as Forest Road 205), following signs to Trappers Lake, and drive 6.6 miles to the Skinny Fish trailhead, with parking on the left (east) side of the road. This is the end of the recommended loop hike, so, if you have a second car, leave it here.

To reach the recommended starting point, continue driving on Road 205 for 1.1 miles to a signed junction immediately beyond Trappers Lake Lodge. Veer left, following signs to Outlet trailhead, and go 0.3 mile to the road-end trailhead.

The Savior of Trappers Lake: Arthur Carhart (1892–1978)

"The cradle of wilderness." That is how the great conservationist and writer Roderick Nash characterized Colorado's impressive Flat Tops region, and specifically the area around Trappers Lake. This evocative statement is true almost solely because of the work of Arthur Carhart, a tremendously important, but now largely overlooked, figure in the environmental movement.

At a time when nearly all employees of the Forest Service actively resisted managing their lands for anything other than timber production and grazing, Arthur Carhart was hired as a "recreation engineer," the agency's first employee whose job was primarily focused on outdoor recreation. He began his work in Colorado, where he saw how in just a few short decades that state's pristine beauty had been transformed into mostly denuded wastelands by unregulated mining, rampant overgrazing, and widespread logging that fueled the local steel industry. To Carhart's eye, the watersheds were in particularly terrible condition. With the land almost treeless, erosion was a huge problem; hence the region suffered from devastating floods.

Receiving virtually no attention or money from the federal bureaucracy, he determined the only practical way to restore the denuded watersheds was to involve local communities. Writing a series of articles drawing attention to this problem, he began working with the San Isabel Protection and Recreation Association, a small group of concerned citizens in Pueblo, Colorado. They provided local capital to restore watersheds, replant forests, and created recreational opportunities for city residents. With their help, Carhart designed and built Squirrel Creek Campground, the first car campground in National Forest history, as well as the first trails specifically designed for recreational purposes. These recreational facilities became extremely popular, and over time the program helped to restore large parts of the magnificent Sangre de Cristo Mountains.

As part of his job, Carhart traveled widely to national forests in many parts of the country, almost single-handedly spurring recreation and forest recovery efforts throughout the National Forest system. However, one location had special significance. In the summer of 1919, he went to Trappers Lake in northwest Colorado on an assignment to survey a road and to plot out an area for 100 summer homes, a marina, and two commercial sites. But Carhart fell in love with the beauty of the place and determined that the lake and watershed would not be able to handle the waste produced by the planned development. He returned to his boss with an entirely different recommendation. His plan involved halting the road well before the lake, perhaps developing a car campground nearby, but keeping the lake and surrounding lands preserved as wilderness. This was a radical idea. In fact, such a plan from a Forest Service official was completely unprecedented. Fortunately, Carhart's boss, Carl Stahl, was sympathetic and helped implement the idea. Decades were required to finalize his dream, and Carhart would still be fighting for Trappers Lake for much of the rest of his life, but the lake was eventually preserved. The surrounding Flat Tops region received "primitive area" status in 1932 and became an official wilderness by act of Congress in 1975.

Significantly, Carhart's unusual recommendation for Trappers Lake was sent out to district rangers around the country, coming to the attention of another Forest Service official, Aldo Leopold. Eventually becoming one of the giants of the conservation movement, Leopold was soon on a train north from New Mexico to meet with Carhart and Stahl.

Carhart was given the assignment of recording the ideas discussed at this important meeting, and his words became both prophetic and inspirational. He wrote, "There is a limit to the number of lakes in existence; there is a limit to the mountainous areas of the world; and . . . there are portions of natural scenic beauty which are God made, and . . . which of a right should be the property of all people. There is no question in my mind but that there is a definite point in different types of country where man-made structures should be stopped." Clearly inspired by Carhart's initiative, Leopold returned to New Mexico and was largely responsible for setting aside the world's first large wilderness area, the Gila Wilderness in southern New Mexico in 1924.

Although Carhart left the Forest Service after only a few years, his initiatives and influence helped change the culture of that organization from one of strictly maximizing resource extraction to including recreation and watershed protection as part of its mandate. The long-term impact of this change, which influenced the management of hundreds of millions of acres of public land, is hard to overstate.

Carhart went on to become a leader in a number of important conservation causes. He was honored as one of the most important people behind the efforts to protect the Boundary Waters Canoe Area in Minnesota. He took on the Bureau of Reclamation and US Army Corps of Engineers over what he saw as a number of ill-conceived dam projects around the American West. He successfully worked to stop what were unneeded and inappropriate roads through Colorado's Sangre de Cristo Mountains. He was the national leader in the fight against special-interest groups wanting to privatize cattle grazing rights on public lands, resulting in death threats from some of his opponents. As the Forest Service dramatically increased logging in the 1950s and 1960s, Carhart outspokenly called for more attention for recreation and watershed protections before cutting began. He also brought attention to, and largely helped to curtail, massive clear-cutting schemes on National Forest lands in the East and Rocky Mountain states. Finally, he was a prolific author who became the most popular nature writer of the mid-twentieth century, writing thousands of articles on everything from gardening to hunting and fishing, as well as authoring twenty-four books.

So why have you probably never heard of him? Despite his strong conservation beliefs, Carhart always remained a maverick, an independent thinker, and even referred to himself as a "raging moderate." In our political system, moderates aren't celebrated, and usually are not even remembered.

Although he frequently supported candidates from both parties, Carhart was a life-long Republican. He disliked bureaucracies, and unlike most of his conservationist contemporaries, he greatly distrusted having Washington-based federal bureaucrats in charge of overseeing distant wilderness areas and making public land decisions. He was willing to work with timber companies and felt they had a legitimate place in using public lands on a sustainable basis. He saw an important place for man in wildlands and believed that since Native Americans had lived on the land for thousands of years, the idea of protecting "untouched" wilderness was naive. He happily enlisted hunters, dude ranchers, businesspeople, fiscally conservative taxpayers, and many other nontraditional groups into conservation issues. His independent streak and friendships with people on both sides of the political spectrum kept many organizations wary of him; as a consequence, he was never asked to be on the board of any significant conservation organization. In the end, he even opposed the Wilderness Act of 1964, concerned, among other things, that it would lead to all nonwilderness land being handed over to other interests with no thought for the overall health of the forest. As he wrote (in his usual colorful language), the attitude would be that "we've stripped out the tenderloin; here's the rest of the carcass—you do what you want with it." His opposition to this landmark legislation sealed his fate of being effectively written out of the history of the conservation cause in America.

His legacy has fared somewhat better with government agencies, which belatedly embraced Carhart as one of their own, conveniently forgetting he fought long and hard against government bureaucracies to achieve his goals. In 1985 the hiker's route around Trappers Lake was renamed the Carhart Trail, and in 1993 the Arthur Carhart Wilderness Training Center was opened in Montana.

In the environmental community, we regularly (and quite correctly) extol the virtues of men such as John Muir, Bob Marshall, or Edward Abbey, offering praise for their passion and their willingness to fight for wilderness and the environment at any and all costs. At the same time, we rarely remember, or perhaps deliberately ignore, the work and achievements of more pragmatic individuals such as Arthur Carhart. Although he was without question a firm believer in the value of wilderness, he regularly crossed ideological lines to work with people with whom he disagreed. He frequently served as a vital go-between for the more radical people on both sides.

As you hike the trail named after Arthur Carhart, and enjoy the spectacular scenery still unblemished by roads and vacation homes around his beloved Trappers Lake, take a moment to remember this overlooked man. This place was definitely worth the fight.

Trip Description: The well-signed trail begins in the middle of a huge ghost forest of silvery snags from a massive 2002 forest fire and gradually takes you up an open hillside. Numerous wildflowers take advantage of the sun to offer colorful blossoms in July. After just 0.2 mile, you reach the top of the rise where you enter the Flat Tops Wilderness and enjoy a tremendous view across huge Trappers Lake to an unnamed mesa-shaped peak to the south (Peak 11,369).

Veer right at a fork onto the Carhart Trail, and soon cross a wooden bridge over the lake's clear outlet stream. The trail then travels around the lake for 0.3 mile to a fork. Keep right and, just 200 yards later, turn left where a side trail veers right toward the access road into Trappers Lake Campground. For the next mile the path goes past lovely ponds and meadows and through the partially burned forest west of Trappers Lake on the way to another junction.

Go right on Wall Lake Trail #1818 and make a steady climb, which takes you on a tour of sloping meadows, a mosaic of burned and unburned forests, and rocky viewpoints overlooking the Trappers Lake Basin, crossing several small creeks along the way. The path eventually leads up a wide canyon just northwest of cliff-edged Peak 11,369. As you approach the head of the canyon, leave the old fire scar and ascend four

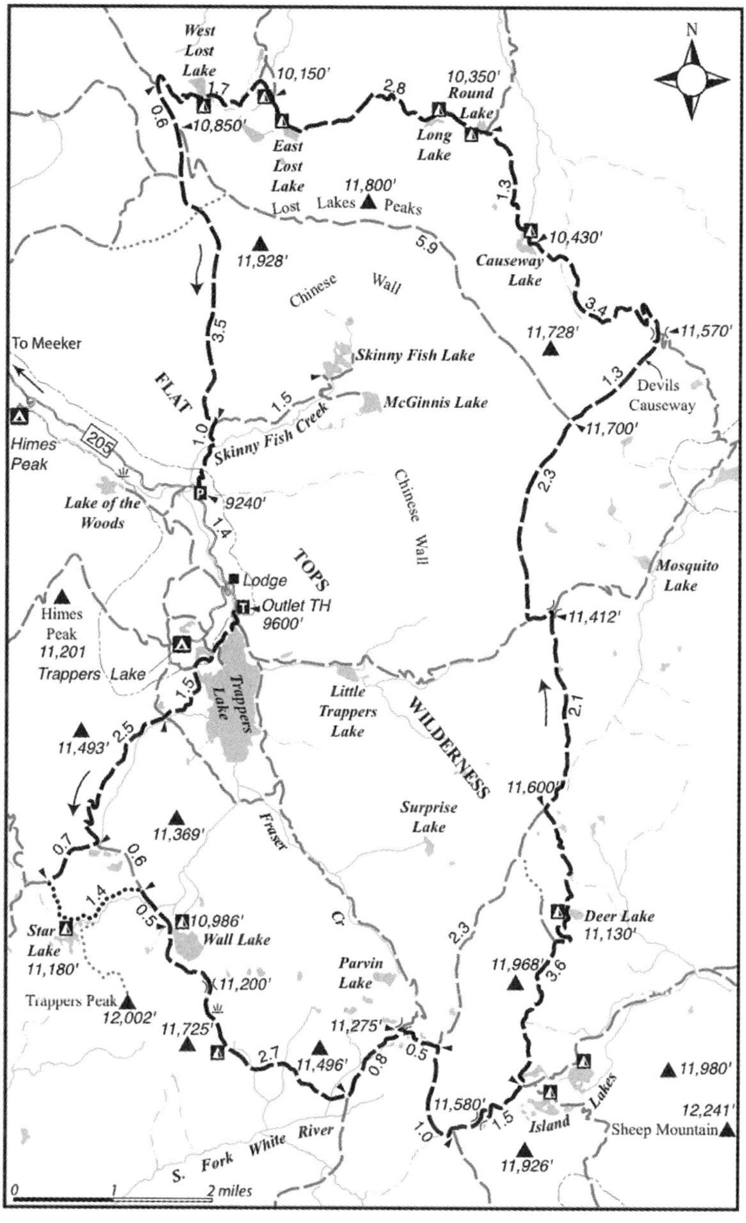

Trappers Lake–Devils Causeway Loop

short switchbacks and then some long uphill traverses to a junction at the top of a relatively flat mesa. Directly ahead is a cluster of pretty but unnamed lakes.

The shortest and most direct route is to go left on the Wall Lake Trail. However, if the weather is decent, a more scenic and secluded off-trail alternate is a better choice: go right at the junction on Oyster Lake Trail #1825. Now atop the extensive high-elevation mesas for which the Flats Tops are known, the hiking is both beautiful and very easy with only limited changes in elevation. The landscape is sublime, mostly rolling meadowlands with lots of wildflowers, scattered trees, and views extending for miles. After 0.7 mile, come to a meadow where the trail curves to the right (west). Leave the trail at this point, and follow an angling line to the south-southeast. This simple cross-country route leads up a meadow-filled gully and over a low rise before heading down to very scenic Star Lake. The convoluted shoreline of this large lake offers numerous excellent campsites with views of Trappers Peak to the southeast. The lake is also an excellent jumping-off point for hikers who want to make the steep but worthwhile scramble to the fine views atop Trappers Peak, one of the highest points in the Flat Tops Wilderness.

To continue the trip, walk along the north shore of Star Lake and then follow an intermittent use path roughly paralleling the lake's trickling outlet creek. This sketchy route descends through brush and beautiful meadows for about 0.6 mile until rejoining the Wall Lake Trail in a meadow. Turn right here and walk another 0.5 mile through gorgeous meadows to deep and scenic Wall Lake, where signs remind visitors that campfires are not allowed within 100 feet of any lakes, streams, or trails in this wilderness. Setting up your tent without a campfire is still a highly desirable option, as there are several good sites near the lake's outlet with awesome views of the cliffs and buttes surrounding this mountain gem.

The trail climbs away from the south side of Wall Lake, goes through a minor pass, and then makes a wide loop around the south side of a large marshy meadow. Still in an alpine wonderland, you descend a bit

View toward Distant Trappers Peak from Pond to the East

to cross several small creeks feeding the headwaters of the South Fork of the White River, and then reach a junction.

Turn left at the junction onto Trappers Lake Trail #1816 and gradually ascend through similarly attractive high country scenery. After passing several small ponds, you reach a junction at the wide divide separating the drainages of the North and the South Forks of the White River.

Turn right on Island Lake Trail #1812, and follow this circuitous but mostly level path past several more ponds for 0.5 mile to a junction with Chinese Wall Trail #1803. The fastest route to complete the loop turns left here. But a better option, with more lakes and better camping prospects, goes right. This trail heads very gently uphill through rolling above-timberline meadows with excellent views, especially to south-southwest of distant and distinctive Shingle Peak. Eventually the trail angles a bit uphill and to the left before reaching a signed junction with the very faint W Mountain Trail. Keep straight on the main trail, and climb a bit more to a beautiful little alpine pond almost right atop a pass. From here you can look down into the scenic basin holding the several Island Lakes.

The trail descends into the Island Lakes Basin via a series of short but steep switchbacks. At the bottom of the descent and on the approach to the west end of a large lake, reach a junction with Deer Lake Trail #1802.

To explore the Island Lakes Basin, go straight and then take off on any of the many official and unofficial paths leading to the numerous lakes in this area. You'll find all of the lakes to be very scenic and most of them have nice campsites.

After exploring the Island Lakes, return to the Deer Lake Trail and go north rounding the base of a striking reddish-colored butte. The generally uphill tread takes you past a small cave just below and to the left of the trail and then through a series of sloping basins beneath a line of rugged cliffs. At about 1.7 miles from Island Lakes, and at a high point where you can see down to Deer Lake, is an unsigned junction. The more obvious trail goes left (uphill). This unofficial trail offers a higher-elevation shortcut to the recommended route, but is more exposed to the weather and misses Deer Lake.

For most hikers the better choice is the indistinct official trail, which goes to the right, through some brush then past a marshy little pond to a stunning cliff-edged overlook. From there the trail switchbacks to the left and makes a steep and rocky descent to a campsite near nicely swimmable Deer Lake. After a brief visit, the trail climbs steeply away from Deer Lake though a series of gorgeous compact alpine basins. Soon above timberline, you make a short, rocky climb to regain the high alpine plateau. Easy hiking now leads past a shallow lake and a reunion with Chinese Wall Trail #1803, angling in from the left.

Keep straight (north), now on Trail #1803, enjoying excellent views as you cross wide alpine parklands. The next few miles are some of the most scenic on the entire trip, across rolling tundra, over snowfields, and past numerous lovely but austere ponds on a joyous and remarkably easy route. After 2.1 miles, reach a junction with the Stillwater and Bear River Trails. Go left on Stillwater Trail #1814 and gently descend over tundra for 0.25 mile to another junction. If time constraints or inclement weather force you to cut your trip short, then go straight here and make an easy descent past Little Trappers Lake back to Trappers Lake and your car.

The longer and more satisfying loop goes right at this junction, back onto the Chinese Wall Trail. This wildly scenic path climbs gently across spectacular tundra meadows for 2 miles to an obscure junction near a high point marked with a cairn.

Now it's time for an important decision and an honest assessment of the situation. If: (1) the weather is at all questionable, (2) you are not a sure-footed and experienced hiker, and (3) you are in any way afraid of heights, then turn left on the initially obscure continuation of the Chinese Wall Trail. For the next several miles, this outstanding route remains very high with great views and offers a terrific hike.

The more spectacular but exposed alternative goes straight ahead on what appears to be the more heavily used Devils Causeway Trail. This route heads down to a large meadow, then uphill along the top of a brushy and increasingly narrow ridgeline, offering jaw-dropping views both to the north of a long tall cliff above sparkling Causeway Lake and south to Stillwater Reservoir. Cliffs drop off on either side as the ridge becomes even narrower. Finally, you reach the Devils Causeway, a 25-yard long section of uneven boulders where the ridgetop is often less than 3 feet wide. Sheer cliffs, several hundred feet high, drop off dramatically on either side. For experienced hikers, this traverse is not a particularly difficult physical challenge, but can be a tough mental obstacle for many. Fortunately, the ridge eventually widens out past Devils Causeway, and you soon make a steep but not particularly frightening drop to a saddle and a junction with East Fork Trail #1119.

Turn left at this junction and gradually descend this view-packed route, soon returning to forest. A series of irregularly spaced switchbacks and rounded turns lead mostly downhill through the trees and past very scenic meadows set beneath a miles-long line of banded cliffs to the west. In one of these pretty meadows, you rock-hop a seasonal creek and continue another 0.3 mile to Causeway Lake, a very scenic pool set directly beneath the aforementioned cliffs. The lakeshore has numerous excellent campsites, though you'll have to scout around to find them. As this lake is very popular, don't expect solitude. After only a brief view of the lake from the trail, you head away from the water only to reach it again where you cross the lake's outlet. Unless there happens to be a convenient logjam, crossing the stream here requires wet feet.

The trail continues north from Causeway Lake, remaining mostly in forest. There are no views through this section, but the hiking is generally easy with only very minor ups and downs. Careful examination reveals that about a quarter of the trees here have been killed by bark beetles. A larger open area, this one created by a forest fire, can be seen on the lower slopes of the tall ridge to the east.

About 1.2 miles from the outlet to Causeway Lake is a junction beside forest-rimmed Round Lake, with some good but mostly viewless campsites. You go left on Lost Lakes Trail #1116 and in another 0.6 mile reach very scenic Long Lake, which offers better campsites and superior views to those at Round Lake.

The trail now climbs almost 300 feet to crest a forested ridge, and then descends to absolutely gorgeous East Lost Lake and an extremely photogenic view of a rugged line of tall cliffs called Lost Lake Peaks. A short downhill from this lake takes you to a creek crossing and a possibly unsigned junction on the edge of a large meadow. There is a good campsite in this vicinity.

Veer left, and go left again a little over 0.1 mile later when another trail comes in from the right. The trail now climbs beside a small creek and past some large beaver ponds to the good campsites at West Lost Lake. Although pretty and a good swimming lake, this pool doesn't compare to the scenery of its eastern cousin.

The trail soon goes left, away from West Lost Lake, and continues climbing in numerous switchbacks to a ridgetop junction with Chinese Wall Trail #1803. You go left here, staying in forest near the ridgetop for the next 0.6-mile to the next junction (had you skipped the Devils Causeway, this is where you reunite with the high-elevation Chinese Wall Trail).

To complete the loop, bear right at this junction (sharply left, if you took the Chinese Wall Trail) onto Lost Lakes Trail #1812, and traverse a wooded hillside for about 0.4 mile to a signed junction with the faint Picket Pin Trail, which drops to the right. Keep straight on the main trail, and continue traversing either on the level or gaining some elevation for another 0.5 mile to a junction with a very steep stock driveway crossing the route.

Keep straight on the hiker's trail and, following another half mile or so of mostly level hiking, begin a long but generally well-graded downhill. The descent leads in and out of burn areas where deadfall can be a problem, especially early in the summer before trail maintenance is completed. The openings created by the blaze offer some nice views, particularly to the area around Trappers Lake to the south. At the base of an aspen-rimmed meadow is the signed junction with Skinny Fish Trail #1813.

Go straight, and descend through meadows and burned forest to a bridged crossing of good-sized Skinny Fish Creek. Another 0.4 mile of downhill takes you to Forest Road 205 and the Skinny Fish trailhead. Without a car shuttle, it's an uphill but not too difficult 1.4-mile road walk to the Outlet trailhead and your car.

Possible Itinerary

	Camps and Side Trips	Miles	Elevation Gain
Day 1	Outlet TH to Wall Lake	6.6	+1,800/−400
Day 2	Deer Lake	8.5	+1,400/−1,300
Day 3	Causeway Lake	10.7	+1,150/−1,850
Day 4	Out to Skinny Fish TH	10.9	+1,300/−2,500

Giving Back

Colorado Wilderness Network:

WWW.COLORADOWILDERNESSNETWORK.ORG

Maroon Bells–Snowmass Wilderness,
White River National Forest

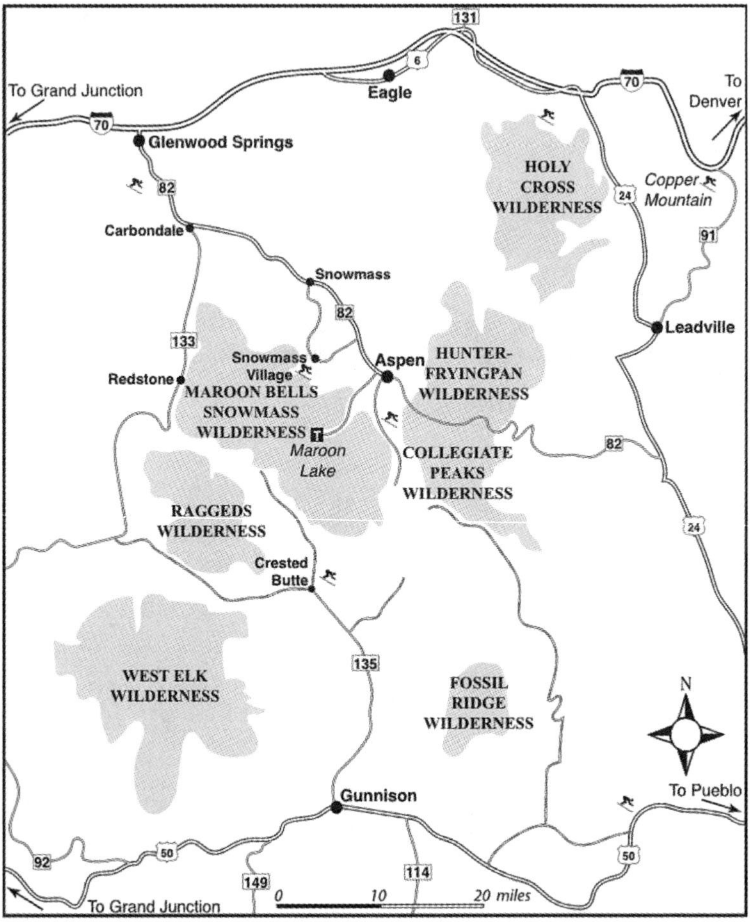

Maroon Bells: Four Pass Loop Location Map

TRIP 13

Maroon Bells: Four Pass Loop

And the Colorado Rocky Mountain high
I've seen it raining fire in the sky
I know he'd be a poorer man if he never saw an eagle fly
Rocky Mountain high
—JOHN DENVER

The Four Pass Loop around the Maroon Bells is justifiably one of the more popular backpacking trails in Colorado, with the picture-postcard view of the Bells from Maroon Lake luring scores of sight-seers, photographers, day hikers, and backpackers every summer day. While this initial scene is a familiar icon to mountain lovers around the world, beauty abounds beyond this heavily viewed Colorado landmark. While some trail runners make the 28-mile circuit in a single day, less hurried recreationists will find plenty of lovely diversions to occupy their attention, including serene lakes, waterfalls, rushing streams, verdant meadows, and colorful wildflowers. As the name indicates, the route crosses four high passes all topping out at over 12,000 feet. Those carrying their belongings on their backs into the backcountry will have to plan ahead to avoid crossing these passes during the usual afternoon thunderstorms.

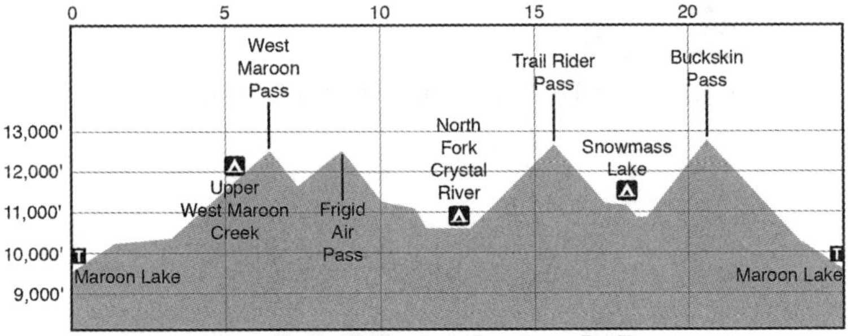

Maroon Bells–Four Pass Loop Profile

Days: 4–6
Distance: 28.0 miles
Type: Loop
Scenery: 9
Solitude: 6
Technical Difficulty: 5
Physical Difficulty: 7
Elevation Gain/Loss: +6,475'/–6,475'

Season: Mid-July through September
Best: Late July
Maps: USGS: *Maroon Bells, Snowmass Mtn.*
Sky Terrain Trail Maps: *Aspen, Crested Butte, Maroon Bells*
Contacts:
White River National Forest
Aspen-Sopris Ranger District
806 W. Hallam
Aspen, CO 81611
303-925-3445

Permits: Self-register at trailhead, no fee.

Regulations: Groups limited to 10 people and 15 stock/pack animals. No campfires at Crater, Geneva, and Snowmass lakes.

Nearest Campground: Maroon Lake—at trailhead (Silver Queen, Silver Bell, and Silver Bar on Maroon Creek Road)
Nearest Airport: Aspen/Pitkin County Airport (ASE)—12 miles
Denver International Airport (DIA)—193 miles

Nearest Outdoor Retailer:
The Ute Mountaineer
210 S. Galena St.
Aspen, CO 81611
970-925-2849

Transportation Logistics: Restrictions on the Maroon Creek Road allow access to private vehicles only before 8 AM and after 5 PM for a $10 recreation fee. Overnight parking near the trailhead is extremely limited, especially on weekends, so you should consider leaving a vehicle in the free parking area at Aspen Highlands and then riding the RFTA bus to the trailhead. Tickets ($6 for adults, $4 for 65 and over, $4 for kids 6–16, and free for children under 6) can be purchased at Four Mountain Sports in Aspen or Aspen Highlands Village. Shuttle buses run every 20 minutes until early afternoon and then every half hour, with service ending at 5 PM. Between 9 AM and 5 PM, a free shuttle bus is available on the Castle/Maroon Bus from the Rubey Park Transit Center in downtown Aspen to Aspen Highlands. Go to www.rfta.com/routes/maroon-bells for more information.

Backcountry Logistics: (A, BB, L, W) Colorado Rocky Mountain thunderstorms are so common in the afternoon that some suggest you could set your watch by them. Plan on hiking over the four high passes on this loop early in the day to avoid being zapped by lightning, or getting drenched by the accompanying heavy rainfall. This is definitely not the place to skimp on rain gear or use flimsy tents.

Amenities and Attractions: As long as you have plenty of cash or a high limit on your credit card, **Aspen** offers nearly unlimited diversions. However, a few activities are worth noting for the less wealthy traveler. Classical music always seems to be in the air here on summer evenings and the mostly belowground **Harris Concert Hall** is the premier venue. The grass-covered slope around the perimeter of the hall is a fine place to set up a lawn chair and enjoy a picnic while listening to the music waft through the opened partitions, all without having to buy a ticket. Summer evenings on the patio at the **Paradise Bakery** (320 S. Galena St.) offer the opportunity to enjoy an ice-cream cone while listening to varied groups of music students performing on their instruments.

Driving Directions to Trailhead: From the town of Aspen, follow State Highway 82 west to a roundabout, and take the second exit onto Maroon

Creek Road (County Road 13). If you're planning on riding the shuttle bus to the trailhead, drive 1.4 miles to the parking lot for the Aspen Highlands Ski Area on the left, park your vehicle, and then wait for the shuttle. Otherwise, before 8 AM or after 5 PM, continue on Maroon Creek Road another 8 miles to the oftentimes full overnight parking lot near Maroon Lake. A $10 recreation fee is required to park here, unless you are the holder of an Interagency, Senior, or Golden Access pass.

Trip Description: The beautiful scenery begins from the very start of the trail, as you follow the Maroon-Snowmass Trail #1975 along the north edge of picturesque Maroon Lake, backdropped by the classic and oft-photographed view of the rosy-hued Maroon Bells (see map of Maroon Bells: Four Pass Loop [East]). Beyond the lake, the trail enters a mixed forest and begins a moderate climb through the canyon of West Maroon Creek. The grade eases, and the forest opens up again on the approach to the loop junction with the West Maroon Trail #1970 just before Crater Lake, 1.8 miles from the trailhead. This trail will be your return route.

Turn left at the junction and wander over to the northwest shore of Crater Lake, where once again the looming Maroon Bells dominate the scene. Enter the Maroon Bells–Snowmass Wilderness at the far end of the lake, where a moderate climb ensues. Pockets of forest appear on the way up the canyon but the topography remains mostly open, which allows for stunning views on the way to the first crossing of West Maroon Creek near 10,500 feet.

Continue climbing, now on the east side of the creek, passing through stands of forest alternating with willow thickets. After about a mile, you cross back over West Maroon Creek (10,880') and then start climbing farther up the canyon and higher above the stream. Reach a willow-fringed bench around 11,650 feet, just below timberline, where campsites will appeal to groups that are not primed to go all the way over West Maroon Pass on the first day.

Beyond the camp area, you enter the alpine realm above timberline and climb stiffly toward West Maroon Pass. Hop over a side stream, usually the last water source below the pass, and follow an angling ascent through rocky terrain sprinkled with clumps of low-growing alpine plants and flowers. A final set of switchbacks followed by a long upward traverse leads to the top of West Maroon Pass (12,500') and a sweeping view, 4.6 miles from the Maroon-Snowmass junction.

A zigzagging descent leads down the far side of the pass and across steep, rocky slopes toward a tributary of the East Fork of the Crystal River. Reach the easier terrain of flower-filled meadows on the way to a junction with the Frigid Air Pass Trail #1974, 1.1 miles from West Maroon Pass. Here the West Maroon Trail continues downstream on a moderate descent, passing through Purity Basin on the way to the East Fork trailhead, 2.3 miles from the junction (see map of Maroon Bells: Four Pass Loop [West]).

Veer to the right at the junction, and follow the North Fork–Fravert Basin Trail on a gently rising traverse across open, wildflower-covered slopes bisected by tiny rivulets. After 1.2 miles, the gentle, view-packed traverse ends at a junction near a small pond with a trail to Halsey Basin.

Turning right, you ascend shortly up a steep slope to gain Frigid Air Pass (12,420') and another sweeping view, which includes the less-seen view of the backside of the Maroon Bells.

Long-legged switchbacks lead down from the pass across more flower-filled slopes to the more sedate topography of Fravert Basin below. As the long descent continues, the return of willows and then conifers corresponds to the drop in elevation. Eventually the trail draws near to the North Fork and follows it downstream through the canyon on a willow-lined path. Shortly after the crossing of a stream, a pair of side trails lead to campsites above the trail, and farther on is a larger campsite right next to the river.

Beyond the last campsite, a series of short switchbacks leads down a steeper slope out of Fravert Basin and onto the floor of the valley below, from where you have a fine view of King Falls. A little over 0.1 mile from where the trail crosses the river, you may notice the faint track of the unmaintained trail heading south into Halsey Basin. Campsites in the open terrain on both sides of the river near the crossing will appeal to

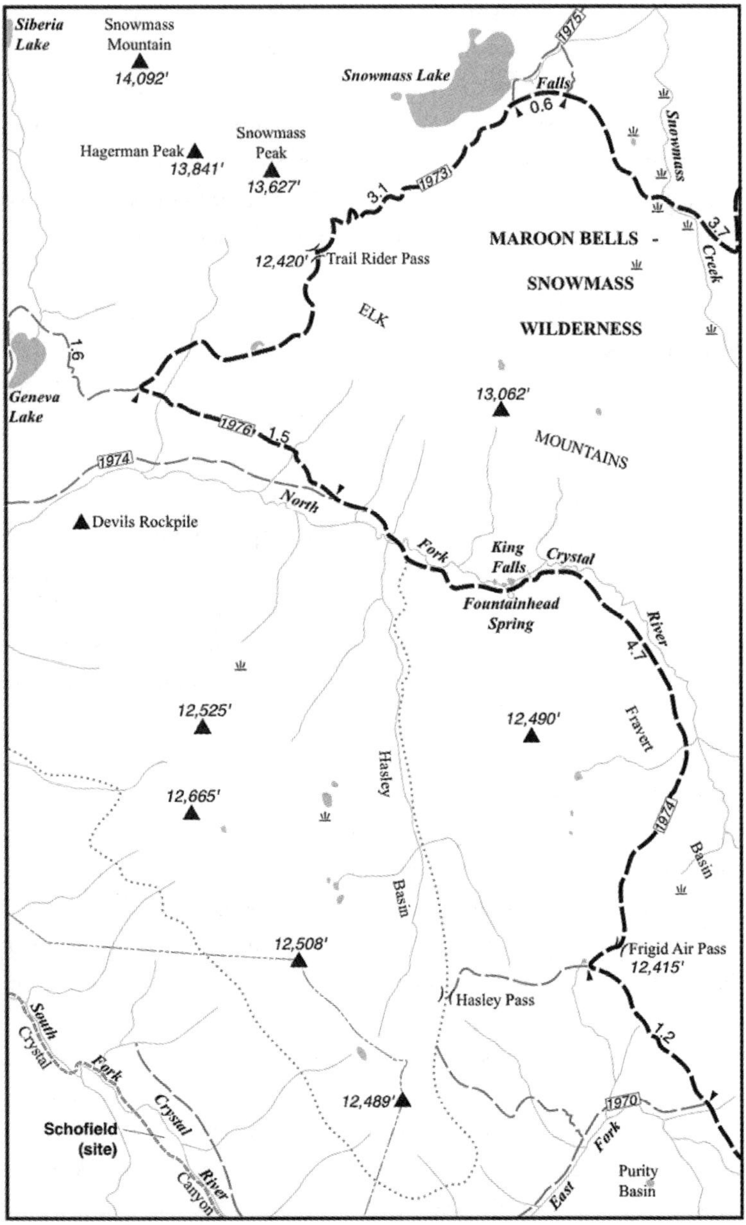

Maroon Bells: Four Pass Loop (West)

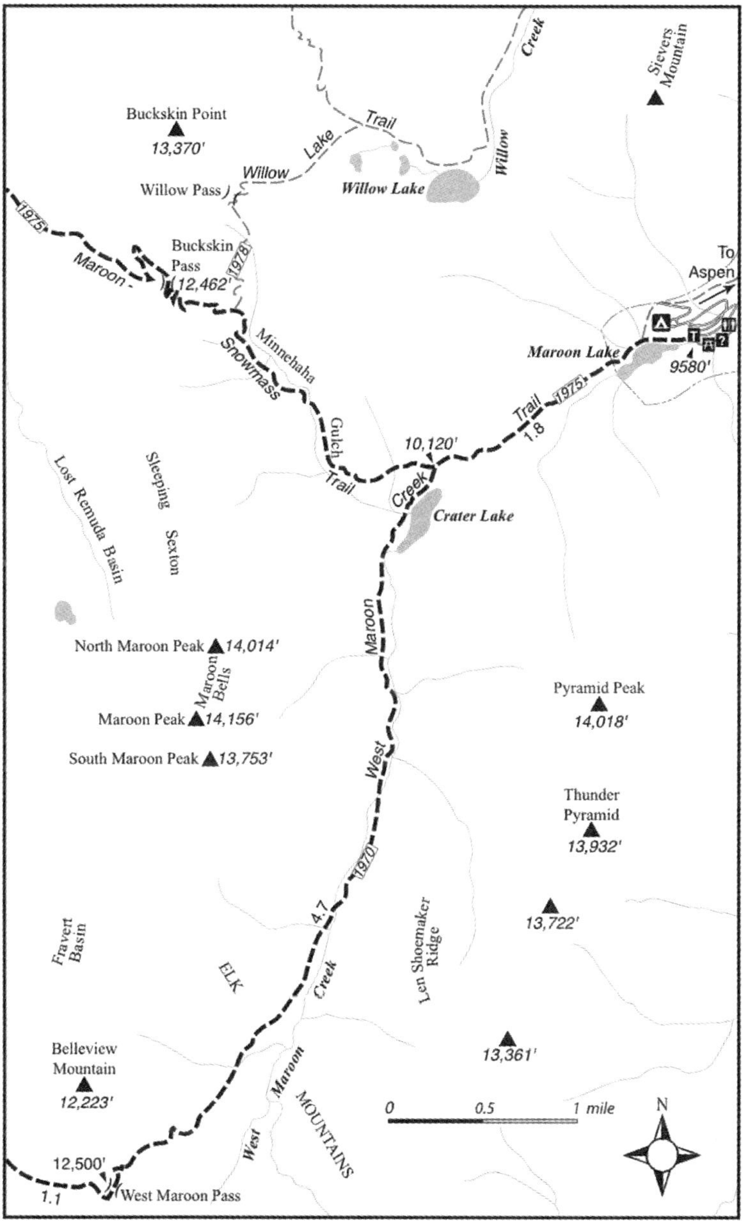

Maroon Bells: Four Pass Loop (East)

those not interested in the climb to Geneva Lake. Continue down the canyon, passing in and out of groves of trees until you reach a junction with the Cutoff Trail #1976, 4.7 miles from Frigid Air Pass.

A steep, zigzagging climb attacks a hillside covered with conifers and then aspens before a long, rising traverse slices across open, wildflower-dotted slopes with fine views of North Fork canyon. After bending into and out of the gash of a gully with a seasonal stream, switchbacks lead up to a junction with Trail #1973, 1.5 miles from the previous junction. A left turn will get you to campsites at Geneva Lake in 1.6 relatively easy miles.

Turning right, you make a moderate ascent toward Trail Rider Pass, soon crossing a usually dry seasonal stream. The grade eases where you enter an upper basin with a small tarn surrounded by widely scattered and stunted firs. While camping here is possible, the lack of protection may discourage the notion. The stiffer climbing resumes at the far end of the basin and eventually leads to short switchbacks just below the pass. You reach Trail Rider Pass (12,420') and another marvelous view, which includes Snowmass Lake immediately below.

From the pass, long-legged switchbacks descend through lush flower gardens on the way toward timberline, with Snowmass Lake constantly in view. Soon small clumps of dwarfed firs appear, and you pass a campsite and keep descending toward the lake. Farther down, a thicker forest obscures the lake views, as you reach a large group camping area near a junction with a half-mile connector to the Maroon-Snowmass Trail, 3.1 miles from the Geneva Lake junction.

Continue ahead on a descent toward the far end of the lake, where a lateral on the left leads to designated campsites nestled beneath the trees at the northeast end. The view is superb, with massive Snowmass Mountain (14,092') rising directly above the head of the lake, while Hagerman and Snowmass peaks top the ridge to the south. A jagged ridge of granite rims the northwestern side of the lake, which reposes majestically in this subalpine bowl.

After your visit to Snowmass Lake is complete, retrace your steps to the main trail and head northeast downstream to a junction with the Maroon-Snowmass Trail #1975. Turn right, cross the outlet from

Backpacker Taking a Break above Snowmass Lake

Snowmass Lake, and begin a downhill romp through moderate forest cover with the aid of some switchbacks to a junction with the connector trail. Breaking out of the forest, you continue the descent through a broad swath of luxuriant meadows down to a log crossing of the main channel of Snowmass Creek.

Across the creek the trail skirts above a large, marshy meadow, created by a beaver dam. A side trail nearby leads shortly to campsites, the last viable ones on this side of the pass. Beyond, long-legged switchbacks climb across mostly forested slopes until the trees start to diminish near the crossing of a pair of seasonal streams. You continue the ascent across open, alpine slopes, getting a short breather on a knoll near 11,600 feet, before the stiff climb resumes. One final, long-legged switchback delivers you to 12,462-foot Buckskin Pass and another stunning, wide-ranging view (see map of Maroon Bells: Four Pass Loop [East]).

A steep, winding descent below the pass leads toward timberline and a junction with Willow Lake Trail #1978 to Willow Pass, 3.7 miles from the junction with the connector trail.

Continue straight ahead at the junction, descending into the forest cover of Minnehaha Gulch on mostly rocky tread. The presence of aspens heralds your eventual arrival at the junction near Crater Lake and the close of the loop, 1.8 miles from the Willow Lake Trail junction. From there, retrace your steps 1.8 miles back to the Maroon Lake trailhead.

Possible Itinerary

	Camps and Side Trips	Miles	Elevation Gain
Day 1	Maroon Lake TH to Upper West Maroon Creek	5.3	+1950/−0
Day 2	Crossing of North Fork Crystal River	7.4	+925/−2,000
Day 3	Snowmass Lake	5.1	+2,100/−1,600
Day 4	Out to Maroon Lake TH	10.2	+1,500/−2,875

Beauty Trumps Misery

First-time visitors to the Rocky Mountains are often struck by the lush wildflower displays of midsummer. My first multiday backpack in the Rockies was unforgettable, when my wife, Robin; best friend, Tic; and a mutual friend, Wayne, took a weeklong excursion in early July on the Highline Trail in the Wind River Range. Two things in particular stand out about that trip—the mosquitoes and the wildflowers.

Having arrived immediately after snowmelt, water was everywhere; creeks were overflowing their banks, meadows were completely saturated, and every low-lying depression became an ephemeral pond. Consequently, the area's fecundity for producing clouds of bloodsucking mosquitoes seemed unprecedented. Never before or since have I experienced these winged pests in such great magnitude. Fully clothed at all times with long pants, long-sleeved shirts, and hats, we dared leave vulnerable only our faces and hands as exposed flesh. The only effective escape was to keep hiking as fast as we could, or to stay in our tents. When standing still, all four of us developed an involuntary wave to keep the mosquitoes off of our faces. To add to the misfortune, these particular mosquitoes seemed immune to any and all repellents. The fight with these insects became an unrelenting and epic battle we were sure to lose.

Oddly enough, when I think back about that trip, the mosquitoes are not the first things that comes to mind. In fact, despite the high index of misery they caused, I fondly remember many other aspects of the hike before reminiscing about the mosquitoes. By far and away, the amazing wildflower displays remain the foremost memory.

In mid-July, several years after that first Wind River trip, I met Tic in Aspen, along with his friend Craig. We were bound for our first backpacking trip in Colorado—the Four Pass Loop around the Maroon Bells. Craig was tall, well over 6 feet and a former basketball player. Currently, he was a pastor at a Covenant church in the San Diego area, so we, somewhat sacrilegiously, made him our unofficial spiritual guide for our trip. The postcard scenery of the Maroon Bells did not disappoint, enhanced tremendously by being there during the peak of flower season. A stunning variety of red, yellow, blue, and white wildflowers, along with the lush green groundcover, created a tapestry of colors that delighted the eyes. The idyllic scenery was enhanced by a string of sunny days without the usual afternoon thunderstorms.

As we rounded a low, forested ridge, we broke out into the open onto a sloping vale bordered by a backdrop of high peaks on three sides. The vale was filled with a field of vibrant wildflowers unlike any we had seen so far. Every inch of ground appeared to be alive with color—we stopped in our tracks, overcome by the beauty of the scene. Our reverential silence seemed to last an eternity until Craig spoke, "God is still the best gardener."—**Mike**

Weminuche Wilderness, Rio Grande and San Juan National Forests

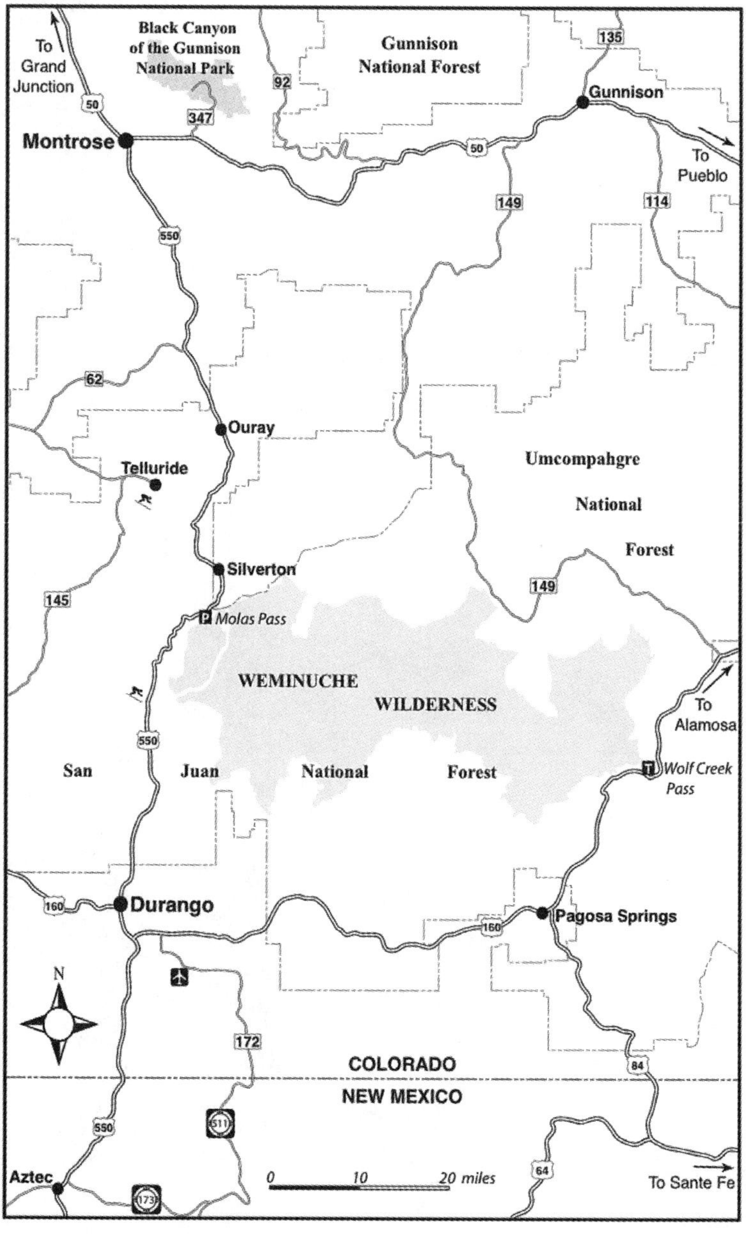

Weminuche Wilderness Traverse Location Map

TRIP 14

Weminuche Wilderness Traverse

> May your trails be crooked, winding, lonesome, dangerous, leading to the most amazing view. May your mountains rise into and above the clouds.
>
> —EDWARD ABBEY, AUTHOR AND ENVIRONMENTALIST

Yeah, I know, this is a book about the "best of the best," so every trip described in these pages is truly outstanding. As a result, superlatives get thrown around pretty freely. But, I mean *really!* The San Juan Mountains of southwestern Colorado are just heartbreakingly beautiful—they may break your heart that you live anywhere else. Even the approach roads through the surrounding valleys feature lush meadows and idyllic ranches that are a joy to drive through. And the mountains? Well, frankly, words fail me. Oh, "sublime" comes to mind, as

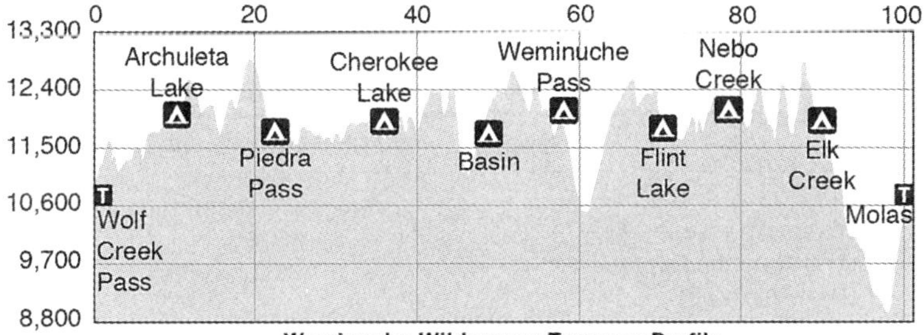

Weminuche Wilderness Traverse Profile

do "spectacular" and "inspiring," but none of these really captures the essence of the place. You'll just have to come up with your own descriptions after you hike here yourself. I know, it's a tough job, but somebody has to do it, and you're elected. Have fun. It would be hard not to.

Days: 8–12

Distance: 102 miles (including only 4.6 miles of side trips, though many more are possible)

Type: Shuttle

Scenery: 10

Solitude: 5

Technical Difficulty: 6

Physical Difficulty: 7

Elevation Gain/Loss: +23,200'/–23,450'

Season: July to October

Best: Mid-July through September

Map: Trails Illustrated—*Weminuche Wilderness*

Resources: *Hiking Colorado's Weminuche and South San Juan Wilderness Areas*, by Donna Ikenberry; *Across the San Juan Mountains*, by Thomas Arthur Rickard

Contacts:

San Juan National Forest
Columbine Ranger District
367 Pearl Street
PO Box 439
Bayfield, CO 81122
970-884-2512

Pagosa Ranger District
180 Pagosa Street
PO Box 310
Pagosa Springs, CO 81147
970-264-2268

Rio Grande National Forest
Divide Ranger District
13308 West Highway 160
Del Norte, CO 81132
719-657-3321

Divide Ranger District
Creede Office
304 South Main Street
PO Box 270
Creede, CO 81130
719-658-2556

Nearest Campground: Although there are no campgrounds immediately near the trailhead, there are several popular campgrounds along the shuttle route between the two trailheads.

Nearest Airports: Durango-La Plata County Airport (DRO)—between the two trailheads
Grand Junction Regional Airport (GJT)—132 miles

Nearest Outdoor Retailers:

REI—131 miles
644 North Avenue
Grand Junction, CO 81501
970-254-8970

Gardenswartz Outdoors
780 Main Avenue
Durango, CO 81301
970-259-6696

Permits: No permits are required.

Regulations: Maximum group size of 15 people or 25 combined people and livestock. Camping is prohibited within 100 feet of all water sources. Camping, fires, and livestock grazing are all prohibited within 300 feet of Archuleta, Flint, and West Ute Lakes.

Transportation Logistics: The easiest way to handle the transportation logistics for this shuttle trip is to have two cars and follow the driving directions below. With some research, finding a commercial taxi or shuttle service to shuttle hikers from Molas Lake to Wolf Creek Pass is usually possible. Contact Animas Transportation Co. at 970-259-1315, or visit their website at www.animastransportation.com.

Backcountry Logistics: (A, L, BB) Thunderstorms occur almost every summer afternoon, so plan to be off the high ridges by no later than 2 PM. Sometimes you will be forced to camp near or above timberline with no trees for cover. Bring a sturdy tent that can survive the hail, rain, and strong winds that often accompany heavy thunderstorms.

Almost this entire hike is above 11,000 feet. As a result, the air is quite thin, especially for those arriving directly from a near-sea-level home. If you are not yet acclimated, it may take a few days of discomfort (headaches, lack of appetite, inability to sleep, and so on) before you start to feel "normal." In a few cases, the symptoms may be so severe that you will be forced to retreat to lower elevations and abandon your trip.

Hundreds of thousands of acres of forest here have been killed in a mountain pine beetle infestation. For at least the first half of this hike, as many as 80 percent of the trees are dead. Expect lots of snags, some deadfall, and marginally less attractive scenery for many years to come.

Attractions and Amenities: Durango is a popular resort community where you'll find a wide selection of quite good (but also quite pricy) restaurants, shops, motels, and related amenities.

The springs just outside of the town of **Pagosa Springs** are a great place to soak after a long hike.

While in this corner of the country, it would be a crime not to check out a few of other nearby attractions. **Mesa Verde National Park** is only 38 miles west of Durango and is well worth a couple of vacation days to see the numerous extraordinarily well-preserved Native American cities and ruins tucked neatly into overhanging caves. The **Durango and Silverton Narrow Gauge Railroad** (durangotrain.com) makes for a fun and scenic ride (or even an alternate way to exit this hike). Finally, to the north, **Black Canyon of the Gunnison National Park** offers stupendous views of a dark, scenic, and very deep canyon, as well as some fine hiking.

Directions to Trailheads: From Grand Junction, drive 65 miles southeast on US 50 to a junction in the city of Montrose, where, following signs to Ouray and Durango, you go south on US 550. This road initially passes through farm and ranchland, but eventually climbs into the mountains and is one of the greatest mountain drives on the continent. The road passes through the former mining towns of Ouray and Silverton, goes over three passes near 11,000 feet, and follows a winding course through some of the finest roadside scenery imaginable. At about 66 miles from Montrose, or 6 miles past Silverton, is a turnoff for the private lodge and campground at Molas Lake. Continue straight on US 550, and after 0.5 mile reach the signed turnoff for the short but bumpy dirt road heading left about 100 yards to the Molas Lake trailhead parking area. This is the recommended ending point of the hike.

To reach the starting point, continue south on US 550 another 0.6 mile to the viewpoint at Molas Pass, then continue for 42.5 miles to the junction of US 160 and 550 in the bustling city of Durango. You turn left (east) onto US 160 and drive 60 miles to a junction with US 89 just east of the city of Pagosa Springs. Continue northeast on US 160 and follow this scenic road for another 21 miles to Wolf Creek Pass. You can either start your hike at this pass, or you can shorten the hike slightly, and save 800 feet of elevation gain, by driving to the higher trailhead at Lobo Overlook. To reach that point, drive about 0.1 mile east of the pass, then turn left onto a possibly unsigned gravel road that begins in a large gravel pullout. This sometimes rough but generally drivable road climbs for 2.1 miles to the end at a wonderful viewpoint called Lobo Overlook. From here a nearly level trail goes west about 0.4 mile to hook up with the Continental Divide Trail (CDT).

Impacts of the Mountain Pine Beetle–Little Bugs, Big Appetites

Many men may be happy to hear this news: apparently there is some truth to what you've heard—size doesn't (always) matter. That is true for *Dendroctonus ponderosae* (commonly known as the mountain pine beetle), a creature no bigger than a grain of rice. People who live or recreate in the Rocky Mountains' forests may refer to this destructive little bug with somewhat harsher language, but that is all part of our story.

The mountain pine beetle is a native resident of western North America, with a preferred habitat of forests of ponderosa, lodgepole, limber, whitebark, and other pines. In an outbreak, a multitude of female beetles lays eggs under the bark of larger trees, which introduces a fungus into the wood that prevents the tree from effectively repelling the beetles with enough pitch flow and also inhibits the tree's ability to transport water and nutrients. This action, along with the feeding of the larval insects, typically kills the host tree in less than a year. Normally, in a healthy forest, these insects exist in relatively low numbers, quietly attacking weak or vulnerable trees, which helps speed forest succession in favor of younger and healthier specimens. Periodically, however, and for reasons that are not entirely clear, this beetle's population explodes and begins attacking and killing large swaths of forests. Such outbreaks are also considered fairly normal—all part of the life cycle of the insect and the forest. Occasional outbreaks have been recorded for as long as people have lived or visited this region, and probably for countless thousands of years before. However, the current plague is anything but normal.

The best estimates put today's ongoing outbreak of mountain pine beetles as approximately *ten times* larger than any known previous event—probably the largest blight of forest insects ever seen in North America. Exactly where and when the population explosion began is hard to determine, because the beetles are always present in some numbers. By 1996, a significant outbreak was in progress in Colorado's Rocky Mountain National Park. As of May 2013, every western state and Canadian province was affected with something close to 88 million acres (an area almost the size of California) devastated at a 70 to 90 percent kill rate, with even more acres impacted at a lesser rate. In Canada alone, over 40 million acres are seriously affected, with enormous swaths of forest decimated. In Colorado, the state's forest service estimates that only 264,000 new acres were badly infested at the start of 2013, down from a peak of 1,150,000 acres in 2008. This sounds like good news, except for the fact that as the report points out, the decrease is almost entirely due to the fact that the beetles *had already killed* most of the available trees and now simply had less to eat. If you drive or hike across enormous areas of Colorado, Wyoming, Utah, or Montana, you can't help but notice hillside after hillside where 80 percent or more of the trees are dead, turning once green mountainsides into at best a patchwork (and often a near monoculture) of brown and gray.

A variety of factors are helping to both cause and prolong this epidemic of hungry bugs. Climate change has produced several years of unusually warm winters and hot, dry summers that have allowed the beetle larvae to survive the winters and provide an optimal breeding season for the adults. The forests are also filled with unusually dense stands of lodgepole and ponderosa pines, due primarily to decades of well-intentioned but overzealous fire suppression. This has resulted in overstocked and crowded forests ripe for beetle infestations. Additionally, drought conditions in many western forests are stressing trees and increasing their vulnerability.

The impacts of this historic outbreak are potentially very widespread. Obviously the views we all enjoy are going to be dramatically altered by a sea of dead trees. Wildlife is heavily impacted, with improvements in conditions for a few, such as woodpeckers, and loss of important habitat for many others. (The beetle-caused death of whitebark pines in the Yellowstone ecosystem, for example, raises concerns that the tree's highly nutritious pine nuts, a vitally important food source for grizzly bears and other animals, will no longer be available.) The tree die-off will directly affect the livelihoods of thousands of people in the lumber and tourism industries. Although the wood from affected trees is structurally sound, the blue stain of the fungus alters its appearance. The timber industry will have to adapt, at *enormous* cost, to producing different wood products from the damaged wood, or to finding a way to use the dead trees for something like biofuels. However, effectively harvesting the damaged trees without creating other undesirable environmental consequences may be problematic. A Harvard study in Montana predicts that due to a combination of the beetles, somewhat warmer summers in recent years, and mismanagement of forests in the last several decades, the state can expect a 200 percent increase in wildfires and an 80 percent increase in pollution from those fires. A Colorado study indicates that the enormous areas of dead forests will result in faster snowmelt, since the shady forest canopy is gone, creating the potential for serious flooding and erosion. According to a Canadian study, the impact could even be global, because by 2020 the beetle outbreak will release some 270 megatons of previously trapped carbon dioxide and dramatically reduce the ability of the now-dead northern forests to play their traditional role of absorbing excess carbon from the atmosphere.

Good solutions to this problem are hard to come by, and even if they arrived tomorrow would be too late to stop an infestation that already seems to be naturally slowing down due to the death of most of the trees. The public land agencies are doing their best, but generally have their hands full with the enormous job of simply removing hundreds of thousands of "hazard" trees from campgrounds and roads, and dealing with local threats of wildfires near populated areas.

The Weminuche Wilderness in southwestern Colorado is typical of many areas in the Rocky Mountains. As you hike along this mostly above-timberline trail you will look down on valley after valley, especially in the eastern part of the wilderness, of mostly dead trees. If you make camp below the tree line, you will find yourself surrounded by mostly dead or diseased pines, something that impacts not just the scenery but creates a potential hazard from falling snags and is a continuing problem for trail crews as they work to keep the route free of deadfall. Backpackers should avoid setting up camp near any of these "widow makers."

The good news is that history shows that over the next several decades, the forests will eventually come back. For the foreseeable future, though, we all must contend with the results of one harmless-looking little bug's *really* big appetite.

Trip Description: From Wolf Creek Pass, pick up the trail at a small gravel parking area where the Continental Divide Trail (CDT) crosses US 160. There is a prominent signboard on the south side of the road.

The trail leaves from the north side of the highway and ascends through a spruce-fir forest with several small grassy meadows that support nice displays of wildflowers. Many (in fact most) of the trees have been killed by a beetle infestation in the last few years—a natural problem that is now plaguing much of the American Rockies. As of 2010 the worst of the problem only went as far west as Weminuche Pass (about halfway through the hike), though it could easily spread over the entire wilderness in the near future.

The trail ascends steadily, but not overly steeply, in mostly rounded switchbacks and turns crossing several tiny seasonal creeks and springs along the way. Decent views extend south-southeast to the Wolf Creek Ski Area. At 1.5 miles you top a ridge where there is an obvious but usually unsigned junction. The trail to the right goes 0.4 mile to Lobo Overlook, the alternate starting point (see Weminuche Wilderness Traverse [Map 7]).

The CDT goes left (straight if you came from Lobo Overlook) and for the next few miles goes mostly west along the ridge on numerous small ups and downs. The views are good especially to the south and southwest down Wolf Creek Canyon toward Pagosa Springs. There are still many scattered trees here, so you have not yet climbed above timberline. At about 3 miles is a sign marking your entry into the Weminuche Wilderness. Now in protected land, you wander through a series of lovely sloping meadows and then switchback up a small ridge with pleasant views. The path then takes you down a bit before climbing past a series of shallow ponds that offer fine reflections of distant rounded mountains and ridges. ***Note:*** *Several of these ponds dry up by late summer, so do not rely on them for water.*

At 6.4 miles you descend to the head of a very lush meadow, where there is a sketchy and unsigned junction. The faint trail to the right offers a pleasant side trip to the two Spruce Lakes: follow this path for about 0.2 mile, and then turn left to climb over a low ridge to the lakes (campsites and decent fishing).

The main CDT loops around the west end of the lush meadow, climbs to the top of a spur ridge, and then contours around the head

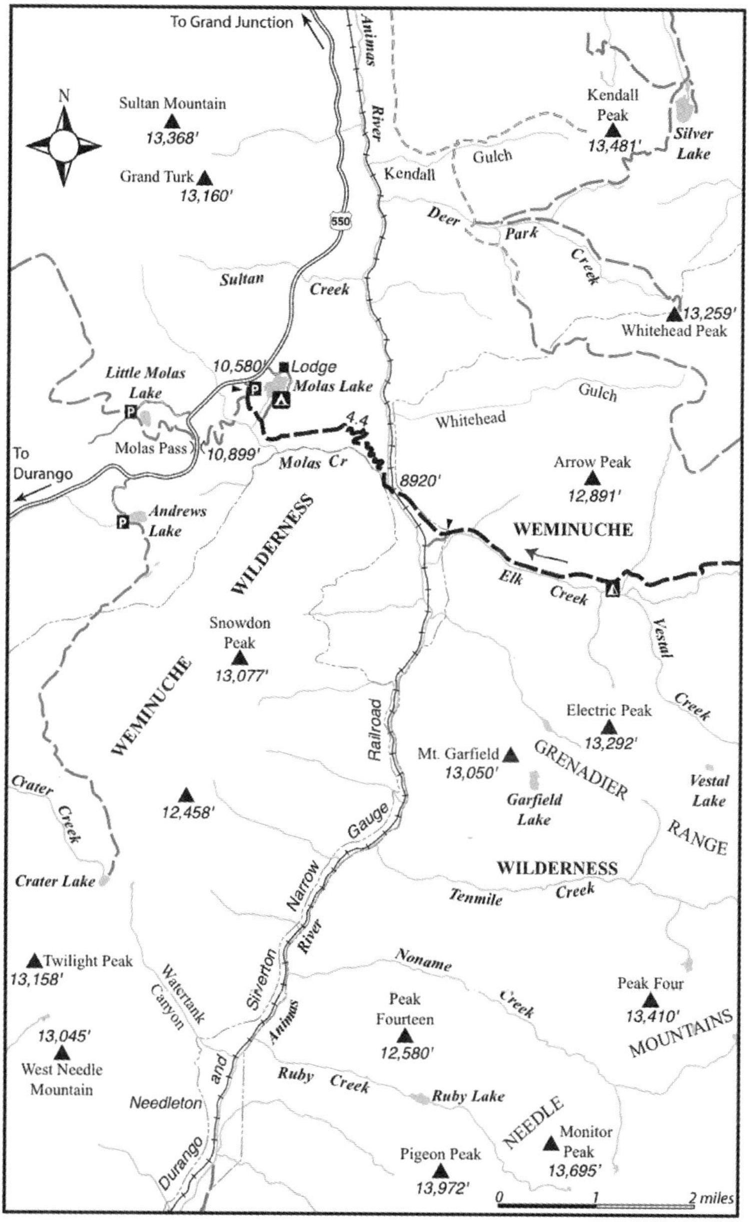

Weminuche Wilderness Traverse (Map 1)

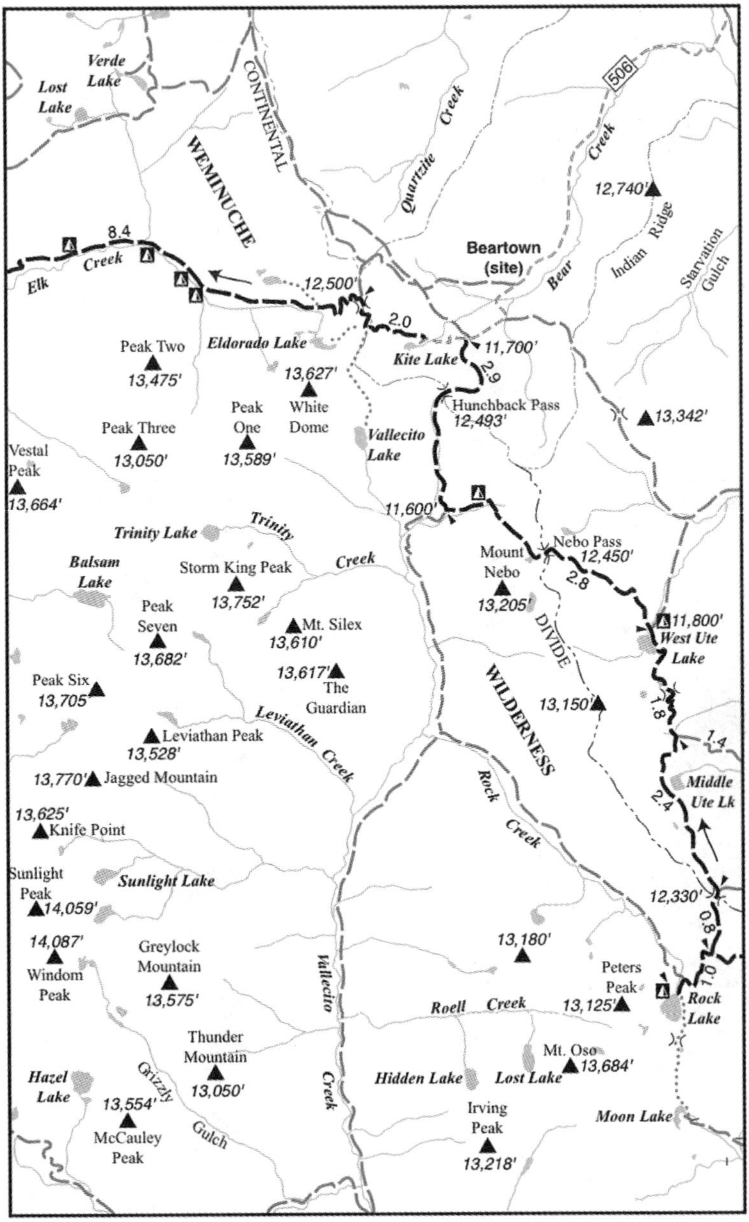

Weminuche Wilderness Traverse (Map 2)

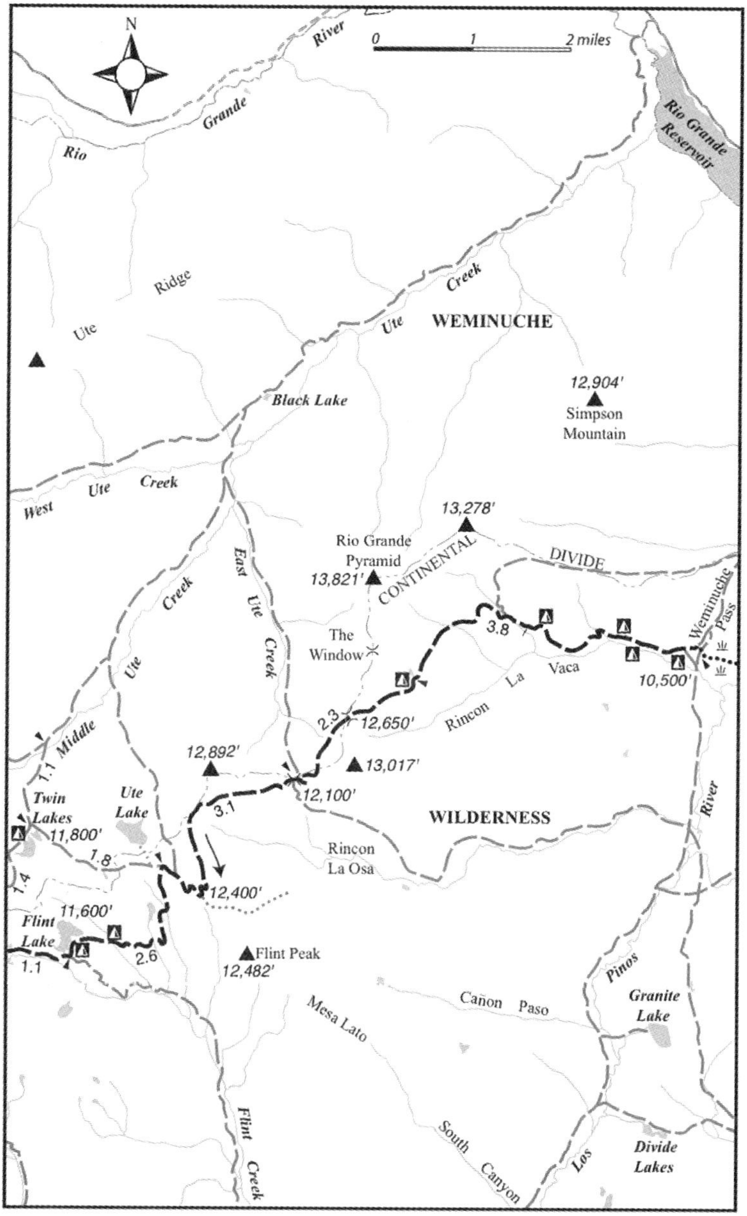

Weminuche Wilderness Traverse (Map 3)

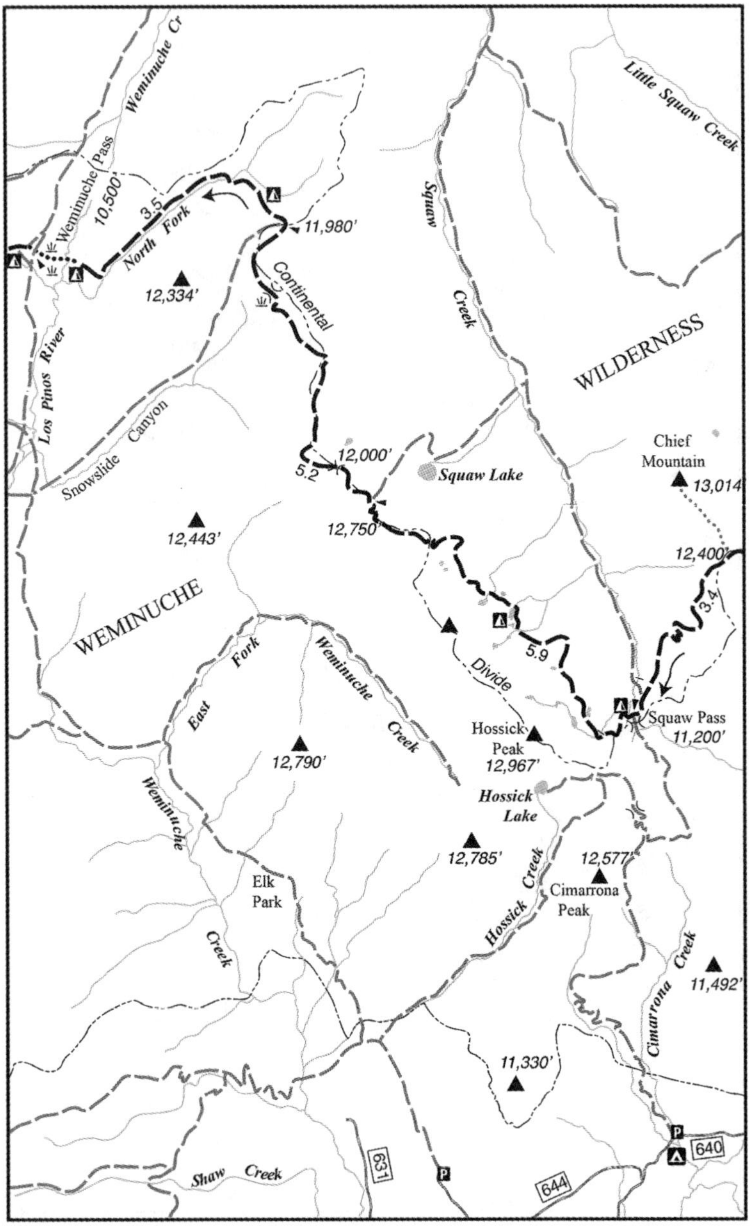

Weminuche Wilderness Traverse (Map 4)

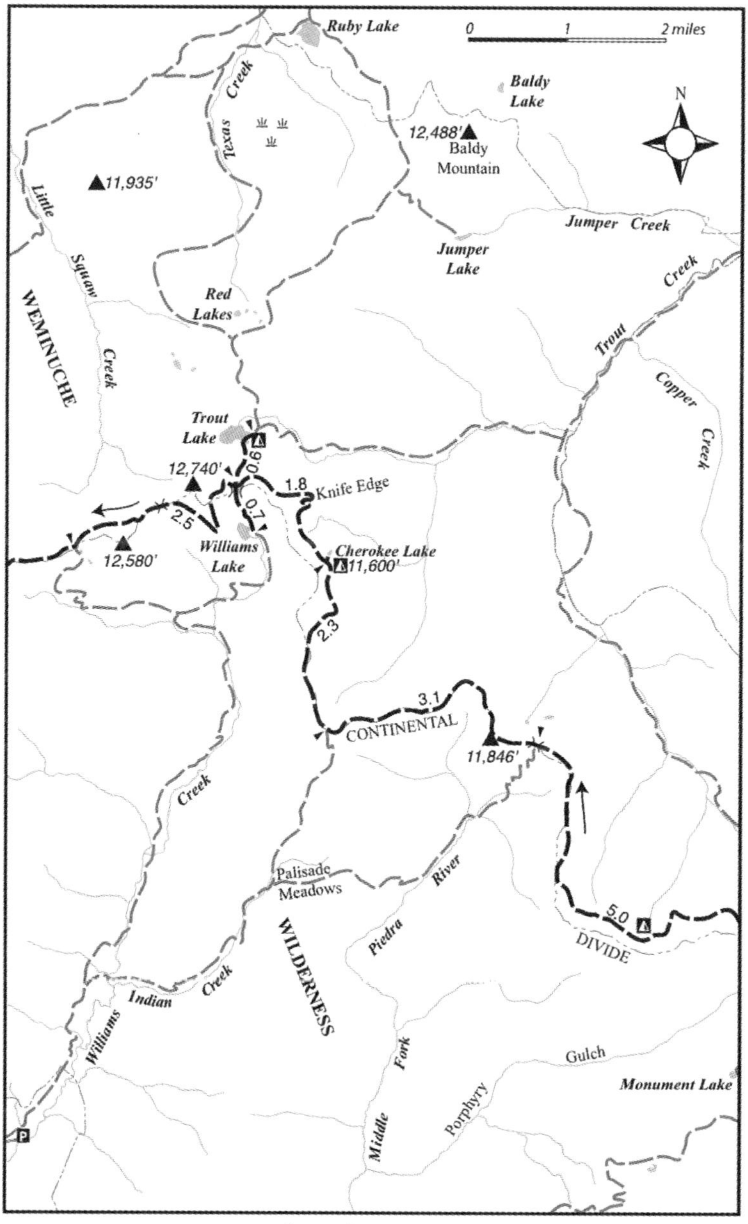

Weminuche Wilderness Traverse (Map 5)

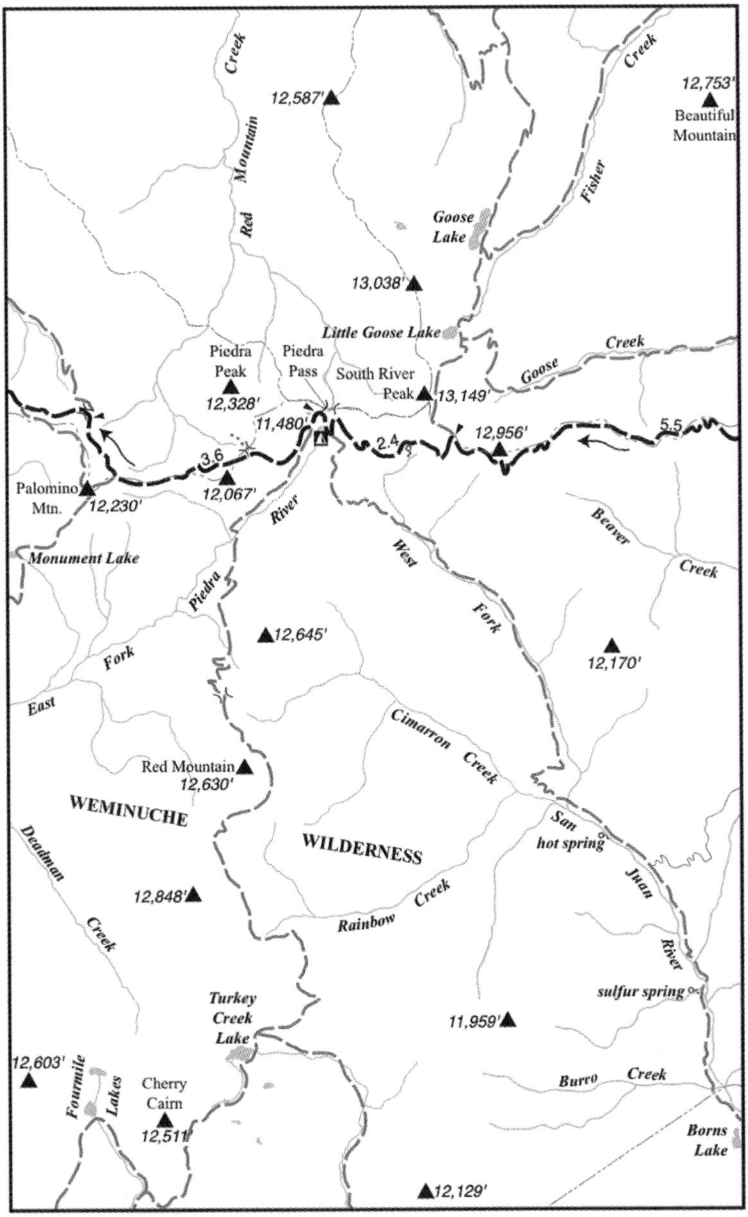

Weminuche Wilderness Traverse (Map 6)

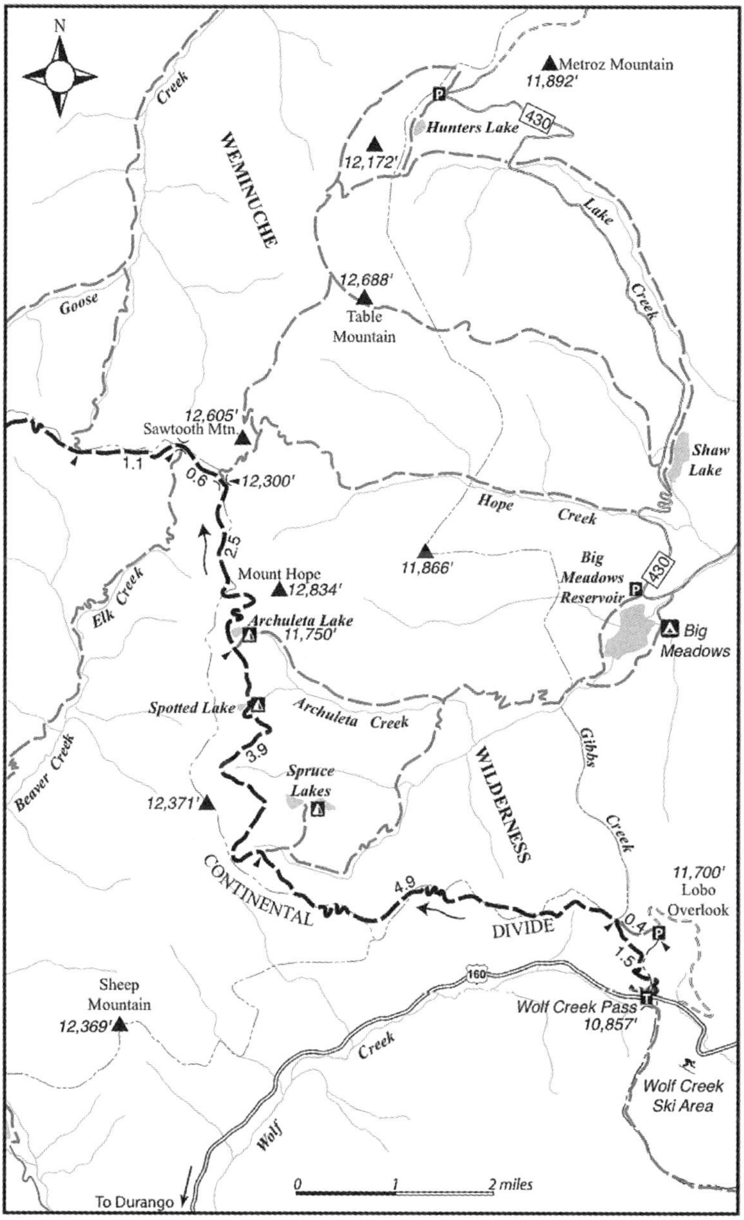

Weminuche Wilderness Traverse (Map 7)

of a creek basin. After passing over another spur ridge, you descend one switchback to reach lovely Spotted Lake (good campsites). This meadow-rimmed jewel has two strikingly distinct color tones: brown near the shallow shore and green-blue in the deeper middle of the lake.

The trail climbs away from Spotted Lake, ascending through a large meadow to the top a low rise before reaching larger and very scenic Archuleta Lake. This beautiful lake (good campsites) sits in a wildflower-covered basin beneath the slopes of Mount Hope. To protect the fragile location, camps are required to be at least 300 feet from the water and virtually all livestock are banned from any activity near the shore. ***Warning:*** *Be sure your water bottles are full when you leave Archuleta Lake, because this is likely to be your last reliable water source for the next 10.5 miles.*

Go straight at an obvious but unsigned junction just south of Archuleta Lake and follow the CDT as it crosses the brushy slope above the lake. The trail then ignores a promising-looking pass just west of the lake and instead makes an uphill traverse to the northeast. After the traverse, seven long switchbacks lead all the way to the top of a rocky above-timberline ridge nearly level with the adjacent summit of Mount Hope. The route then proceeds downhill and follows the high Continental Divide ridgeline north of Mount Hope, providing continuous far-ranging views of peaks, ridges, and valleys for many miles in all directions.

At a saddle 2.5 miles from Archuleta Lake, you come to a fork. The Highline Trail angles to the right (uphill), but you veer left (slightly downhill) staying on the CDT. For the next several miles this top-of-the-world path goes up and down along the divide sometimes down among short, wind-blown trees but more often amid the rocks, grasses, and wildflowers above timberline. The scenery is superb, but do not plan to hike this high route in the afternoon during the summer thunderstorm season.

At a saddle about 0.6 mile from the Highline Trail junction is an unsigned and easily missed junction with a trail that goes south (left) down Elk Creek. You keep straight on the main trail and 1.1 miles later reach a signed junction with the Goose Creek / Sawtooth Trail, which

Backpacker Walking past Archuleta Lake

goes downhill to the right. Again remain straight on the CDT, sticking with the high ridgeline. After a short stretch at somewhat lower elevation in beetle-killed forest, the trail climbs a set of switchbacks and then stays well above timberline on a wide, grassy ridge with superb views especially to the west of the area around South River Peak (see Weminuche Wilderness Traverse [Map 6]). Another tough uphill in four switchbacks takes you to the highest point of this hike and within an easy 50-yard scramble of an unnamed 12,956-foot peak. Needless to say, the views from this grandstand are extensive and superb. From the high point it is another 0.8-mile alpine section of up and down to the next junction.

Side Trip to South River Peak

If the weather is cooperating, an excellent side trip goes right here and in just 0.6 mile provides access to a short and fairly easy cross-country scramble to the top of South River Peak. At 13,149 feet, the view from the top of this peak is outstanding, encompassing a large percentage of the Weminuche Wilderness as well as countless peaks and valleys beyond.

The CDT goes left at the junction and descends steadily over open slopes in a long switchback to a sloping alpine basin. Except in late summer of particularly dry years, there are usually small springs and creeks in this basin, making this the first generally reliable on-trail water since Archuleta Lake. The trail continues downhill for another 1.4 miles, returning to forested terrain and coming to a signed junction with the West Fork Trail just above Piedra Pass. You go straight and almost immediately reach the two shallow ponds, small creeks, exposed camps, and lovely meadows at Piedra Pass. The pass has good views, but also lots of mosquitoes, so be prepared.

At the pass the CDT makes a curve to the south beside what appears to be an old road. After only 0.1 mile, you come to a signed junction. The Turkey Creek Trail goes straight, but you turn right on the CDT and very gradually climb past a metal shed that acts as a gauging station to a wide, forested saddle. A well-traveled game trail forks to the right at this saddle, but you keep left, climb a bit in forest, and then cross a large talus slope on the north side of an unnamed 12,067-foot butte.

From here the trail descends through meadows and forests and then makes a steep climb up a ridge leading to timberline high on the slopes of orange-tinged Palomino Mountain. Here a faint and unsigned alternate trail veers left near a large cairn and climbs nearly to the top of Palomino Mountain before going up and down above timberline for 1.9 miles and reuniting with the CDT.

Meanwhile, the more heavily used and less demanding CDT angles to the right at the unsigned junction on the slopes of Palomino Mountain, maintaining a generally constant elevation as it travels through meadows and past a narrow creek canyon lined with rocky pinnacles. At 0.8 mile from the Palomino Mountain junction is another unsigned junction about 150 yards before an obvious pass. Keep left (uphill), climb through the pass, and then make a gradual but rocky ascent to a ridgetop, where the faint trail over the top of Palomino Mountain reunites with the CDT.

Here you begin an extended section of minor ups and downs remaining just below timberline, as you travel beneath the impressive cliffs and talus slopes on the north side of the ridge forming the Continental Divide. Water can sometimes be obtained from springs, tiny ponds, or lingering snowfields along this stretch. Pass by several potential camp areas, although no established tent sites. The ridge then turns north and the trail follows suit, eventually traveling right on top of the rounded, up-and-down divide. At the west end of a grassy saddle, about 8.6 miles from Piedra Pass, is an unsigned junction with an obscure and easily missed trail on the left heading down the forested valley of Middle Fork Piedra River (see Weminuche Wilderness Traverse [Map 5]).

Keep straight on the CDT, and for the next 3.1 miles continue following the ridgetop with many small dips and high points along the way. The first 1.2 miles along this ridge are forested but then it transitions to an open, windy, and view-packed ridge with extensive vistas. You keep straight at an obvious junction marked only with a cairn, and then continue hiking along the open windswept divide for another 1.2 miles, where the trail veers to the right (northeast), away from the suddenly steepening ridgetop, and generally contours across the steep slopes on the east side of the divide. About 1.1 miles after leaving the ridgetop, the trail passes less than 150 yards above small and circular Cherokee Lake. A fluted, reddish-colored cliff backs this scenic pool on the north side. There are some adequate campsites on the eastern shore.

The CDT climbs away from Cherokee Lake and then crosses a scenic alpine basin before climbing to the top of Knife Edge, which, as the name suggests, is a very narrow rocky ridge. Staying high, the trail contours across the very steep slopes on the north side of Knife Edge. As you hike this high route you'll be treated to excellent views of large Trout Lake, filling almost the entire scenic basin to the northwest. At 1.8 miles from Cherokee Lake is a four-way junction amid the tundra of a wide pass.

Side Trips to Trout and Williams Lakes

Two not-to-be-missed side trips take off from this pass, and both are relatively short. To the north a trail drops 350 feet in 0.6 mile to large and marshy Trout Lake, with good fishing and campsites. The other side trip goes south from the pass and descends for 0.7 mile past a shallow pond to Williams Lake, a dramatic spot set beneath a rugged cliff.

The CDT goes straight at the pass, initially on a sketchy tread where cairns help to keep you on course. The path then makes a long, tough climb up a big alpine wall. At the 12,400-foot top of the wall you are rewarded with marvelous 360-degree views encompassing more deep canyons and tall peaks than could be easily listed.

The trail now descends across steep, treeless slopes to a slight dip in the divide, and then climbs a bit before cutting across the wildflower-covered slopes on the north side of an unnamed 12,580-foot peak. From here you'll have terrific views to the north of the dramatic U-shaped glacial valley of Little Squaw Creek.

At the end of this section is a "low" point in the ridge (about 12,000 feet) beside a shallow marshy pond. A tall cairn here marks the junction with Trail #587. You go straight (uphill), still on the CDT, and make a view-packed climb of 450 feet to the top of the high ridge south of Chief Mountain (see Weminuche Wilderness Traverse [Map 4]). As always, the views from this high point seem to stretch for eternity. The 13,014-foot summit of Chief Mountain is an enticing goal from this spot, and the ascent is not technically difficult.

From here you face a long downhill, descending some 1,200 feet in 1.5 miles. Much of the route is eroded and rocky, so watch your step. After losing most of the elevation, you hop over a small, wildflower-banked creek, and then angle to the left on a contour to the southwest leading to wide Squaw Pass. On the way, you'll stroll past an assortment of brushy meadows and a small waterfall, while enjoying good views looking west up to Hossick Peak. About 0.2 mile prior to reaching the pass, an unsigned but obvious trail goes sharply right on the way down Squaw Creek. Go straight and soon come to the grassy pass. At one of the several posts that are in place to mark the route, you may notice a faint trail on the left heading to the Cimarrona trailhead. Keep straight, soon jump over a small branch of Squaw Creek not far downstream from a round metal gauging station, and 50 yards later come to a nice campsite, though unfortunately located right on the trail.

The trail winds uphill to a gorgeous meadow in a basin below Hossick Peak. Here you cross what's left of Squaw Creek right beside a small waterfall, and then wander past a shallow rock-lined pond. The trail then climbs over and around a spur ridge before heading gradually downhill on very rocky tread to a second lovely basin. Here are several beautiful ponds and small lakes reflecting fine views of the peaks and cliffs rising to the south and west. The good campsites in this basin require some effort to locate.

Just 0.5 mile beyond this basin is a third, smaller basin with a sparkling lake beneath an old moraine and an unnamed, craggy, reddish peak. After contouring across the slopes just to the west of a fourth lovely alpine basin (although this one only has some marshy ponds and no lake), the trail ascends three long switchbacks to a ridgetop. From here, turn onto the ridge and continue gradually uphill across tundra expanses nearly to the top of a rounded butte, topping out at close to 12,750 feet. Bird lovers should try to tear their eyes away from the grand views to look for water pipits and well-camouflaged white-tailed ptarmigans, as both of these hearty species nest in this harsh above-timberline location. Perhaps the views draw them here, including northwest to the distant and distinctive Rio Grande Pyramid. This towering landmark will be a major part of your vistas for the next couple of days.

Descending from the high point, you follow nine short switchbacks to a junction, marked with a post, with a very faint trail that goes to the right on its way down to Squaw Lake.

From the junction, the wildly scenic CDT continues downhill to a treeless pass then ascends some 400 feet to a wide alpine plateau. The view-filled trail stays atop the nearly flat tundra and rocks for almost a mile before making a fairly long and gradual descent through brush to another high saddle, this one holding several meadows and ponds. A gentle, 0.4-mile climb leads to a ridgetop and a junction with a well-used trail on the left toward Snowslide Canyon.

You go straight, still on the CDT, and immediately begin a long downhill. The trail enters forest just below the ridgetop and stays amid the beetle-killed trees most of the way down this 1,500-foot descent. Shortly after reentering the forest, you approach the North Fork Los Pinos River (a rather lofty name for what is just a small creek) and come to a nice campsite. About 0.4 mile later the trail crosses the stream on an easy rock-hop. The trail then generally stays on the partly forested slope well above the stream, except for where you closely approach the water beside a large beaver dam. Just before the bottom of the long downhill, you cross a possibly dry canal, and immediately thereafter come to the huge open meadows just south of Weminuche Pass. There is a great view here looking west to Rio Grande Pyramid and a closer unnamed peak. Good campsites can be found near where you enter the meadow, not far from the North Fork Los Pinos River.

Your goal from here is to reach the trail heading up the canyon of Rincon La Vaca, which you can see directly across the meadow to the west (see Weminuche Wilderness Traverse [Map 3]). Unfortunately, trails tend to disappear in this meadow, so the best solution is to walk straight across the meadow aiming for the right side of your destination canyon. There are supposed to be posts marking the correct route, but they are hard to find. Still, navigation is pretty straightforward as the goal is always in sight. Be prepared to ford a slow, but sometimes deep, creek along the way and to get wet from the dew-covered grasses as you cross the meadow. Once on the west side of the meadow, you'll come to a trail crossing your route just as you leave the grasses and enter slightly higher terrain covered mostly with sagebrush. Cross this trail, then pass over another dry canal to your desired trail, which is just a few yards into the forest on the other side.

Follow well-defined tread uphill for 0.5 mile to a second higher meadow, where there are several good campsites, as well as views to the west-northwest to Rio Grande Pyramid and an obvious squared-off notch in the ridge called The Window. About 2.2 miles above Weminuche Pass, your gradual, steady climb leads to a small creek in a lush little meadow with a small but attractive campsite in the trees on the west side. About 0.2 mile past this camp, you begin a steep climb beside a boulder field and past a small waterfall that takes you up to an obvious but unsigned junction just before a creek crossing. The uphill trail to the right is a newer ridgetop path not shown on most maps.

Go left at the junction, and almost immediately hop over the small creek you have been paralleling during the climb. Look upstream here for an exceptionally photogenic view of massive Rio Grande Pyramid.

The trail climbs a bit more, and then makes an exceptionally scenic crossing of a relatively level alpine bench with stupendous views of both Rio Grande Pyramid and The Window, both very close by. At the south end of this section you pass a lovely little lake, then curve to the southwest and ascend to a 12,650-foot pass with the trip's first really good views looking west to the rugged Needles Range.

Cutting across an open, wildflower-covered slope, the trail then makes a short, steep descent to a pass with a pair of junctions. The first junction is with a trail on the right down East Ute Creek. Go straight and about 150 yards later reach a second junction, this time with a trail going left toward Rincon La Osa. ***Note:*** *This last trail section is inaccurately shown on the older Trails Illustrated maps.*

The CDT goes right (slightly uphill) at the second junction and begins a gradual uphill traverse around the south side of a 12,892-foot mountain. ***Note:*** *Older maps show the CDT not going around this mountain, but over the top of it. If that ever were the case, it is no longer true.* The trail offers excellent views back to Rio Grande Pyramid and down to the meadow of Rincon La Osa, as it curves south and comes to the top of a narrow ridge. From here you can look down and northwest to large Ute Lake and west to the very rugged range centered on Peters Peak and Mount Oso (pictured in figure 14.4).

The trail descends a series of switchbacks from the ridgetop and soon passes an abandoned trail heading to the left back toward Rincon La Osa. More downhill takes you to an obvious but unsigned trail fork about 0.8 mile from the ridgetop. The trail going uphill to the right heads over the ridge a little east of Ute Lake and then down Ute Creek. Keep left, and after another 0.2 mile of winding downhill reach a signed junction. Here you face a choice.

CDT Alternate

The CDT goes straight, passes above Ute Lake, and then gradually descends across open terrain to a junction just north of Twin Lakes. From there, turn right (downhill) and descend for 1.1 miles to a junction beside Middle Ute Creek. The CDT goes left here and climbs back up into meadows to a junction about 0.4 mile north of Middle Ute Lake and a reunion with the alternate route. Although this 4.3-mile section of the CDT is very pretty, it's not as scenic as the alternate route.

Flint Creek Trail Alternate

The alternate trail to reach this same junction is 2.6 miles longer and more challenging, but is also more scenic and offers a wonderful side trip option to spectacular Rock Lake (pictured in figure 14.4). To take this trail, turn left at the junction southeast of Ute Lake onto the Flint Creek Trail. This sometimes muddy and very circuitous route winds up and down past marshy ponds and over rocky ridges for 2.4 miles until reaching the shores of large Flint Lake. Signs inform you that camping, campfires, and livestock are prohibited within 300 feet of this popular lake.

The trail descends 0.2 mile from the lake to a junction, where you turn right. This path climbs past ponds and campsites for 1.1 miles to a pass and, just 50 yards down the other side, comes to an unsigned junction. The trail to the right is the return route to the CDT.

Side Trip to Rock Lake

A great side trip is in order from this junction. Your goal is Rock Lake, which you can see shimmering in a spectacular cirque basin a little less than 1 mile to the southwest. Drop your heavy pack, take out your camera, and continue straight from the junction, losing about 250 feet on a winding route. After 0.7 mile, watch carefully for a faint unsigned path heading uphill to the left. (If you come to a crossing of Rock Creek, then you've gone about 100 yards too far.) Follow this indistinct route for 0.3 mile, and you'll arrive at Rock Lake. Camping here is too exposed for comfort, but the views of Peters Peak, Mount Oso, and the other rocky peaks surrounding the lake are outstanding. Excellent cross-country routes radiate from this lake up to ridges and hidden lakes in several directions. At the end of your visit, retrace your steps to the junction.

After returning from the Rock Lake side trip, go north from the junction and walk past several ponds that beautifully reflect the surrounding craggy peaks before ascending an open slope to a pass and an unsigned junction just down the other side.

From this pass you have another choice. If you prefer well-maintained and obvious trails, then go straight and descend to a reunion with the CDT just past Twin Lakes. Descend from there to Middle Ute Creek, turn left, and climb back up to a junction north of Middle Ute Lake.

Hikers who don't mind some route finding on a higher and more scenic route should veer left at the unsigned junction just below the pass onto the sometimes faint tread of the Middle Ute Lake Trail. This sketchy route generally stays high in wildflower-covered meadows on a gradual descent past a small pond and through some brushy areas to a slope just above Middle Ute Lake. Travel around the west side of the lake's basin and then climb a bit to a reunion with the CDT. ***Note:*** *This description ignores the fact that the tread tends to disappear frequently, so be prepared to study the map and possibly wander around a bit while you are searching for the correct route. If you lose the route altogether, just make your way north-northwest until you can see Middle Ute Lake, and then scramble over rocks and brush to the north until you pick up the obvious tread of the CDT.*

On the distinct tread of the CDT, make a short, switchbacking ascent to a pass from which you can look down on West Ute Lake and all around to seemingly infinite sky-scraping peaks—some of the most spectacular views in all of the American Rockies. The trail then descends open, view-packed slopes in long lazy traverses and switchbacks to sparkling and deservedly popular West Ute Lake (see Weminuche Wilderness Traverse [Map 2]). Wilderness regulations prohibit camping, campfires, and bringing livestock to within 300 feet of this fish-filled lake. There are some excellent legal campsites a little below the lake on the right (east) side of the lake's outlet creek.

Just 80 yards below West Ute Lake, the trail forks, where the West Ute Trail goes right, but you bear left on a newer section of the CDT not shown on most topo maps. You immediately splash across West Ute Creek and then contour across a wooded slope for about a half mile. Beyond, you return to alpine country, as the trail steadily ascends through very scenic and open terrain to Nebo Pass. Not surprisingly, the views from here are stupendous, especially looking east to Rio Grande Pyramid and The Window, and west to the extremely rugged

Needles country and Grenadier Range. There are two small but striking lakes on the west side of the pass. The first is larger, deeper, and has a rocky island, while the second is more of a shallow pond.

On the west side of the pass the trail is rocky and quite steep descending into the canyon of Nebo Creek. About 80 yards after the third easy rock-hop creek crossing of this stream, you'll come to a nice campsite in some trees just to the right of the trail. Just 0.2 mile past this campsite is a signed junction with Vallecito Creek Trail.

Turn right and soon climb back out of the forest onto open, brushy slopes. Before long the trail returns to the land of tundra and rocks as you climb steeply to the top of Hunchback Pass, an appropriate name for hikers who have hauled their heavy packs this far.

The trail meanders gently downhill from Hunchback Pass through lovely alpine terrain and back down into a landscape of a few scattered trees. At 1.4 miles from the pass is a remote trailhead on a 4 × 4 mining road. Here you face a choice of routes. The eastbound Colorado Trail, another long-distance route that travels all the way across the Centennial State, follows the road downhill to the right. The CDT also goes right, but after just a few yards bears off to the left across the rolling basin of Bear Creek.

The recommended and most scenic route is to go left (uphill) on the mining track, which steeply climbs a mostly open hillside. After about 0.4 mile the road levels out about 200 yards before you reach the basin of Kite Lake, where an unsigned path forks to the right (uphill). This path is the continuation of your route. However, before going that way, a very short side trip to the end of the road at Kite Lake is a worthwhile diversion. Here you'll find a wooden mine building beside the lake, which is well situated for soaking in the dramatic setting of the lake in a colorful glacial cirque. ***Warning:*** *At the west end of the lake is a large pile of bright yellow and orange mine tailings, which should be warning enough that drinking water from this lake, even if it is filtered, is not recommended.*

After backtracking 200 yards to where the faint trail goes uphill, you turn onto this path, which soon becomes obvious as the rocky tread steeply climbs the hillside north of Kite Lake. Near the pass at the top of this tiring 750-foot climb are several short switchbacks, but they do little to reduce the steepness. Extremely generous compensation for your work comes once you finally reach the top. The view from here is, arguably, the best of the entire trip (or in the entire American Rockies, for that matter). Peaks and ridges crowd the skyline in every direction, but the most dramatic scene is looking west and southwest over to White Dome and down to sparkling Eldorado Lake at its base. Lunch spots simply don't get any better than this!

Trails go both left and right from this pass, which at over 12,800 feet is the second highest elevation reached along this trip. The trail to the left is an unofficial path that heads for the climber's route up White Dome and a scramble route down to spectacular Vallecito Lake. Another option is a very faint trail that goes down the slope in front of you to Eldorado Lake. Although finding this route on the ground is difficult, those with an understandable urge to visit this lake needn't worry, as the way down is quite apparent and relatively easy over open tundra and rocky slopes.

To continue the hike, turn right (north) at the pass, gain a few more feet along the ridgetop, and then steeply descend a set of rocky switchbacks. The trail goes a short distance along the rounded top of the divide, with jaw-dropping views of the extremely deep canyon of Elk Creek to the west. The ridgetop here also holds a riot of colorful wildflowers in mid to late July. You soon come to an important junction atop the ridge. Going straight here would take you to a junction with the CDT in about 0.5 mile.

For the recommended route, turn left (downhill) at the junction onto the westbound Colorado Trail heading for Elk Creek. This incredibly scenic route descends more than two dozen well-graded switchbacks across a wildflower-covered hillside, and then goes more steeply downhill beside a tiny creek to an old miner's cabin that is a real "fixer-upper." Here an unofficial use path goes northwest toward a pair of scenic but unnamed lakes.

Your trail continues downhill soon entering the very deep and steep-sided defile at the head of Elk Creek's canyon. The trail's next section is extremely steep with lots of loose gravel, so watch your footing. The scenery is excellent and quite distracting, but careful foot placement is crucial to avoid a nasty fall, so try to pry your eyes away from the nearby cliffs and peaks long enough to remain safe. The grade eases off after about 0.5 mile, becoming only intermittently steep as you make your way down the north side of the canyon. The canyon walls are impressively tall, and waterfalls streaking down add to the lovely scenery. When the canyon floor finally starts to level off, the forests return and inviting campsites start to appear. The first good site is almost directly opposite Peak Two to the south, but you'll pass many more in the next several miles (see Weminuche Wilderness Traverse [Map 1]).

At about 4.4 miles from the top of the divide, you pass a large and pretty meadow with numerous excellent campsites. Below this point the forests are increasingly filled with quaking aspens, making for a fine color show in late September. After an extended, fairly level stretch near the meadow, the trail makes some intermittently steep descents intermixed with level stretches and even a couple of short uphills. About 1.6 miles below the meadow, you pass the last good campsite. Continue another 2.4 miles to a signed junction.

Alternate Exit via the Durango and Silverton Railroad

The trail going downhill to the left soon leads to the Elk Park railroad stop. This is a possible exit route for hikers who are willing to flag down the train, who left a car at the train depot for the Durango and Silverton Narrow Gauge Railroad, and who want to avoid the long climb back up to Molas Pass.

For those hiking, rather than taking the train out of this wilderness, keep straight at the junction and follow the hillside above the slightly silty Animas River and the narrow-gauge train tracks paralleling the stream. After 0.7 mile, you come to the tracks and follow them north for about 80 yards. The trail then veers left away from the tracks and soon comes to a large wooden bridge spanning the rushing Animas River. You cross the bridge, then walk upstream 0.1 mile, being constantly wary of the stinging nettles hidden amid the riparian vegetation, to a log crossing of Molas Creek.

Now begins the trip's last, and perhaps longest, sustained uphill. In the next 3 miles you'll go from the hike's lowest elevation, of less than 9,000 feet, to the Molas Lake trailhead, at about 10,600 feet, so settle in for a long and often hot ascent.

Parallel Molas Creek for just under 0.1 mile and then follow a series of ten short switchbacks up a rocky slope studded with quaking aspens and Douglas firs, with fine views looking south down the Animas River Canyon to the rugged Grenadier Range. Beyond, longer-legged, well-graded switchbacks zigzag up an increasingly forested ridge. The forest not only gets denser, but it also gradually changes into the higher elevation's mostly spruce and fir forests that have characterized the majority of this trip.

After twenty-six more switchbacks, the grade eases and you wander through rolling meadows with lots of cinquefoil, flax, and other wildflowers, enjoying fine views of several nearby mountains, ignoring unsigned game trails branching off to the left. After about a half mile through the meadow, the trail makes a brief climb and reaches a fork. The trail to the right goes to the private campground at Molas Lake, but your trail heads left, following signs for the Colorado Trail. Walk 0.3 mile to a second fork, where this time the Colorado Trail goes left, but you branch to the right and reach the Molas Lake trailhead 0.1 mile farther.

Possible Itinerary

	Camps and Side Trips	Miles	Elevation Gain
Day 1	Wolf Creek Pass to Archuleta Lake	10.3	+2,500/−1,600
Day 2	Piedra Pass	12.1	+2,800/−3,050
Day 3	Cherokee Lake	14.0	+2,800/−2,700
Day 4	Basin north of Hossick Peak	10.8	+2,600/−2,300
	Side trip to Trout Lake	1.2	+300/−300
	Side trip to Williams Lake	1.4	+350/−350
Day 5	Weminuche Pass	11.4	+1,900/−3,300
Day 6	Flint Lake	11.8	+3,050/−1,950
Day 7	Nebo Creek	8.7	+2,350/−2,150
	Side trip to Rock Lake	2	+400/−400
Day 8	Elk Creek at meadows	9.5	+2,150/−3,750
Day 9	Out to Molas TH	8.4	+2,000/−1,600

Giving Back

San Juan Mountains Association: www.sjma.org

Young and Foolish

Many baby boomers can look back at their childhoods and wonder how they survived into adulthood. Unlike the norm of today, our mothers would gladly shoo us out the door in the morning when school was not in session for an entire day of unsupervised play, and our only directive was to be back for lunch, after which we'd resume our activities until called for dinner. Although our usual pursuits were fairly benign, such as pickup games of baseball, football, or street hockey; building forts; role playing, sometimes they involved more risk than our parents would have approved—had they known.

Some of our less well-thought-out plans on the edge of the Portland suburbs included building ramps in the woods for bike jumps, which became higher and higher with each level of success. We'd make increasingly longer approaches on our one-speed Schwinns in order to increase our speed to go higher and farther until someone invariably would get hurt, which would usually happen conveniently right about lunchtime. Of course, these were the days when no one wore a helmet, or knee or elbow pads, or any form of protection whatsoever. After lunch, we'd all regroup for some less hazardous game or activity, but we'd eventually resume the bike jump later that week after the bruises and scrapes had healed. Another suspect activity with our bikes involved pushing them up to the top of Mt. Scott and gleefully roaring downhill to the bottom, reaching speeds beyond the posted speed limit for cars, again without helmets or any other protection. One errant rock in the road could have maimed the blissfully ignorant for life, or simply killed us outright.

Having successfully survived those early years, I set off for Colorado one July to meet Dave for a backpacking trip in the San Juans. As twenty-somethings, I'm not sure we had completely evolved much beyond adolescence, which shall become clear as this story unfolds. Married and working full time, I had some extra funds but Dave, a graduate student at New Mexico Tech, had nothing you could term as disposable income. Consequently, rather than coughing up the funds for an enjoyable ride on the Durango & Silverton Narrow Gauge Railroad to the trailhead at Elk Park, we drove my car to Molas Pass and hiked the extra 4 miles to reach our starting trailhead instead. We had a very enjoyable time backpacking in the shadow of the Continental Divide, with fantastic mountain scenery as our constant companion.

Somewhat limited by time constraints and without the utility a second vehicle would have provided for arranging a point-to-point trip, we determined a turnaround spot at a campsite along Vallecito Creek. With one extra day for a day hike before we'd have to start retracing our steps, we set our sights on an area renowned for outstanding mountain scenery, Chicago Basin, where a horseshoe of 14,000-foot peaks rimmed an alpine vale. The only problem was that the basin was a long way from our present location—almost 20 miles. Although we were young and in very good physical condition, why hiking nearly 40 miles in a single day didn't seem outlandish to us at the time is now hard to comprehend. I certainly don't recall any concussions from one of those preadolescent bike jumps.

The morning of our proposed hike dawned fair and clear and we hit the trail reasonably early, knowing we were in for a long day. From camp the hiking was easy, as we headed downstream along Vallecito Creek for several miles to the junction with the Columbine Pass Trail. Now the trail started a long climb toward the pass. The weather was still accommodating, without the buildup of clouds preceding the customary Rocky Mountains afternoon thunderstorms and we were feeling good, so optimism reigned for the time being about our likely success of reaching Chicago Basin. Much later, approaching Vallecito Basin to the east of Columbine Pass, I started to gauge my reserves and calculated the energy expenditure required for completing the entire trip. Requesting a short confab, I told Dave I was worried about not having the resources for continuing the steepening climb to the pass, dropping into the basin, climbing back over the pass, and then going all the way back to camp. Sometime that afternoon (we didn't have watches and GPS units, and cell phones had yet to be invented), we parted company, as I headed back to camp and Dave pressed on, determined to reach Chicago Basin.

I returned to camp very late in the afternoon, tired but not to the point of collapse, and settled in to wait for Dave. The hours steadily ticked by, as I occupied myself with a good paperback and by performing some necessary camp chores. Sometime after sunset, the attempt of waiting for Dave before cooking dinner eventually was thwarted by my increasing hunger. I ate my portion and reserved the rest to be reheated when my partner arrived. Now it was completely dark, and the hours continued to go by with no sign of Dave. Falling temperatures eventually drove me into the tent and my sleeping bag after I put some more logs on the fire as a beacon for Dave, but an active mind concerned with his lateness was not going to allow any sleep that night. Alone in the tent, I experienced more time elapse with no sign of my friend. Sometime well after midnight, Dave stumbled into camp near exhaustion. He ravenously consumed the unheated dinner, while briefly grunting out the tale of successfully reaching Chicago Basin, proclaiming it to be as beautiful as billed.

After a half night's sleep, we broke camp and loaded our packs onto our backs for the trip out toward the Molas Pass trailhead. Totally thrashed by the death march of the previous day, Dave walked down the trail like a cowboy after a forty-eight-hour horseback ride. Tired, stiff, and sore, he willed himself back over Hunchback Pass and down to a camp at Kite Lake. The next day we climbed back over the Continental Divide and then followed the Elk Creek and Molas Trails back to the car. Incredibly grateful for the luxury of motorized transport, perhaps Dave more than I, we headed for home, never again to consider hiking almost forty miles in a day.—**Mike**

APPENDIX

Best Times by Season

JULY THROUGH SEPTEMBER

- Trip 12. Trappers Lake—Devils Causeway Loop

MID-JULY TO EARLY AUGUST

- Trip 3. Crazy Mountains Traverse
- Trip 4. Spanish Peaks Loop
- Trip 8. Solitude Trail Loop

MID-JULY THROUGH AUGUST

- Trip 9. Wind River Highline Traverse
- Trip 10. Cirque of the Towers Loop

MID-JULY TO EARLY SEPTEMBER

- Trip 11. Glacier Trail to Gannett Peak

MID-JULY THROUGH SEPTEMBER

- Trip 14. Weminuche Wilderness Traverse

LATE JULY

- Trip 13. Four Pass Loop

LATE JULY TO EARLY AUGUST

- Trip 5. The Beaten Path

LATE JULY TO MID-AUGUST

- Trip 7. Teton Crest Trail

AUGUST

- Trip 1. Ptarmigan—Glenns Pass—Highline Loop

AUGUST TO EARLY SEPTEMBER

- Trip 2. Gunsight Pass Traverse

LATE AUGUST THROUGH EARLY SEPTEMBER

- Trip 6. Bechler River Trail

About the Authors

Doug Lorain began hiking at age four, and until recently had always managed to hike his age in miles in a single day. (Upon turning 41 several years back, he switched to kilometers.)

His first backpacking trip was at age twelve with his father—a miserable mosquito-infested affair about which the nightmares have yet to subside—and he has since logged well over 33,000 trail miles pursuing his favorite activity all around the American and Canadian West.

Over time, he has been charged by grizzly bears (*twice!*), been bitten by a rattlesnake, spat upon by a llama, gotten stuck in quicksand, suffered through a nasty bout of *giardia,* was shot at by a hunter, been nearly washed away in river fords, and survived enough Pacific Northwest storms to turn the Sahara into a rainforest, but has also been blessed to see some of the most beautiful scenery on Earth.

He is the nationally award-winning author of eleven previous hiking and backpacking guidebooks with plans for several more, assuming his knees hold out. Although he considers his real home to be on the trail, those days he is forced to spend indoors he spends in Hamilton, Montana, with his wife, Becky Lovejoy.

Top Trails Olympic National Park & Vicinity
One Best Hike: Mount Rainier's Wonderland Trail
Backpacking Wyoming
One Night Wilderness: Portland

Backpacking Idaho
100 Classic Hikes in Oregon
Afoot & Afield Portland/Vancouver, 2nd Edition
Backpacking Washington, 2nd Edition
Backpacking Oregon, 2nd Edition
Best Backpacking Trips in California and Nevada
Best Backpacking Trips in Utah, Arizona, and New Mexico
100 Classic Hikes in Montana

Mike White grew up in Portland, Oregon, from where he began adventuring in the Cascade Range. He obtained a BA from Seattle Pacific University, where he met and married his wife, Robin. The couple lived in Seattle for two years before relocating to Reno, Nevada, where Robin had been accepted to medical school. For the next fifteen years, Mike worked for a consulting engineering firm, journeying to the Sierra Nevada and other areas of the West as time permitted. During that time, the couple had two sons, David and Stephen, and Robin completed school and residency, and then went into private practice as a pediatrician. Upon leaving the engineering firm, Mike became a full-time writer, eventually authoring or contributing to numerous outdoor guides, as well as articles for magazines and newspapers. A part-time community college instructor, Mike is also a featured speaker for outdoors and conservation organizations.

The Trinity Alps & Vicinity, 7th Edition
Nevada Wilderness Areas
Snowshoe Trails of Tahoe, 2nd Edition
Snowshoe Trails of Yosemite
Backpacking California, 2nd Edition
Best Snowshoe Trails of California
50 Classic Hikes in Nevada
Backpacking Nevada
Sequoia National Park
Kings Canyon National Park
Sierra South, 8th Edition
Sierra North, 9th Edition
Sequoia & Kings Canyon National Parks, Your Complete Hiking Guide

Top Trails Northern California's Redwood Coast
Top Trails Lake Tahoe, 3rd Edition
Afoot & Afield Reno-Tahoe, 2nd Edition
Lassen Volcanic National Park, A Complete Hikers Guide, 5th Edition
Top Trails Sequoia and Kings Canyon National Parks, 2nd Edition
Best Backpacking Trips in California and Nevada
Best Backpacking Trips in Utah, Arizona, and New Mexico
50 Best Strolls, Walks, and Hikes around Reno
50 of the Best Snowshoe Trails around Lake Tahoe

Index